Emotionally Intelligent School Counseling

Emotionally Intelligent School Counseling

Edited by

John Pellitteri
Queens College, CUNY

Robin Stern
*The School at Columbia University
and the Woodhull Institute for Ethical Leadership*

Claudia Shelton
The Hopewell Group, LLC

Barbara Muller-Ackerman
Parsippany Counseling Center

 LAWRENCE ERLBAUM ASSOCIATES, PUBLISHERS
2006   Mahwah, New Jersey   London

KH

Lawrence Erlbaum Associates, Inc., Publishers
10 Industrial Avenue
Mahwah, New Jersey 07430
www.erlbaum.com

Cover design by Kathryn Houghtaling Lacey

Library of Congress Cataloging-in-Publication Data

Emotionally intelligent school counseling / edited by John Pellitteri ...
[et al.].
        p. cm.
    Includes bibliographical references and index.
    ISBN 0-8058-5034-1 (cloth : alk. paper)
    ISBN 0-8058-5035-X (paper : alk. paper)
    1. Educational counseling. 2. Emotional intelligence.   I. Pellitteri, John.
    LB1027.5.E45   2005
    371.4'22—dc22

                                                    2004061928
                                                           CIP

Books published by Lawrence Erlbaum Associates are printed on acid-free
paper, and their bindings are chosen for strength and durability.

Printed in the United States of America
10 9 8 7 6 5 4 3 2 1

6/12/06

Contents

PART III: APPLICATIONS IN SCHOOL SETTINGS

PART IV: APPLICATIONS WITH SPECIFIC GROUPS

PART V: APPLICATIONS WITH SPECIAL MODALITIES

PART VI: SUCCESS STORIES

Detailed
Table of Contents

PART III: APPLICATIONS IN SCHOOL SETTINGS

PART IV: APPLICATIONS WITH SPECIFIC GROUPS

PART VI: SUCCESS STORIES

Foreword

Peter Salovey
Yale University

Typically, emotions are aroused through interactions or anticipated interactions with other people. They are part of the landscape of an organism's social environment. One would think that an intelligence guiding such an important aspect of the human psyche would be well understood, but investigators historically have been reluctant to consider the emotions seriously. Now, in the middle of the first decade of the 21st century, the idea of an emotional intelligence has come into its own. There are formal theories of emotional intelligence in the scientific literature, methods for measuring it as a set of abilities; and studies of the importance of these skills and competencies in school, work, and social relations appear every day. It would seem natural that the implications of emotional intelligence for school counselors would be important to identify, and this volume provides a significant seminal discussion of emotional intelligence in this educational domain.

Emotional intelligence encapsulates the idea that students, teachers, and counselors can be "smart," in part, by understanding their emotions and the emotions of other people. My collaborators and I believe that there is an intelligence involving the processing of affectively charged information (e.g., Mayer, Salovey, & Caruso, 2004; Salovey & Mayer, 1990). We define *emotional intelligence* as involving both the capacity to reason about emotions and to use emotions in order to assistance reasoning. We believe emotional intelligence includes abilities to identify emotions accurately in oneself and in other people, understand emotions and emotional language, manage emotions in oneself and in other people, and use emotions to facilitate cognitive activities and motivate adaptive behavior. The classroom learner faces tasks nearly every day that draw on these skills. And so do teachers and counselors. These emotion-related skills could be grouped into four clusters or "branches" (Mayer & Salovey, 1997): (a) perceiving emotions, (b) using emotions to facilitate thought, (c) understanding emotions, and (d) managing emotions in a way that enhances personal growth and social relations. And it is not difficult to imagine how such skills inform the counseling relationship and could predict the success of counseling interventions.

The chapters in this excellent book explore the role of emotions and emotional competencies in various aspects of school counseling. Depending on the chapter, the vantage point varies—from the counselor, to teachers, to students, and to interactions among any of these actors. A developmental perspective is obvious in the progression of the chapters, and the desirability of focusing on students with different kinds of needs is apparent as well. Some of the chapters provide suggestions for cutting-edge applications of emotional intelligence such as in work with music or with computers. In the next century, the school day will not look much like the traditional set of classes and periods we experienced in our 20th-century educations. Rather, the role of the school in creating not just an educated populace but also prosocial citizens who can contribute to society's greater good will increasingly dictate the activities of teachers and counselors. Whether this trend is desirable or not is neither the focus of these remarks nor of this volume; nonetheless, the salience of emotion-related skills in the mission of schools of the 21st century would seem undeniable.

REFERENCES

Mayer, J. D., & Salovey, P. (1997). What is emotional intelligence? In P. Salovey & D. Sluyter (Eds.), *Emotional development and emotional intelligence: Educational implications* (pp. 3–31). New York: Basic Books.

Mayer, J. D., Salovey, P., & Caruso, D. R. (2004). Emotional intelligence: Theory, findings, and implications. *Psychological Inquiry, 15,* 197–215.

Salovey, P., & Mayer, J. D. (1990). Emotional intelligence. *Imagination, Cognition, and Personality, 9,* 185–211.

Contributors

Jennifer Allen, M.A.T., is an educational consultant who works in public and private schools both nationally and internationally to address issues and concerns related to school climate. The focus of her work is largely on creating a safe and supportive school climate in order to promote students' academic achievement. Former Director of Education and Consultation and currently Senior Project Director at the Center for Social and Emotional Learning, Ms. Allen is the lead investigator on the development of ASSESS, a series of surveys designed to provide data regarding student, staff, and parent perceptions of school social and emotional safety as the basis for school improvement. She has likewise served as director of the organization's annual national/international summer institute, Educating Minds and Hearts: Safe Schools, Healthy Character Development, Academic Success, and Social Emotional Education. A former high school English teacher and high school assistant principal, she was a middle school principal for more than 10 years, where she and her staff were recipients of extensive grant funding for their comprehensive school reform efforts related to school climate. She is the co-author of the *New York State Interpersonal Violence Prevention Education Guidelines* (2002), and is currently a doctoral candidate at Teachers College, Columbia University, where her research is focused on the relationship between school climate and academic achievement.

Jennifer Lauren Axelrod, PhD, is a Project Director at the Collaborative for Academic, Social and Emotional Learning. In that role, she provides consultation and technical assistance to Chicago Public Schools, implementing social and emotional programs. Dr. Axelrod also works to integrate services for children at-risk for social, emotional, and academic difficulties with the development of comprehensive, coordinated social and emotional programming. Prior to joining CASEL, Dr. Axelrod was an assistant professor at the University of Maryland, School of Medicine and the Associate Director of the Center for School Mental Health Assistance (CSMHA). In addition to her research interests in social and emotional learning and school mental health, Dr. Axelrod is a licensed psychologist and a nationally certified school psychologist.

Kevin P. Brady is presently an Assistant Professor in the Graduate Program in Educational Leadership at The City University of New York (CUNY)–Queens College. Dr. Brady received his PhD in 2000 with a concentration in educational policy studies and school law from the University of Illinois at Urbana-Champaign. His current research focuses on emotional intelligence for school leaders, equity issues in school law and finance, and training school leaders in educational technology. His most recent publications appear in *West's Education Law Reporter, Children's Legal Rights Journal, Reading and Writing Quarterly*, and the *Brigham Young University Education and Law Journal*.

Sheila Brown has been a guidance counselor in District 2 in New York City for the past 15 years. She has developed and implemented a mentoring program for district guidance counselors and has planned and organized staff development for counselors. Sheila was instrumental in instituting Community School District Two's Crisis Team. For the past 3 years, she has been the Director of Project EXSEL, a social emotional learning pilot project funded by the Department of Education.

Linda Bruene Butler, M.Ed., has worked in the area of research, development, and dissemination of school-based programs in social and emotional learning for more than 20 years. Currently she is the director of the Social Decision Making/Problem Solving Program (SDM/PS) at the Behavioral Research and Training Institute at UMDNJ, University Behavioral HealthCare. She has also served as an adjunct faculty at the Department of Psychology at Rutgers University while in the role of Research Coordinator for the Improving Social Awareness/Social Problem Solving Project at Rutgers University, which was a NIMH grant funded project for the initial research and development of what is now The Social Decision Making/Problem Solving Program. Ms. Bruene Butler has been the primary trainer/consultant for four of the demonstration sites of New Jersey Center for Character Education, has trained and consulted in the area of social emotional learning to hundreds of school districts throughout the state and nationally, has published and lectured extensively in the social problem solving area, and has trained many others to become SDM/PS consultants and trainers. Ms. Bruene Butler co-developed the program's training manual for teachers and certified trainers. She was a major contributor and site visitor for the monograph entitled *Promoting Social and Emotional Learning: Guidelines for the Educator* that was published by the Association for Supervision and Curriculum Development in 1997. Her current area of interest is the use of technology to network school districts with advanced level SEL programming, to enhance pre-service and in-service professional development activities and as tools for internal district trainers, which she sees as a critical component of sustained program institutionalization.

Michael Dealy, PhD, is the headmaster of Bay Ridge Prepatory High School in Brooklyn, N.Y. and an adjunct associate professor at the New York University, Department of Applied Psychology. He holds a doctorate degree in Educational Psychology from Fordham University. Dr. Dealy is a New York State licensed psychologist, a certified school psychologist, and has permanent state certification as a teacher. He has worked for more than 35 years in the education and mental health fields in various capacities. He has taught students at several grade levels from K–12 and was an adjunct professor of psychology at Pace and Fordham universities. Dr. Dealy has expertise in learning disabilities, psychoeducational evaluation, crisis intervention, and suicide prevention. He has extensive clinical experience treating adolescents with depression and other forms psychopathology, children with terminal illness, and families in crisis. Dr. Dealy has several publications on the psychosocial functioning of children as related to bone injuries (in the *Handbook of Pediatric Orthopedic Surgery*) and chronic obstructive pulmonary disease (in *Pulmonary Rehabilitation* edited by John Bock, MD). Other publications include emotional intelligence and reading disabilities (forthcoming in the *Reading & Writing Quarterly*) and a book on Martial Arts Therapy. Dr. Dealy maintains a private practice in psychology.

Maurice J. Elias, PhD, is a Professor in the Psychology Department, Rutgers University, and Leadership Team Vice-Chair for the Collaborative for Academic, Social, and Emotional Learning (www.CASEL.org). He is the co-author of *Emotionally Intelligent Parenting* (2000), *Raising Emotionally Intelligent Teenagers* (2002), *Engaging the Resistant Child Through Computers and Social Problem-Solving Interventions in the Schools* (www.nprinc.com), and *Building Learning Communities with Character* (ASCD, 2002), as well as *Bullying, Peer*

Harassment, and Victimization in the Schools: The Next Generation of Prevention (Haworth, 2004). Dr. Elias is a licensed psychologist and an approved provider of professional development for educators in New Jersey. Dr. Elias is married and the father of two children.

Charles Fasano holds a PhD in School Psychology and a masters degree in Special Education. He is the executive director and founder of Bay Ridge Preparatory School, a K–12 school located in Bay Ridge Brooklyn. Dr. Fasano is a licensed psychologist and a specialist in learning disabilities. He has been a school headmaster for the past 10 years and has worked in the field of education as a teacher and school psychologist for more than 20 years. Dr. Fasano is certified by New York State as a trainer in violence prevention and child abuse prevention. He was a crisis counselor in a psychiatric residential program and has developed and directed several youth intervention programs in New York City. He was also a staff psychologist in a hospital setting providing psychoeducational evaluation and counseling to children and families.

Julaine E. Field, PhD, LPC, is an Assistant Professor in the Department of Counseling and Educational Psychology at Slippery Rock University. She received her PhD in Counselor Education at North Carolina State University, Raleigh, North Carolina. Her counseling career has included work as an elementary and high school counselor, social work case manager and therapist, college counselor, consultant and trainer for a domestic violence and sexual assault shelter, and therapist in private practice serving children, adults, couples, and families. Her primary research interests include counselor advocacy and gender identity, and gender roles of females.

Brian S. Friedlander, PhD is a licensed and certified school psychologist with expertise in the area of assistive technology. Dr. Friedlander maintains an assistive technology practice, which provides assessments, workshops, and individual training in the area of assistive computer technology. He is an adjunct faculty member at the College of St. Elizabeth and at Lesley University, where he teaches courses in educational technology. Dr. Friedlander is also the co-author of *Engaging the Resistant Child Through Computers: A Manual to Facilitate Social Emotional Learning* (Maurice J. Elias, Brian S. Friedlander, and Steven E. Tobias, New York: National Professional Resources, 2001). Dr. Friedlander is the publisher of *Inclusion Times*, a nationally distributed special education newsletter that is published by AssistiveTek, LLC. He also moderates the Assistive Technology eGroup, which can be accessed by going to http:// groups.yahoo.com/group/attechnology. Dr. Friedlander is a frequent presenter on the topic of assistive technology at National and State Conferences. Dr. Friedlander can be reached at brian@assistivetek.com.

Lauren Hyman is a consultant and speaker in the field of social emotional learning, emotional intelligence, and violence prevention. She is a past teacher and has experience directing training institutes and providing on-site technical assistance for administrators, counselors, teachers, and parents at public and independent schools across the country. She is a certified consultant to the U.S. Department of Justice, Office for Victims of Crime, and a Grant Reviewer for the U.S. Department of Education. She has an M.A. in school counseling from New York University. She is an adjunct faculty member in the Steinhardt School of Education at New York University, an instructor at Bank Street College of Education in New York and The City University of New York. She is the co-author of *RESPECT: Interpersonal Violence Prevention Resource Guide for Parents and Educators* (New York State Department of Education, 2002).

Jered B. Kolbert, PhD, is an Assistant Professor in the Department of Counseling and Educational Psychology as Slippery Rock University. He obtained his doctorate in counseling from The College of William and Mary, Williamsburg, Virginia. He has worked as a school counselor, marriage and family counselor, and substance abuse counselor. His primary research interests include bullying prevention and gender issues.

Courtney E. Martin is a writer, teacher, and film maker living in Brooklyn, New York. She teaches English at Brooklyn College, writes freelance for a variety of local and national media, and makes documentary films on cross-cultural dialogue and feminism. She has worked with the Social and Emotional Learning program at The School @ Columbia University since its inception and is also the Editorial Director of Star Factor, a consulting firm devoted to coaching educators, business leaders, and entrepreneurs in Emotional Intelligence.

Maria McCabe, MA, NCC, NCSC, LPC, is a practicing elementary school counselor at Meadowbrook School in Northbrook, Illinois. In that capacity she has been responsible for designing and implementing a school-wide social emotional learning curriculum. She is an appointed member of the Children's Mental Health Partnership. She is also a member of the Executive Committee of the Partnership and serves as the co-chair of the School Age subcommittee. Prior to joining the Children's Mental Health Partnership, Ms. McCabe participated in the Children's Mental Health Task Force and helped to write the legislation that led to the passage of the Children's Mental Health Act 2003. She also served as the President of the Illinois School Counselor's Association and over the past 10 years helped with many initiatives to promote the role of the school counselor in Illinois.

Karen Mildener, M.S.Ed., has been employed by the New York City Department of Education for 7 years. She worked for 2 years as a Substance Abuse Prevention and Intervention Specialist in elementary schools before entering the Graduate Program in Counseling at Queens College, City University of New York. Ms. Mildener piloted an elementary school counseling grant, Project EXSEL, for Community School District 2 in Manhattan for 3 years. She is experienced in teacher partnerships and SEL program development. Ms. Mildener currently works at P.S. 89, an elementary school that stands in the shadow of what was the World Trade Center.

Barbara Muller-Ackerman, MA, LPC, NCC, NCSC, has been a practicing counselor in New Jersey for the past 13 years. She is the immediate past Elementary Vice-President for the American School Counselor Association (2000–2002), after serving for 2 years as ASCA's Public Relations Chair. During her tenure in national leadership, she edited *A Year of School Counseling: Tools & Techniques for K–12 Themes Throughout the Year* and the *Public Relations Toolbox: A Collection of the Best Practices for School Counselor* (both by Youthlight, 2002). She has been active on the state level, in the New Jersey School Counselor Association, as President (1996–1997), and on numerous committees. She has served on the Advisory Board of the New Jersey School Counseling Initiative and has authored *A-Z Advocacy: A Primer for Promoting Your School Counseling Program* (NJSCA, 1995). Barbara currently moderates an online community for elementary school counselors, elementary-counselors@yahoogroups.com, and hosts the school counselor chats on Tapped In, the Global School Network's forum for educators. She writes for the Internet with articles published by *Education World*, the *Family Education Network*, *Home School Learning Network*, and *Teachers First*.

John Pellitteri, PhD, is the director of the Graduate Program in Counseling at Queens College, City University of New York. He holds a doctorate degree in Counseling Psychology from New York University and an MEd in School Counseling from Teachers College, Columbia University. He is a licensed psychologist, a certified school counselor, and has degrees and certifications in Music Therapy and Music Education. Dr. Pellitteri has worked for more than 20 years with children and adolescents in numerous general and special education settings. He was a school counselor for the Archdiocese Drug Abuse Prevention Program and a teacher at various private schools. He has extensive clinical experience as a music therapist in such agencies as the Northside Center for Child Development, Jewish Board of Family & Children Services, and the Heartsong Music & Art Therapy program. In addition, he has experience as a counselor in hospital and residential settings for mentally ill adults. Dr. Pellitteri has conducted research studies on the assessment of emotional intelligence and on its relationship to adaptive personality functions. He has publications, has served on advisory boards, and has made numerous presentations on emotional intelligence. Dr. Pellitteri maintains a private practice in psychology providing psychotherapy, testing, and consultation services in the Brooklyn, New York area.

Victoria Poedubicky, BS, holds state certification in Student Personnel Services from The College of New Jersey, has 25 years in education and is currently a school counselor at Bartle Elementary School in Highland Park, NJ. Her expertise is in the implementation of social and emotional learning in educational settings and its application in the counseling field. She serves as a presenter, trainer, and supervisor of the Social Decision Making Lab and has published several articles most recently, *Students and Teachers Both Win When Social-Emotional Learning/EQ and IQ are Combined in Education* (NJJSCD 2002) and co-author of a book chapter entitled *Social Decision Making/Problem Solving: A Theoretically Sound, Evidence-Based Framework for SEL Programming* forthcoming in a book on emotional intelligence in the classroom published by Corwin Press to be released in 2005.

Cristi Riccio Keane earned a Masters of Arts in Organizational Psychology and an Ed.M in Counseling Psychology from Teachers College, Columbia University. She worked in the design and implementation of a Social and Emotional development program, Project EXSEL (Excellence in Social and Emotional Literacy), in the NYC school system. The program design was based on Emotional Intelligence theories and sought to provide elementary school students with tools to strengthen their social and emotional skills. Mrs. Keane has also worked providing individual and group counseling services to at-risk youth in the NYC schools.

Claudia Shelton is President of the Hopewell Group, LLC, providing guidance to businesses and schools on personal and professional development. Previously a school counselor and teacher, Shelton co-authored *Understanding Emotion in the Classroom* (2004). She is a nationally certified psychologist, a licensed and nationally certified professional counselor, and a frequent keynote and seminar speaker throughout the US and abroad. For more info and published articles see www.claudiamshelton.com.

Joseph Sperlazza, PsyD, holds a doctorate in organizational psychology from the Rutgers University Graduate School of Applied and Professional Psychology and currently serves as Assistant Professor with the Fairleigh Dickinson University School of Education. There he serves as co-coordinator of Fairleigh Dickinson University QUEST teacher preparation program. His past professional experience includes serving as the Supervisor of Programs and Services for the (32,000 student) Jersey City, New Jersey Public Schools where he developed and managed a number of student support services programs such as social emotional learning, character education, sudden traumatic loss, crisis intervention, comprehensive guidance and counseling, school and community agency partnership, and alternative education programs. Before assuming his district supervision responsibilities, Dr. Sperlazza served as a school psychologist, as an alternative education program teacher and developer, and as a regular education teacher in the Jersey City district.

Robin Stern, PhD, is an educator, psychotherapist, and consultant in New York City. She teaches on emotional intelligence, communication, gender and technology at Teachers College, Columbia University and is the Social-Emotional Learning Specialist at The School @ Columbia University. Additionally, Dr. Stern has worked as an SEL consultant with Project EXSEL, senior supervisor at the Hunter College School of Education Leadership Center and a member of the facilitation team of Project Renewal, all efforts to enhance the lives of educators and educational leaders in New York City. Robin holds a masters degree in Personality and Social Development, a doctorate in Applied Psychology and Research Design, as well as a post-doctoral certificate in Psychoanalytic Group Psychotherapy. Robin is also a consultant at the Children's Advocacy Center in the area of emotional abuse. Additionally, she serves on the board of Educators for Social Responsibility. Finally, Robin was one of the founding board members of The Woodhull Institute for Ethical Leadership and has two amazing children, Scott and Melissa.

Susan Stillman, NCC, NCSC, LPC, has been the sole school counselor in a K–8 school in Bolton, CT for many years, and has been instrumental in establishing a social emotional learning initiative at the school. She has presented throughout the state on social emotional learning and school counseling. The school counseling program that she designed and implemented received a Professional Recognition Award from the Connecticut School Counseling Association for a Comprehensive Guidance and Counseling Program. She has served a 1 year appointment as Assistant Professor in the Department of Counseling and School Psychology at Southern Connecticut State University, and currently is an Adjunct Professor in the Department. Ms. Stillman is President-Elect of the Connecticut School Counseling Association. She is a doctoral student in Educational Leadership and Change at Fielding Graduate Institute in Santa Barbara, CA.

Steven Tobias is the director of the Center for Child & Family Development in Morristown, NJ. He is also a co-author of *Emotionally Intelligent Parenting,* and *Raising an Emotionally Intelligent Teenager.* He provides consultation to schools and workshops to educators and parents regarding social and emotional development.

James Tobin, PhD, is a consultant with a specialization in social emotional learning, conflict management, and organizational change. He has worked with school systems and colleges throughout the United States and in the Netherlands. He currently teaches at Ramapo College of New Jersey but has also taught at Adelphi, Hampton, and New York University. A former staff developer and Coordinator of Administrator Training for the Resolving Conflict Creatively Program in New York City, Dr. Tobin has trained thousands of principals, teachers, parent, and student mediators in social emotional skills. As a curriculum writer, he has written reading materials for such publishers as Harcourt Brace, Macmillan, and Scholastic and has produced curricula for adult learners in the workplace. His most recent publication is the book *SMART School Leaders: Leading with Emotional Intelligence* (Kendall Hunt Publishing, 2003), which he co-authored with Dr. Janet Patti of Hunter College of the City University of New York.

Toni Tollerud, PhD, is a professor of Counseling at Northern Illinois University, DeKalb, Illinois. For more than 15 years she has coordinated the school counseling program and has assisted in promoting school counseling with the Illinois State Board of Education by chairing the committee that developed new state standards for school counselors in 2002. Dr. Tollerud has also been President of the Illinois Counseling Association, Illinois School Counselors Association and Illinois Counselor Educators and Supervisors. She has won numerous awards as an advocate and leader. From 1999 to 2004 she was the Executive Director of the Illinois School Counselors' Academy, which provided state-wide professional development to counselors on a wide variety of topics including career development, academic achievement, and social/

emotional literacy. She is part of the Illinois Children's Mental Health Task Force and Partnership that mandated social/emotional literacy in all schools. Currently she is part of the state standards writing team and consults with school counselors in the design and implementation of comprehensive pro-gramming for all students.

Acknowledgments

I thank my colleagues, Jesse Vazquez and Howard Margolis, for their support, wisdom, and guidance in the world of academia. Thanks also to my students, Rachel Goodman and Ben Laudicina, for their assistance in reviewing the book manuscript. I also thank my wife, Leda Sabio, for her support during the endless hours of work on the project, and my children, Alexander and Maya, for the joyous emotions that they bring to me. I acknowledge the memories of my father, Mario, and my sister, Joan. A special thank you goes to my good friend and mentor, Michael Dealy, for his guidance and support throughout the years and for the emotional intelligence that he has developed in myself and in others.

—J. P.

With great appreciation I thank all of the counselors whose meaningful work in schools continues to ease the way for students and enhances their emotional lives. I acknowledge the leaders in the field of emotional intelligence, whose inspirational work launched this important movement in education: Daniel Goleman, Maurice Elias, Linda Lantieri, Linda Bruene, Janet Patti, Cary Cherniss, Richard Boyatzis, and Deborah O'Neil. In particular, I thank the whole Project EXSEL team, both those who created it and those who carried it out: Sheila Brown, Marjorie Robbins, Barbara Leventer Luque, Donna Klein, Jim Tobin, Pat Hunter, Christi Riccio-Keane, Karen Mildener, and our amazing web designer, Mauricio Miraglia, and web masters, Angela Peng, Rushika Sah, and Kate Casano. I thank my co-editors, John, Claudia, and Barbara, for collaborating on this important project. I thank my brilliant research assistant, Courtney Martin, who keeps me organized and sane. Most of all, I thank my emotionally intelligent children, Scott and Melissa, and my loving partner, Frank, for their continuous love and support of my work.

—R. S.

I thank all those people who shaped my own understanding of emotionally intelligent education. Jay Cherry, Janine Roberts, and Jack Wideman at the University of Massachusetts provided early guidance and training and a philosophy of caring. Jane Shipp and Marg Ayres of Renbrook School are educators with intelligence and sensitivity who helped me greatly in developing my own approaches to working with children. Linda Lantieri has been a model and friend in sharing her own vision of emotionally intelligent education. To all the colleagues, peers, friends, and schools around the country who opened their classrooms and thoughts, I am most grateful. Finally, to my family—Jim, Chris, Ryan, Kim, Kathleen, and Randy—I am thankful for their unending support, encouragement, and love.

—C. S.

I offer heartfelt gratitude to all the school counselors I have had the privilege of working with, sharing with, and learning from. Given the honor of association leadership positions in this wonderful field has allowed me to travel and meet more than most; learning from some incredibly talented and dedicated professionals who are in schools each day doing the work that is making a difference in the lives of our nation's children. I offer appreciation to my mentors in counseling; Jane Runte, Betty Caccavo, Drew Cangelosi, and Phylis Philipson, who nurtured my growth and encouraged me along this path. Thanks to Jane Bluestein and Josh Freedman for so many lessons about emotional intelligence, not only in the work they do but most especially in being who they are. To my co-authors, I thank you for your patience, for your wisdom, for your sharing, and your modeling of the content of this book throughout its writing. Thanks to my family—my husband and best friend, Mike; my children, Jaime and Allison; and my mother, Rosalind Perlish Muller—for being there with endless encouragement, steadfast support, and much love.

—B. M. A.

I

INTRODUCTION

The introductory chapter in this section discusses the premise that emotional intelligence is inherently part of the professional counseling tradition and is consistent with the current roles of school counselors. It introduces the notion of counselors as the "emotional centers" in the school. It then presents an overview of the chapters and the range of theoretical and professional topics that are covered.

1

The Emotional Intelligence of School Counseling

John Pellitteri
Queens College, CUNY

Robin Stern
*The School at Columbia University
and the Woodhull Institute for Ethical Leadership*

Claudia Shelton
The Hopewell Group, LLC

Barbara Muller-Ackerman
Parsippany Counseling Center

There has always been a natural connection between emotional intelligence and the work of the professional school counselor. Long before the term *emotional intelligence* was used by Peter Salovey and Jack Mayer in 1990, school counselors were focused on the social-emotional development of students (Sink, 2005; Smith & Mink, 1969). The interpersonal dynamics that characterize the counseling process rest on the emotional interactions of the counselor and client. Whether the school counselor is working with an individual student, facilitating a group, teaching a class, consulting with a parent or teacher, or intervening in a whole ecological system, the emotional aspects of human relationships come into play. Human relationships are the medium in which counselors work. It is through interpersonal relationships that counselors can effectively facilitate positive change at different levels in a school.

Effective counselors are inherently emotionally intelligent, whether they know of the term or not. Many are already are aware of the concept and seek to integrate it into their own practice and their school communities at large.

The development of emotional intelligence is of the utmost importance in the lives of school counselors for a number of compelling reasons. Counselors not only face a range of emotional issues in the students and parents they serve but also in the administrators and teachers with whom they collaborate and consult. Counselors are in the unique and challenging position of balancing the perspectives, wants, and needs of all of these parties, essentially serving as the "emotional center" of the complex system of the school community. Consequently, counselors can become increasingly pressed to manage not only the emotions of the people around them but their own emotions as well. As the school's emotional center, it is essential that they develop the foundational skills of emotional competence, which begins with self-awareness. The emotional intelligence of the counselor not only sets a necessary example of leadership but supports the counselor's own well-being and personal adjustment to a challenging work environment.

School counseling is an emotionally demanding, dynamic, and fast-paced profession that can be inspiring and rewarding as well as discouraging and taxing. Many counselors recognize the unique importance of their work and the necessity to address the emotional needs of others. However, some of the empathetic and caring individuals who are drawn to this humanitarian career unfortunately end up burning out or losing the driving spirit that once motivated them. This may occur for a variety of reasons, which might include the need: to feel successful, to recognize their impact on others, to be appreciated by others, or to actualize one's self-concept and uniqueness as a person. Our careers and work roles are tied to our identities and form a significant aspect of life's meaning (Super, 1990). When positive emotions become associated with our professional work, our careers become more meaningful and satisfying. Successfully meeting the challenges in the school counseling profession, therefore, can have a larger significance for the individual counselor.

Emotional self-awareness is essential for counselors to recognize and to meet the range of personal and professional demands in today's schools. When counselors access and maintain connections with their emotional resources, they can begin to establish themselves as sustainable and inspired emotional leaders. They can also find deeper meaning in the quality of the human relationships that are a part of their work. This book is a testament to the importance of the school counselor and to the inherently humanistic and emotionally based nature of the profession.

THE HUMANISTIC PSYCHOLOGY
OF EMOTIONAL INTELLIGENCE

Humanistic views have become deeply embedded in the defining characteristics of professional counseling (Gelso & Fretz, 2001). Carl Rogers was a major historical influence and established a person-centered approach that has become a cornerstone of counseling (Nystul, 1999), even for counselors who favor other clinical orientations. Rogers' (1961) core conditions, considered to be necessary elements for therapeutic change, include empathy, genuineness, and unconditional positive regard. *Empathy* is a cornerstone of emotional intelligence in that it requires the perception and awareness of another's feeling states and an ability to create sensitive responses that communicate an understanding of those feelings. *Genuineness* means being an authentic person, which requires self-awareness and openness to understanding the range of our emotions. *Unconditional positive regard* means maintaining flexibility, optimism, and a positive affective state, in order to find positive aspects of the clients.

When a student experiences these core conditions, he or she begins to thrive as a person and can increase emotional intelligence. The experience of empathy not only establishes the therapeutic alliance but can lead a student to develop greater self-awareness and emotional knowledge through an acknowledgment of reflected feelings. When the counselor is genuine, he or she becomes trustworthy and has a deeper impact on the student, who in turn may become more genuine and insightful as well. When a student receives unconditional positive regard from a counselor, he or she may increase in self-acceptance and positive self-worth. The core conditions create potential for the development of a person's identity integration, which in turn increases the potential of that person to be better adjusted to the social world. Improvement in a student's social-emotional functioning usually involves, in some way, a qualitative improvement in these core human qualities. A counselor needs to have these qualities developed in his or her self to create these conditions for change in students, teachers, and other school personnel. It is essential, then, that counselors actively work toward developing their own emotional intelligence.

It may be challenging at times to sustain these conditions when a student exhibits disruptive behaviors, shows resistance toward receiving help, or is confrontational. Such student responses can activate biases and strong negative reactions in the counselor and other school personnel. The emotionally intelligent counselor, however, does not become a victim to negative emotions (whether within the self or in others). The counselor uses emotional intelli-

gence abilities to remain centered in the midst of conflict, to maintain a positive and flexible stance, and to see beneath the student's "symptoms" to
understand the underlying affective processes. Effective professional counselors not only understand the emotional worlds of their clients/students but also
direct the student's emotional energy toward positive channels that facilitate
growth and development. This is the essence of unconditional positive
regard—to separate the worth of a person from the consequences of his or her
behavior. Emotional intelligence comes into play when the counselor resists
the tendency to be judgmental and maintains appropriate and "effective" emotions toward the person while understanding the intrapersonal and
interpersonal factors that influenced the student's behavior.

THE WORK OF THE SCHOOL COUNSELOR

Emotional intelligence is relevant not only for the social-emotional aspects of
school counselors' work but for the academic and vocational aspects as well.
School counselors are continuously faced with issues of student motivation,
learning difficulties, and special needs. Developing emotional intelligence in
students increases their flexibility, persistence, frustration tolerance, impulse
control, and optimism. To the extent that emotional factors influence self-efficacy and achievement motivation, emotional intelligence is essential for
academic success. Likewise, career development involves deeply personal self-
examination and complex decision-making processes. Using emotions in an intelligent manner is important in making career choices. Satisfaction in career
and college decisions depends in part on self-awareness, which is the foundation of emotional intelligence development.

   In addition to work with students, professional school counselors work with
teachers, administrators, parents, and the whole school ecology. Empathy, genuineness, and unconditional positive regard are also important conditions for
the personal and professional development of school personnel. The interpersonal relationships a counselor develops with colleagues and school staff are essential in creating an emotionally intelligent school environment. When a
counselor understands the emotional world of other educators, he or she can
better support them in their own process of self-awareness and social awareness. This effort increases the "critical mass" of emotionally intelligent participants in the system, which in turn increases emotional sensitivity in the school
environment as a whole. If students are to develop emotional intelligence,
then their environments must provide the conditions to support that development. Emotionally intelligent school counselors should think like social psychologists in working not only at an individual or small group level but by

addressing the social-emotional dimensions of the school ecology as a whole (Aubrey & Lewis, 1988).

An important role of the professional school counselor is that of an educational leader. The school counselor is in a unique role in that he or she consults with administrators, teachers of all grade levels, support service personnel, parents, and outside agencies. In this position the counselor can facilitate school-wide efforts to incorporate emotional intelligence into the classroom, the curriculum, and the general environment. An effective leader possesses the qualities of emotional intelligence and motivates others toward higher goals. It is through direct and indirect leadership roles that a counselor can influence the school ecology. An emotionally intelligent school counselor works to develop a mindset or framework for administrators and teachers that is sensitive to the emotional needs of the students and personnel alike. A focus on the emotional dimensions of the school ecology can bring a humanistic tone into the school. Good leaders lead by example. In this way, a counselor inspires others to be more emotionally intelligent by the effects of his or her own emotionally evolved model of awareness and management.

School counseling is a dynamic profession that encompasses multiple roles and responsibilities (Davis, 2005). Emotional intelligence is a "core condition" necessary for the professional to be effective. Emotionally intelligent counselors have flexibility, adaptability, a positive attitude, and balanced sensitivity. Areas of knowledge other than emotional intelligence are also important for school counselors such as developmental psychology, the organizational dynamics of the school, instructional and learning practices, and programmatic needs. When a counselor uses emotional intelligence abilities, however, he or she enhances the quality of the work and taps into a deeper, more meaningful dimension.

For example, a brief encounter with a student regarding a program change may at times have the potential for the counselor to assist the student beyond the simple need of a schedule. The emotionally intelligent counselor may sense something unsettled within the student or within their interpersonal interactions. The emotional perception of the counselor is important in uncovering the "tip of the iceberg" and the possibly troubled world of a desperate student seeking help. At other times a pleasant and encouraging encounter with the student can be the basis of a connection that, a year later, may become a counseling relationship. The positive emotional tone of the counselor makes him or her approachable, sets up the counseling office as a supportive place, and establishes the counselor's reputation in the collective consciousness of the student body as an adult who genuinely cares. The emotionally unintelligent counselor merely sees a program change, misses this deeper dimension, and does not use

the windows of opportunity for connection. The attention to a student's underlying affect enables the counselor to focus on prevention by detecting problems
before they begin or at an early stage of formation.

Like the counseling profession, the field of emotional intelligence is in dynamic development. Different theories provide contrasting definitions of emotional intelligence and measurement instruments rest on different conceptualizations with inconsistent results. While theorists and researchers push the
emotional intelligence construct into a next generation of its evolution, numerous school-based programs move ahead with the enthusiasm of this popular idea. It is critical, however, for professional school counselors to be
knowledgeable about the various models and to use existing emotionally
intelligent measures in appropriate and effective ways.

THE BRIDGE BETWEEN THEORY AND PRACTICE

This book is applicable for school counseling practitioners, counseling psychologists, counselor educators, and counselors in training, as well as for
other educational professionals who may wish to gain useful perspectives on
incorporating emotional intelligence into their work. The book attempts to
bridge the gap between theory and practice, between the academician and
the practitioner, and between the graduate school classroom and the school
counselor's consultation room. Without an organizing theoretical framework
and an empirical psychological foundation, the work of the counselor can become misguided, ineffective, and frustrating, despite the real-world experiences and best intentions of the professional. However, if theoretical models
are not actively processed by the practitioner and adjusted to the situation,
they run the risk of becoming dry and disconnected sets of concepts that lose
their relevance to clinical work. The professional counselor and graduate student alike must understand that theoretical models will not perfectly fit the
real-world scenarios. The use of models and concepts must be flexible and
adaptive and may only partially explain behaviors. Theory can guide clinical
interventions to a limited degree. The real-world examples and vignettes,
however, are not mere stories of successful counseling. Counseling interventions must be understood in the context of emotional intelligence (or other
psychological) models to appreciate the importance and depth of the intervention. Understanding one's clinical work within a larger framework creates
meaning and integrates the various tasks of the professional. Table 1.1 outlines the theoretical models and concepts as well as the professional issues
and applications that are referred to in each chapter.

One way that this bridge between theory and practice can be built is for the reader to reflect on his or her own emotional world and affective processes. Self-awareness is a foundation of emotional intelligence. Counselors must develop their own emotional awareness to effectively apply the principles and methods of emotional intelligence to school settings. It is the practitioner who makes the translation of theory into clinical practice by first "practicing" on oneself. In this way the theoretical models of emotional intelligence can come to life and have personal relevance for the counselor. Counseling is an art as well as a science (Nystul, 1999). The professional school counselor must be creative and flexible to use the principles of emotional intelligence in a manner that is best suited for the particular situation. It is an artistic endeavor to meet the various needs of diverse people in a school setting, to perceive the larger picture that connects seemingly unrelated events in an integrative manner, and to direct the emotional energies of students, teachers, and administrators toward a greater good.

This book seeks to present both the art and science of emotionally intelligent school counseling. It offers theoretical models and empirically supported interventions that can frame the way a counselor thinks and works. It also offers case examples and stories of emotionally oriented counseling in the schools that illustrate the wisdom and experience of practitioners. The reader may choose to focus on the chapters that are most relevant to his or her purpose. It is important in the counseling profession, however, to find a balance between conceptual frameworks and practical clinical application.

OVERVIEW OF THE BOOK

The organization of the book includes a foundation section and four application sections. The foundation section (chaps. 2–4) sets the groundwork for understanding the school counselor and emotional intelligence. Barbara Muller-Ackerman and Claudia Shelton, in chapter 2, give a historical perspective on the evolving roles of school counselors and the recent national standards of the profession. They emphasize the importance of counselors as facilitative leaders and the skills required to support the personal-social, academic, and career development of all students. John Pellitteri, in chapter 3, describes and compares the major emotional intelligence theories and measurement approaches. He addresses the importance of being cautious when using emotional intelligence tests as the different models and their respective measures are notably distinct. In chapter 4, Robin Stern, Lauren Hyman, and Courtney Martin emphasize the importance of self-awareness, a foundation of emotional intelligence, in the personal and professional work of the school counselor. In their chapter they offer practical suggestions for using journals as a means of self reflection.

The first applications section (chaps. 5–8) addresses school environments and particular issues at each of the different school levels (elementary, middle school, and high school). Charles Fasano and John Pellitteri, in chapter 5, present three methods—teacher modeling, productive discipline, and psychology instruction—that can increase emotional awareness and positive interactions throughout the school's ecology. In chapter 6, Barbara Muller-Ackerman and Susan Stillman present the professional functions of elementary school counselors in supporting the school and the developmental foundations of its students. They consider the powerful benefits that arise from an integration of social emotional learning (SEL) concepts into a comprehensive developmental school counseling program. Claudia Shelton and Jennifer Allen, in chapter 7, focus on how self-awareness and the concept of "innersense" can aid in adolescent identity development and adjustment to middle school challenges. They offer techniques such as relax, temperament watch, and reflective feedback along with a needs vocabulary that give students tools to have dialogue about their emotions. Finally, in chapter 8, Michael Dealy and John Pellitteri describe the steps of how the counselor can map out the emotional dimensions of the school ecology and recognize the affective potential in each individual's life space. They offer stories that illustrate emotionally intelligent interventions for facilitating the environment as a resource for the teenager's journey through the high school years.

The second applications section (chaps. 9–12) focuses on specific groups within the schools. Victoria A. Poedubicky, Linda Bruene Butler, and Joseph Sperlazza, in chapter 9, present the application of the social decision making/problem solving approach to counseling special need students. They describe the various social-emotional tools and illustrate, through three case studies, how these techniques can improve listening, self-control, and emotional regulation. In chapter 10, Karen Mildener and Cristi Riccio-Keane describe their collaborative and educational work with teachers in elementary schools. They illustrate the issues and challenges of developing and implementing an SEL curriculum. In chapter 11, Kevin Brady discusses leadership styles and their relation to emotional intelligence. He notes the impact that a school administrator's emotional resonance has on the school and how counselors can build bridges with administrators in promoting emotional intelligence. Julaine Field and Jered Kolbert, in chapter 12, emphasize the importance of parent's emotional intelligence and their impact on the child's development and the family system. They describe how counselors can use consultation, brief family counseling, and presentations to parent groups as a means to facilitate emotional intelligence.

The third applications section (chaps. 13 and 14) focuses on special modalities. In chapter 13, John Pellitteri describes the links between music and emotions and presents adaptations of music therapy methods for facilitating emotional learning. He describes how the counselor can incorporate these experiential methods in individual and group counseling as well as in consultation with music educators. Maurice Elias, Brian Friedlander, and Steven Tobias, in chapter 14, discuss how computers and digital technologies can be used and integrated with social skills development. They offer examples of software programs and activities that can be used to develop goal setting and planning for student portfolios.

The final section (chaps. 15–17) presents applications of emotional intelligence at the school, district, and state levels. Linda Bruene Butler, Victoria A. Poedubicky, and Joseph Sperlazza, in chapter 15, present case studies of SEL through comprehensive school counseling at the Bartle School in New Jersey. They describe structures that are established with the integration of research-based SEL programs. In chapter 16, Sheila Brown, James Tobin, and Robin Stern present the development of the districtwide project EXSEL (EXcellence in Social-Emotional Learning) that targeted several New York City elementary schools. They describe how counselors were chosen as the centerpiece for the program and how the project became essential in responding to the student and community needs after September 11. Finally, Maria McCabe, Toni Tollerud, and Jennifer Axelrod, in chapter 17, present the development of professional counselors in Illinois and the recently created Children's Mental Health Act. They highlight the inclusion of counselors in the legislation and the importance of SEL in state policies on mental health and school districts educational programming.

As one of the purposes of the book is to bridge the gap between practitioners and academicians, Table 1.1 is presented to give a context to each of the chapters. This table assists in providing an overview of the range of topics covered in the book. It lists the theories and concepts and/or the professional issues and applications that are emphasized or at least referred to in the chapters. Column 1 notes whether the chapter topics are based, directly or indirectly, on any of the three major models of emotional intelligence. Column 2 notes whether related emotional-intelligence models and concepts are the focus of the chapter. Column 3 notes whether the chapter emphasizes or refers to other psychological theories and concepts that are not explicitly based on emotional intelligence. It is important to understand the theoretical basis of the chapter topics to compare, integrate, and more fully conceptualize these ideas. With regard to

counseling applications, if a chapter refers to general issues, roles, and/or functions of professional school counseling, these topics are listed in column 4. If
the chapter refers to methods of application and/or particular techniques to be
used by practitioners, these are listed in column 5. The last column lists any
groups or settings that are illustrated in a particular chapter. This table can be a
guide for readers who seek particular topics or for graduate course instructors
who wish to focus student's learning.

REFERENCES

Aubrey, R., & Lewis, J. (1988). Social issues and the counseling profession in the 1980's and
    1990's. In R. Hayes & R. Aubrey (Eds.). *New directions for counseling and human develop-
    ment* (pp. 286–303). Denver, CO: Love Publishers.
Davis, T. (2005). *Exploring school counseling: Professional practices and perspectives.* Boston:
    Houghton Mifflin.
Gelso, C., & Fretz, B. (2001). *Counseling psychology* (2nd. ed.). Belmont, CA: Thomson/
    Wadsworth.
Nystul, M. (1999). *Introduction to counseling: An art and science perspective.* Boston: Allyn &
    Bacon.
Rogers, C. (1961). *On becoming a person.* Boston: Houghton Mifflin.
Salovey, P., & Mayer, J. (1990) Emotional intelligence. *Imagination, Cognition, and Personal-
    ity, 9,* 185–211.
Sink, C. (2005). *Contemporary school counseling: Theory, research and practice.* Boston:
    Houghton Mifflin.
Smith, C. E., & Mink, O. (1969). *Foundations of guidance and counseling: Multidisciplinary
    readings.* Philadelphia: Lippincott.
Super, D. (1990). A life-span, life-space approach to career development. In D. Brown & L.
    Brooks (Eds.), *Career choice and development: Applying contemporary theory to practice*
    (2nd ed., pp. 197–261). San Francisco: Jossey-Bass.

TABLE 1.1
Chapter Topics

Chapter	Major EI Model	Related EI Models and Concepts	Other Psychological Theories and Concepts	Professional Issues	Professional Applications and Techniques	Populations and Settings
1		Self-awareness	Humanistic psychology	Counselor roles and functions		
2	Mayer and Salovey			History of counseling; professional standards; counselor roles and functions		
3	Mayer and Salovey; Goleman; Bar-On			Measurement applications		
4	Mayer and Salovey; Goleman	Self-awareness		Counselor development	Journals for self-reflection	
5		Self- and other awareness	Social learning; moral development	Psychoeducation; Consultation	Student discipline; psychology instruction	Middle/high schools
6	Goleman	Social-emotional learning		Counselor roles and functions		Elementary school
7		Temperament; self-awareness	Identity development	Developmental guidance	Feedback and self-regulation techniques	Middle school
8		Social awareness	Ecological systems/field theory		Systems interventions; human relations	High school

(continued)

13

TABLE 1.1 *(continued)*

Chapter	Major EI Model	Related EI Models and Concepts	Other Psychological Theories and Concepts	Professional Issues	Professional Applications and Techniques	Populations and Settings
9	Goleman	Social decision making/problem solving	Reality therapy; cognitive-behavioral therapy		Counseling interventions; social skills training	Special needs students
10	Goleman	Social-emotional learning		Consultation; psychoeducation	Teacher collaboration	Elementary school; Teachers
11	Mayer and Salovey; Goleman;	Multiple intelligence	Leadership styles	Consultation		Administrators
12	Mayer and Salovey; Goleman		Family systems	Consultation		Parents/Families
13	Mayer and Salovey		Music psychology; music therapy	Consultation psychoeducation	Relaxation techniques; Group counseling	Music educators
14		Social decision making/problem solving			Incorporating technology; portfolio activities	
15		Social decision making/problem solving		Consultation	Collaboration	Schoolwide program
16		Social-emotional learning		Consultation; psychoeducation	Collaboration; crisis intervention	District program
17		Social-emotional learning		Advocate for policies		State education department

14

II

FOUNDATIONS

This section presents some of the basic and elemental foundations of the book on which subsequent chapters may be built. Chapter 2 describes the history and professional roles of school counselors, as it is important for practitioners and students to understand the evolving role of counselors toward more broad-based systemic interventions. Chapter 3 presents the theories and measurement tools of emotional intelligence to develop a deeper understanding of the concept and its issues, controversies, and challenges. Chapter 4 focuses on self-awareness, which is a central facet to both counseling and emotional intelligence. As is reiterated throughout the book, for a counselor to implement emotional intelligence in a school setting, he or she must develop emotional intelligence in the self.

2

Practitioners' Perspective on School Counseling and Emotional Intelligence

Barbara Muller-Ackerman
Parsippany Counseling Center

Claudia Shelton
The Hopewell Group, LLC

As we examine how the concept and theories of emotional intelligence apply to school counseling, we as practitioners thought it was important to take perspective on several key questions: What do we see as the role and priorities of today's school counselor? What added value do concepts of emotional intelligence bring to this emerging role? What fundamental questions should school counselors and academicians be asking together to shed light on shared concerns? Does study of theories of emotional intelligence prepare counseling students to understand better the changing demands of their profession? These are not simple questions, and the answers are also complicated. However, we believe that their consideration brings to light why the material in this book is relevant to counselors and why the partnering of academicians and practitioners on these subjects is important to all of us.

HISTORICAL PERSPECTIVE ON THE ROLE
AND PRIORITIES OF SCHOOL COUNSELING

In the past 20 years, the school counseling profession has gone through a series of shifts and turns in response to the introduction of different counseling theories, changing national educational priorities, state and local school needs, and the needs of the students themselves. All these dynamic factors have added new dimensions to the school counselor's role and functions. The counselor's role has in fact continually evolved since the position's creation more than a hundred years ago.

In the early 20th century, school counseling didn't exist; vocational education, oriented to lead students into the world of work, was one of many tasks assigned the classroom teacher. In 1958, with the passage of the National Defense Education Act (Nystul, 2003), use of guidance counselors on a full-time basis in high schools became a common part of the educational landscape. As the United States sought prominence in the space race, guidance counselors were used in a limited role to place students who showed particular talent in math and science into postsecondary opportunities. Specific funding through the National Defense Act provided training in the college admissions process for counselors. Counselors' training in human development and counseling theory was relegated to use only in remediation or crisis counseling to help students successfully move onto their postsecondary education. Counselors concentrated on this population in the high schools and saw few others. Since the 1970s, however, the idea of developmental counseling has come into prominence. Within the scope of a school counseling program, professionals began focusing on developmental activities for all students.

In the past 20 years, the role of guidance counselors and the functions they perform have been more clearly established. Counselors' responsibilities grew, as did the skills counselors use in performing their jobs. Counselors were used for identifying those students at risk or with special needs, for facilitating career development, for academic counseling, and for intervening with issues of attendance and behavior. As the focus on the counseling functions being added to the job description increased, the term *guidance* was removed from the job title. Those who worked in a school setting were then called *school counselors*.

In the 1980s the middle school and elementary school counselor came into being to provide the comprehensive developmental models of school counseling that were being advocated by Bob Myrick, Norm Gysbers, and others. School counseling programs, which were planned and systematic though without uniform standards, were emerging throughout the nation.

In 1997, the American School Counselor Association (ASCA) published the National Standards for School Counseling Programs, written by Carol Dahir and Cheri Campbell. In the document, Dahir and Campbell, and the professional association for school counseling, defined the primary goal of the school counseling program to "promote and enhance *student learning* through the three broad and interrelated areas of *student development*" (ASCA, 1997, p. 11). These standards, and the competencies detailed in the National Standards, defined what students who experienced a Kindergarten through 12th-grade school counseling program should "know and be able to do" within the three domains of academic, career and personal/social development. In a time when each of the academic disciplines had created, or were creating, their national standards and frameworks, the school counseling profession offered their own, which are detailed in Figs. 2.1 to 2.3

States and their counselors either embraced or wrestled with the adoption of the National Standards. Some states, such as Utah and Arizona, had been

---

Standard A: Students will acquire the attitudes, knowledge and skills that contribute to effective learning in school across the life span.

Standard B: Students will complete school with the academic preparation essential to choose from a wide range of substantial post-secondary options, including college.

Standard C: Students will understand the relationship of academics to the world of work and to life at home and in the community.

FIG. 2.1.   Academic development standards.

Standard A: Students will acquire the skills to investigate the world of work in relation to knowledge of self and to make informed career decisions.

Standard B: Students will employ strategies to achieve future career success and satisfaction.

Standard C: Students will understand the relationship between personal qualities, education and training and the world of work.

FIG. 2.2.   Career development standards.

Standard A: Students will acquire the attitudes, knowledge and interpersonal skills to help them understand and respect self and others.

Standard B: Students will make decisions, set goals, and take necessary action to achieve goals.

FIG. 2.3.   Personal/social developmental standards.

working closely with career development competencies from the National Occupation Information Coordinating Committee (NOICC) to write their program models. Other states found that the common language of the National Standards added continuity to the field that had not existed before this time. Although education and business praised the standards, and although the "Sharing the Vision" document (ASCA, 1997) identified the Standards within a comprehensive developmental program, criticism was leveled that they did not go far enough in creating a complete and common model for school counselor practice.

In 2002 school counseling field leaders Myrick, Johnson, and Gysbers met with leaders in education reform, counselor educators, and counseling practitioners. ASCA convened this summit to discuss what a national model needed to include. One vision resulted from that collaboration, and in 2003, ASCA introduced the National Model for School Counseling Programs, written by Judy Bowers and Trish Hatch. The National Model described a comprehensive school counseling program, uniform in its approach and components: Each of the pieces of a school counseling program were detailed along with the additional skill sets, or themes, important to implementing that model. It is in this new model that counseling, consultation, and coordination, always taught to and learned by pre-service counselors, are given equal importance with Johnson's results-based approach and education reform's insistence on academic rigor, equity and access for *all* students.

TODAY'S CHALLENGES

What did this 20-year journey yield for the current practice of school counseling professionals? In essence, the counselor's role was defined to incorporate responsibility for the academic, career, and personal-social development of students. In addition, the profession made a commitment to demonstrating the effectiveness of its efforts in terms of measurable skill building of all students.

This is the contemporary charge to all school counselors. So, how are school counselors responding to this call to action? What forces are at work that reinforce or diminish the mission of the profession?

Local Needs Dictate Priorities

At their best, school counselors are backed by a well-defined, developmentally focused school counseling program. In such situations, a counselor–principal agreement sets forth the time counselors spend in each area of function, from program management to program delivery. Quasi-administrative functions are decreased.

In many districts, however, counselors continue to be utilized for test coordination; for master schedule creation; for bus, parking lot, and lunch duties; for handing out student discipline; and for substituting in classrooms to provide preparation periods for teachers. Many are without clerical assistance and taxed with numerous clerical duties such as entering grades into cumulative folders, sending out mailings, creating brochures and fliers, and other tasks that could be accomplished by secretarial support.

The needs of an individual district, often driven by economic factors, still take precedence in determining how a school counselor's practice finally looks. Grant funding, which is used to hire many new counselors, can proscribe how the counselors' time is used. For example, in many large urban communities, counselors may have been hired with Title I funding to do Individual Education Plan (IEP) mandated counseling. Creating and providing a comprehensive, developmental program serving all students becomes impossible when so much time is spent in one-on-one intervention.

We believe that the transition to a well-defined, developmentally focused school counseling program takes time and talent. Counselor and administrator training in comprehensive emotional intelligence skill building and related models for schoolwide programs will assist more schools to strengthen their developmental focus.

No Child Left Behind

With the heavy focus on academic performance, measured by the continuous expansion of high-stakes testing from grade level to grade level, school counselors have needed to align their work with the academic mission of their schools. Although counselors' hearts may be strongly centered on the mental health of their students, it is not mental health that is being tested. Counselors ensure their place in the educational process by being one of many on a team committed to the academic success of their students. Counselors can take a lead here in understanding and advocating the strong relationship between academic learning and emotional learning.

Clearly, students who are emotionally motivated and able to manage their attention in the classroom are the ones who achieve academically. Conversely, students who cannot manage their impulses and stay motivated to academic tasks are the ones who underperform in the classroom. SEL programs such those featured in this book demonstrate the important role the counselor can play in emotional and social skill building throughout the academic program.

Diverse Professional Approaches

The brief history we provided about the evolution of school counseling revealed the mix of professional backgrounds of those entering the school counseling profession: vocational counselor, mental health counselor, academic counselor, or facilitative leader of students across all three roles. Each grouping has its own counseling approach, priorities, standards, and proponents. As a result, preservice counselor education has varied greatly depending on the professional background of the department and its commitment, or lack of commitment, to staying current with the ever-changing standards. It should be no surprise, therefore, that the current level of professional skills and professional expectations of counselors across the country vary widely.

From Good Intentions to Accomplishments

As specified in the ASCA National Model (2003), there is a shift for school counselors from good intention to accomplishments, from hard work to effectiveness. The National Model also asks counselors to recognize and embrace a paradigm shift to "not only monitor process and measure services but measure the results of our programs" (p. 9). Programs of merit, such as the social decision making model presented in the chapters by Breune Butler (chaps. 9 & 15), show results of their programs to get that designation. School counseling programs, too, must show the results they have measured to answer the salient question posed throughout the presentation of the National Model, that is, "How are students different as a result of having participated in a school counseling program?" Unfortunately, it is often easier to measure simple yardsticks such as attendance, report card grades, conflict-resolution incidents, numbers of mediations conducted, numbers of students who can recite policies on sexual harassment, and so forth, than to take on the complex measurement of the social-emotional growth of students. Hopefully, over time assessment tools will be developed that support counselors in this challenge. This is certainly a fruitful area for academicians to provide support and research.

SKILLS REQUIRED TO SUPPORT
THE EVOLVING ROLE OF COUNSELORS

Clearly the field is in professional evolution. Are there some overall observations we can make about the state of skill development? What directions should we be providing to counselor educators who are now preparing the next generation of school counselors?

As those who study math chose to become math teachers, today those who are committed to understanding the human dimension of people have chosen counseling. For school counselors, many of whom had a teaching background as a requirement of certification, it was affective education and the other side of the report card, more than any content area, that drew them to the field. The counseling process and the dimensions of human development, human wellness, and human empowerment are at the core of training for counselors.

However, the emerging challenges facing the school counselor and the increasing emphasis on responsibility for the results of their programs require a broadened skill set. Clearly, understanding of the counseling process and an ability to be an outstanding counselor will continue to be a core skill of the school counselor. Many counselors, by district mandate, may continue to focus their work on crisis counseling or IEP programs. However, many others who are trained in and advocating for the recently defined role set out in the ASCA National Model are taking on additional responsibilities that require additional skills.

As we consider the ASCA National Model, we can envision the changes in the school counselor's role as going from being an individual contributor of counseling services to being a manager of the system of learning that integrates academic growth of students with their personal-social and career development. The school counselor's new role involves both activities related to the student and activities related to the school system and its stakeholders.

According to the National Model (ASCA, 2003, p. 29), the four theme areas necessary to support the role of today's counselor include a) Leadership, b) Advocacy, c) Collaboration and Teaming, and d) systemic change. Clearly, the National Model suggests that the school counselor use each of these thematic areas to support the student's development, and success in academics, personal-social development and vocational development.

1. **Leadership:** This role involves setting direction systemwide to ensure student success. Counselors promote student success by closing the achievement gaps found among students of color, poor students, and under-achievers. Effective leadership involves working with other professionals in the school to implement systemwide changes and reforms. Counselors work at the school, district, and state levels.

2. **Advocacy:** Counselors advocate for students' educational needs and ensure these needs are met at every school level. School counselors support and promote every student's goals for success and helps remove barriers that inhibit learning. School counselors exercise their leadership to advocate for high standards for every student—providing equity through access to quality curriculum. Results must be measurable and are expected to increase the number of students completing school and choosing a wide variety of postsecondary options.

3. **Collaboration and Teaming:** Counselors need to work with others inside and outside the school to support the development and implementation of educational programs that support achievement of goals identified for every student. School counselors encourage genuine collaboration among school staff toward common goals including equity, access, and academic success for every student. Data analysis to identify where educational programs need to be changed is part of this goal.

4. **Systemic change:** School counselors have access to data about academic success or failure and they use these data to advocate for every student. Data from the school and relevant community sources can be analyzed to understand better what contributes to student success. Systemic change occurs when policies and procedures are examined through data analysis, with the involvement of all critical players—often led by school counselors.

When leadership, advocacy, and collaboration are done together, systemic change can occur. It involves seeing the system of interconnectedness of things around them and viewing the environment in terms of patterns of events (Carey Dimmett School Counseling Leadership Institute, 2003). This creates an ability to see and feel a connection to the whole school, not just one piece of it. It reinforces the ability to see the school and its constituencies as able to make changes effectively. It encourages people to examine their belief systems and operating philosophies to consider alternative ways of doing things.

ROLE OF EMOTIONAL INTELLIGENCE

Theories and practices of emotional intelligence support the emerging roles of counselors and relates to the four theme areas of leadership, advocacy, collaboration, and systems change. First, building emotional intelligence abilities strengthens the counselor's skills for the four themes. Second, the research-validated models used to build schoolwide SEL programs offer results-based approaches toward systemic change and address the increasing need for accountability.

Common emotional intelligence abilities within the four theme areas include "emotional perception ... [and the] ... reflective regulation of emotions in others," which are the first and fourth branches, respectively, of the Mayer and Salovey (1997) model of emotional intelligence (p. 11). In advocating, leading, and collaborating, the counselor must be aware of others' emotions and be able to influence them. Goleman (1995) offered other relevant traits including persistence, zeal, self-motivation, empathy, and social deftness, which are also beneficial to the skills of school counselors. These theorists are contrasted in Chapter 3.

Systemic change requires school counselors to not only build their own emotional intelligence skills but to be able to engage students, administrators, and faculty members to develop these skills for themselves. This calls on school counselors to provide leadership in implementing an integrated approach to the social and emotional activities of the school. It means incorporating principles of emotional intelligence in providing professional development for teachers as well as in consultation and collaboration.

Those who are committed to the study of SEL can also provide useful tools for understanding and integrating the role of emotions in learning. As recent brain research reveals, the experience of emotion is central to the process of learning (Goleman, 1995). The feelings we experience in learning environments influence our intellectual processes. To ask students to ignore their feelings as they approach academic subjects results in shutting down an important part of the brain's capacity to learn. Emotions provide motivation, engagement and important problem-solving input for the learner (Shelton & Stern, 2004).

THE IMPORTANCE OF LEADERSHIP

Given the importance of leading a school to set new curriculum objectives in response to the National Model, it should be clear just how critical the role of leadership is for the counselor. One method for assessing leadership effectiveness is the Hogan Personality System (1992), which is a research-validated, gender, and racially neutral system for evaluating important skills that predict leaders' success. It has been used with hundreds of thousands of individuals across diverse, international organizations. We see four of these skills clearly representative of emotional intelligence.

Adjustment refers to the degree to which persons are calm or moody and volatile in accomplishing their work. Are they able to experience confidence, resilience, and optimism or tension, irritability, and negativity? Are they able to reduce stress in themselves and others, or do they internalize stress within themselves, thereby raising the stress levels of those around them?

Ambition evaluates the degree to which persons seem leader-like and value achievement. Do they seem hard working and assertive or unassertive and not interested in achievement? Are they comfortable being the center of focus in engaging others to follow their direction?

Sociability assess the degree to which persons appear socially self-confident. Do they appear outgoing or reserved and quiet? Are they able to reach out to other people and engage them in task?

Interpersonal Sensitivity reflects tact and perceptiveness. Do they appear friendly, warm, and popular or independent, frank, and direct? Are they able to read the reactions of other people effectively so they can "listen" to the nonverbal as well as verbal cues that others communicate?

Consideration of a counselor's leadership effectiveness is important in becoming change agents within a school and effective advocates for student success. The emotionally intelligent counselor who takes on the role of a leader also becomes the emotional center of the school and influences all participants in the system through the affective dimensions of the environment.

COLLABORATION BETWEEN ACADEMICIANS AND PRACTITIONERS

We have briefly touched on the importance of emotional intelligence skills for the school counselor. Throughout the book we build on this premise. It is fair to observe that, to a large extent, school counselors and academicians live in two very different worlds. The academician is looking at theoretical models, empirical research, and long-term perspectives; the school counselor is pressed to focus on the next school period and be expected to show results of the past hour. Yet, effective counselor education and the preparation of a new generation of counselors require that counseling practitioners and educators work together to find meaningful dialogue that reinforces each other's work. We suggest a number of areas of mutual interest where increasing the dialogue between academicians or researchers and school counseling practitioners can benefit both groups. This book can be a starting point for fruitful discussions of these topics.

1. How can emotional intelligence and SEL programs be applied in school, district and state educational systems?

2. What emotion-related research can improve classroom environments, learning processes, and instructional applications?
3. What are new ways of meeting the special challenges of students at different stages of academic, social-personal ,and career development?
4. What are the best methods of professional counselor training that prepare new counselors to meet the demanding educational roles in preventing violence, mediating conflict, and addressing the needs of special groups?
5. How can emotional learning enhance skill building in counselor education?
6. How can technology be integrated into the teaching of emotional intelligence skills?

THE LOOK OF COLLABORATION

When we lay out a focus of issues for collaboration between practitioners and academicians, the task seems neat and tidy. As you look through the book, you will see that our experience comes from very different perspectives. Our perspectives and recommendations are sometimes conflicting. You will see that the development of different topics in different geographical locations is diverse. This is not a neat process. However, as practitioners we realize the value of the collaboration to strengthen all our efforts as we grow together if the field of school counseling is to reach its potential in becoming an important center of the school. This book is a first step of many we hope will bring us all closer to that goal.

REFERENCES

American School Counselor Association. (1997). *Sharing the vision: The National Standards for School Counseling Programs*. Alexandria, VA: Author.
American School Counselor Association. (2003). *The ASCA National Model: A framework for school counseling programs*. Alexandria, VA: Author.
Carey Dimmett School Counseling Leadership Institute. (2003). *Systemic change presentation*. University of Massachusetts.
Goleman, D. (1995). *Emotional intelligence: Why it can matter more than IQ*. New York: Bantam.
Hogan Personality Inventory. (1992). Retrieved June, 2004 from www.hoganassessments.com
Mayer, J. D., & Salovey, P. (1997). What is emotional intelligence? In P. Salovey & D. J. Sluyter (Eds.), *Emotional development and emotional intelligence* (pp. 3–31). New York: HarperCollins.
Nystul, M. (2003). *Introduction to counseling: An art and science perspective* (2nd ed.). Boston: Allyn & Bacon.
Shelton, C. M., & Stern, R. (2004). *Understanding emotions in the classroom: Differentiating teaching strategies for optimal learning*. New York: Dude.

3

Emotional Intelligence: Theory, Measurement, and Counseling Implications

John Pellitteri
Queens College, CUNY

THE CHALLENGE OF DEFINITION

The term *emotional intelligence* has had popular appeal in the last decade among professionals and laypeople alike. One reason appears to be the high regard for the concept of intelligence, as it is a desirable quality that is associated with power, expertise, and prestige. The conceptualization and measurement of intelligence has been an important focus in psychology for more than a century. The term *emotional* also has appeal in that emotions are inherent and central to psychosocial functioning, motivation, well-being, and life satisfaction. Emotions make up the fabric of relationships and are embedded to one degree or another in all interpersonal interactions. Emotions have been the subject of philosophical inquiry for many centuries, with alternating views on their importance and value (Solomon, 1993). To have the power and expertise about such a central human quality as emotions would understandably be desirable. The appeal of emotional intelligence, therefore, stems from its inherent relationship to adaptation and optimal social functioning.

When asked "what is intelligence?" most people have some notion of what it means (Sternberg, 2000). Intelligent people are smart, have knowledge, are skillful, and are better than the "average" person. In school settings, the concept of intelligence (and IQ) is closely related to academic performance. Grade point average is often considered an indicator of a student's overall intelligence. Students who struggle with learning disabilities or have other academic difficulties often deal with issues of self-esteem and self-concept because of the implication that their intelligence is reflected in poor academic performance. Heated controversies have surrounded the division of ethnic and other social groups based on IQ, and the use of intelligence testing has been challenged.

It is often assumed that there is one generally agreed-on definition of intelligence. However the construct of intelligence has been defined and redefined for more than a century with no consensual definition. Robert Sternberg (1990), a leading authority in the field, compared expert definitions of intelligence from two symposiums on the topic, one in 1921 and the other in 1986. There were 19 attributes of intelligence mentioned in 1921 and 27 mentioned in 1986. Some of the many descriptions included: "knowledge, ability to learn, speed of mental processing, ability to deal with novelty, academic abilities, 'g' factor, that which is valued by culture, executive processes, not one construct, and metacognition" (Sternberg, 1990, p. 50). Despite the wide diversity of views on intelligence, there was some degree of overlap from the two eras. "Attributes such as adaptation to the environment, basic mental processes, and higher order thinking (e.g. reasoning, problem solving, decision making) were prominent in both listings" (Sternberg, 1990, p. 51).

With the construct of intelligence being defined so diversely, it therefore should not be surprising that the emerging construct of emotional intelligence is also defined differently. The term *emotional intelligence* was originally used by Peter Salovey and Jack Mayer in a seminal article in 1990 to describe a distinct set of emotion-related abilities. The concept became widely popular in 1995 with the publication of a book by Dan Goleman and the claims that emotional intelligence has more predictive power for success than IQ. Working independently, Reuven Bar-On (1996) was developing a measurement instrument, the Emotional Quotient Inventory (EQi), that incorporated aspects of the emotional intelligence construct. The work of these authors—Mayer and Salovey, Goleman, and Bar-On—represents the three major approaches to emotional intelligence theorizing and assessment.

Although there are some areas of conceptual overlap, the three main models have distinct differences. These differences have lead to confusion about the definitions and parameters of emotional intelligence and can obscure research and clinical efforts because what is labeled as emotional intelligence can mean many things. Emotional intelligence can be conceptualized as a set of abilities or as a set of personality traits (Mayer, Salovey, & Caruso, 2000a).

Traits tend to be relatively stable personality structures whereas abilities are tied to fluid psychological processes that are open to modification through learning. The closely related construct of social intelligence has existed for almost a century and includes concepts that are important for adaptation that may or may not be part of one's definition of emotional intelligence. It is essential, then, that counselors and other educational specialists are aware of the current limitations as well as the potential strengths of the emotional intelligence construct. When choosing to work from an emotional intelligence orientation, it is important to have an understanding of the conceptual definitions that form the foundations of the particular model and its assessment measures. There are many familiar concepts (i.e., self-esteem, social skills, ego strength) that are related to emotional intelligence and too often may be confused with it. It is important to know what is and what is not emotional intelligence to target specific areas of intervention and maximize efforts to improve emotional intelligence functioning. At the same time, it is important to understand related concepts that may sometimes be more relevant to counseling interventions than emotional intelligence. One must also be cautious not to get caught up in the exaggerated claims, the hype, and the media appeal about emotional intelligence but rather to root one's work in research-based information and make an "intelligent" application of established knowledge.

In the following section I describe the three major emotional intelligence theories and their respective measurement instruments. In the next section I describe issues of emotional intelligence assessment, and in the following section I compare the major models. In the final section I suggest some implications for adopting an emotional intelligence orientation to school counseling.

THEORIES AND MEASURES
OF EMOTIONAL INTELLIGENCE

Abilities-Based Model (Mayer & Salovey)

Definitions

Salovey and Mayer's (1990) original definition of emotional intelligence proposed a construct with three subcomponents. Subsequently, this model evolved and resulted in a revised definition that consisted of four components (Mayer & Salovey, 1997). The initial definition of emotional intelligence was: "The subset of social intelligence that involves the ability to monitor one's own and others' feelings and emotions, to discriminate among them, and to use this information to guide one's thinking and actions" (Salovey & Mayer, 1990, p.

189). Emotional intelligence is defined more narrowly than social intelligence and in doing so it becomes more easily operationalized and measurable, thus addressing the century-long struggle of defining the social intelligence construct. Inherent in this emotional intelligence definition is the term *abilities* as well as the relationship of emotional information on one's thinking. These key aspects are retained in the revised definition. Emotional intelligence represents the effectiveness of an individual's abilities to understand, control, and use the information inherent in emotional experiences. "[It] involves the accurate appraisal and expression of emotions in oneself and others and the regulation of emotion in a way that enhances living" (Mayer, DiPaolo, & Salovey, 1990, p. 772). The link to adaptation is also a defining characteristic of emotional intelligence. The three components of the 1990 model were: emotional perception, emotional regulation, and emotional knowledge. The new model more clearly describes specific abilities and places greater emphasis on emotion-cognitive interactions: "Emotional intelligence involves the ability to perceive accurately, appraise and express emotion; the ability to access and/or generate feelings when they facilitate thought; the ability to understand emotion and emotional knowledge; and the ability to regulate emotions to promote emotional and intellectual growth" (Mayer & Salovey, 1997, p. 10).

Structural Components

The four-component model includes: (a) emotional perception, (b) emotional facilitation of thinking, (c) understanding emotional knowledge, and (d) reflective regulation of emotions. The differences from the earlier model are essentially that the elements of the emotional knowledge component were divided into a more elaborate emotional knowledge component and the emotional facilitation component. The perception and regulation components, too, were elaborated with more descriptive distinctions of abilities. Table 3.1 outlines the structure of this model with examples of the four clusters of abilities within each of the four main components.

The model also conceptualizes the abilities and components along a developmental structure. The numbering of the components I to IV is a general index of their degree of psychological complexity. For example, Component I, perception, is considered a more basic psychological process that emerges earlier and is less integrated than Component IV, regulation. The abilities within each component are also numbered in a hypothesized order of development. Within Component III, knowledge, for example, Ability 1, labeling emotions, is a prerequisite skills for Abilities 3, understanding blends of emotions, and 4, recognizing transitions. It is important to note that this ordering is conceptual

TABLE 3.1

Structure of the Mayer and Salovey (1997) Model of Emotional Intelligence

---

I.   Perception, appraisal, and expression of emotions
    1. Ability to identify emotion in physical states and thoughts
    2. Ability to identify emotion in other people
    3. Ability to accurately express emotion
    4. Ability to discriminate between honest and dishonest expressions of emotion

II.   Emotional facilitation of thinking
    1. Emotions direct attention and prioritize thinking
    2. Emotions can be generated to aid in judgments
    3. Emotional mood swings can change perspectives
    4. Emotional states encourage specific problem-solving approaches

III.   Understanding and analyzing emotions: Employing emotional knowledge
    1. Ability to label emotions
    2. Ability to interpret the meanings that emotions convey
    3. Ability to understand complex feelings or blends of feelings
    4. Ability to recognize transitions of emotions and intensities

IV.   Reflective regulation of emotions to promote emotional and intellectual growth
    1. Ability to stay open to pleasant and unpleasant feelings
    2. Ability to engage or disengage from emotions
    3. Ability to monitor emotions in oneself and others
    4. Ability to moderate and enhance emotions without repression

---

and has not yet been completely tested. The four-component model, however, has been validated with the use of the second abilities-based emotional intelligence measure, the Mayer–Salovey–Caruso Emotional Intelligence Test (MSCEIT; Mayer, Salovey, & Caruso, 2002).

The Mayer and Salovey (1997) model emphasizes the interaction of emotions and cognitions. This is illustrated for example, by the second component, emotional facilitation of thinking, which considers how emotions and moods influence thinking and judgment. This influence can be positive and enhance intellectual processes which presents a view of emotions that is in contrast to the historical views of emotions being disruptive to reasoning. Mayer, Salovey, and Caruso (1999) view emotional intelligence as related but distinct from IQ as evidenced by moderate correlations between the their first measure, the Multifactorial Emotional Intelligence Scales (MEIS) and measures of aca-

demic intelligence. Their third component, understanding emotional knowledge, illustrates the cognitive dimensions of their emotional intelligence model
in that labeling emotions and interpreting their meanings requires the
intellectual processes also associated with IQ.

Measurement Instruments

The two measures developed by Mayer, Salovey, et al. (1999, 2002) are the
MEIS and the MSCEIT. The paper-and-pencil formats of these tests measure
one's ability to perform particular emotional intelligence tasks. Each test contains 12 subtests that cluster to form, respectively, the components of the original and revised Mayer and Salovey emotional intelligence models. The
emotional intelligence tasks involved in these performance-based measures include: identifying emotions in pictures of faces, artwork, and story characters;
determining concepts about emotional transitions and blends of different emotions; reasoning with emotional information; identifying how a various characters feel in a given social scenario; and determining the effectiveness of
particular actions in a given situation. One of the tasks requires the respondent
to imagine feeling a certain way and then compare that feeling with various
sensory qualities. Another task asks the respondent to rate how a course of action might influence another person given a particular social conflict. The formats of the MEIS and MSCEIT items include Likert scale rating, multiple
choice, and semantic differentials.

Some of the issues that have been raised regarding these measures have
been the criteria for establishing correct answers. As emotional reactions can
vary depending on characteristics of the social situation, it becomes difficult
to determine which responses are more effective than others. Mayer et al.
(2000a) have argued that such criteria can be established. Their ability-based
measures have been designed with three scoring systems. One is based on expert scoring, where experts in the field of emotions have been surveyed and
have reached a general agreement on the correctness of an item response.
Another scoring system, which is more often used, is the consensus scoring,
where item responses are given a certain weight based on normative samples
of the measures. A third scoring system, target scoring, applies to certain
subtests (faces, stories, artworks) where the creator of the story or the person
posing for the picture of the face rates how they were feeling, which becomes
the criteria for the respondents.

Abilities-based emotional intelligence measures, despite their limitations,
come closest to traditional measures of intelligence (i.e., Wechsler Adult Intelligence Scales; Stanford Binet Intelligence Scales). Such IQ instruments in-

clude various subtests that measure respondent's performance on tasks such as assembling blocks and puzzle designs, determining the meanings of words and concepts, identifying details in pictures, and solving arithmetic problems. One major difference, however, is that abilities-based emotional intelligence measures are paper-and-pencil formats that can be administered in groups and computer scored, whereas the standard IQ tests need to be administered and scored by an individual examiner.

Mixed Model (Goleman)

Definitions

In his original publication, Goleman (1995) defined emotional intelligence as the "abilities such as being able to motivate oneself and persist in the face of frustrations; to control impulses and delay gratification; to regulate one's moods and keep distress from swamping the ability to think; to empathize and to hope" (p. 34). Goleman's initial presentation of emotional intelligence included five components: self-awareness, self-regulation, self-motivation, empathy, and social skills.

In collaboration with Richard Boyatzis on the creation of a measurement instrument, Goleman's model has developed and shifted its focus to the manifestation of emotional intelligence performance. His revised descriptive definition is that "emotional intelligence is observed when a person demonstrates the competencies that constitute self awareness, self management, social awareness, and social skills at appropriate times and ways in sufficient frequency to be effective in the situation (Boyatzis, Goleman, & Rhee, 2000, p. 344). There is an emphasis on competencies and on their effectiveness in the social situation. The revised definition also outlines the altered componential structure of his model, which consists of two dimensions: self–other and awareness-management.

Structural Components

The four components that result from the combination of these two dimensions are (a) self-awareness, (b) self-management, (c) social awareness, and (d) social skills. The new four-component model differs from the original model in that it combines self-motivation with self-regulation. Each component consists of several competencies that are outlined in Table 3.2. The Emotional Competence Inventory (ECI; Boyatzis & Goleman, 2001) is based on this four-component model and has been used in various business settings to assess managerial effectiveness and leadership.

TABLE 3.2
Structure of the Goleman Model of Emotional Intelligence
(Boyatzis, Goleman, & Rhee, 2000)

I. Self-awareness cluster	II. Social-awareness cluster
Emotional self-awareness	Empathy
Accurate self-assessment	Organizational awareness
Self-confidence	Service orientation
III. Self-management cluster	IV. Social skills cluster
Self-control	Leadership
Self-control	Leadership
Trustworthiness	Communication
Conscientiousness	Influence
Adaptability	Change catalyst
Achievement orientation	Conflict management
Initiative	Building bonds
	Teamwork and collaboration
	Developing others

"If defined as a single construct, the term emotional intelligence might be deceptive and suggest an association with cognitive capability … this association has not been substantiated when empirically studied" (Boyatzis et al., 2000, p. 344). Goleman indicated that his model of emotional intelligence as measured with the ECI is unrelated to cognitive abilities and therefore separate from IQ. He also implied that emotional intelligence is multifactorial and not a single construct. Boyatzis et al. (2000) noted associations between their competency-based model of emotional intelligence and the widely recognized "big five" model of personality traits, which includes extroversion, neuroticism, agreeableness, conscientiousness, and openness (McCrae & Costa, 1990). Within the structure of personality, such traits combine with motivational drives, neurological and hormonal bases, and philosophical and value foundations in the development of competencies. The Goleman model of emotional intelligence therefore purports to involve several behavioral manifestations of the whole personality.

Measurement Instruments

The ECI–University Edition is a 63-item self-report test. It requires respondents to rate statements about their own behaviors on a 5-point Likert scale. The test items are similar to statements such as: "I listen closely to others" and "I respect and relate well to different people." The results can be self-scored and yield ratings for each of the 21 competencies. There is also a 360 degree format of the ECI that incorporates self-report with reports of peers and supervisors. This assessment structure allows for data not just from the individual but also from others in the environment, thus providing an external measure of the individual's effectiveness to be compared with the self-reports. The 360 degree assessment format is the only method that incorporates data from the person's environment. This method, however, limits the ECI application to the particular environment under study, which makes the ECI most applicable to work contexts.

Mixed Model (Bar-On)

Definitions

Bar-On (1997) defined emotional intelligence as, "an array of personal, emotional, and social competencies and skills that influence one's ability to succeed in coping with environmental demands and pressures" (p. 3). His model of emotional intelligence grows out of his development of the EQi (Bar-On, 1996). His work on this instrument began in the 1980s as an attempt to identify aspects of social and emotional functioning that are associated with psychological well-being (Bar-On, 2000). His research on the validation of the EQi has been extensive and has included studies in 15 countries with numerous comparisons with various psychological concepts.

Structural Components

The model has five broad components that organize 15 subscales. The five components are: (a) intrapersonal, (b) interpersonal, (c) adaptability, (d) stress management, and (e) general mood.

The 15 specific factors subsumed within these broad categories are outlined in Table 3.3. Bar-On (1997) used the metaphor of human anatomy to organize these factors by systems and by topography. The five components in Table 3.3 represent the systems view where similar functions are grouped together. For example, problem solving, reality testing, and flexibility work together to enable individuals to adapt to their environment. In the topographic ordering, factors are listed as core factors that interact with supporting factors and lead to resultant factors. For example, "Supporting Factors, like Optimism and Stress Tolerance, combine with Core Factors, like Reality Testing and Impulse Control, to facilitate [the Resultant Factor] efficient Problem Solving" (Bar-On, 1997, p. 7).

TABLE 3.3
Structure of the Bar-On (2000) Model of Emotional Intelligence

I. Intrapersonal component	II. Interpersonal component
Self-regard	Empathy
Emotional self-awareness	Social responsibility
Assertiveness	Interpersonal relationship
Independence	
Self-actualization	
III. Adaptability component	IV. Stress management component
Reality testing	Stress tolerance
Flexibility	Impulse control
Problem solving	
V. General mood component	
Optimism	
Happiness	

Bar-On (1997) emphasized the comprehensive and multifactorial nature of his model and noted that it relates to "the potential to succeed rather than success itself" (p. 3). In a more recent definition, he stated that the EQi "may more accurately be described as a self report measure of emotionally and socially competent behavior that provides an estimate of one's emotional and social intelligence" (Bar-On, 2000, p. 364). The Bar-On model, therefore, is not a pure emotional intelligence model in that it also includes the construct of social intelligence. The broad conception of emotional intelligence to include social skills along with emotional skills and personal factors places Bar-On's model in line with various conceptualizations of personality, as has been confirmed by numerous validation studies that show high correlations between the EQi and existing personality measures (Bar-On, 1997, 2000). In addition the EQi yielded low and nonsignificant correlations, respectively, with measures of IQ and cognitive reasoning, thus illustrating Bar-On's conceptualization of emotional intelligence as noncognitive (Bar-On, 1997).

Measurement Instruments

The EQi is a 133-item self-report measure that requires respondents to rate statements on a 5-point Likert scale. The respondent must rate the degree to which the statements are "true of me." The tests items are similar to statements such as: "I can be impatient," "I don't stay in contact with friends," and "I am aware of how I feel." The results are computer scored and yield ratings for the 5 composite scales and the 15 subscales that constitute them. There are also validity scores that consider omission rate, an inconsistency index, and positive–negative impressions. The extensive validation studies with numerous international samples, as well as factor analytic and internal consistency methods, support the EQi as a psychometrically sound instrument. A children's version of the EQi and a 360 degree format for the EQi are under development (Bar-On, 1997).

THE CHALLENGE OF MEASUREMENT

Comparison of Measurement Methods

Empirical research and clinical application of emotional intelligence is dependent on the limits of the existing measurement instruments. As with the IQ construct, concepts and measures are intertwined as each shapes the other. The distinctly different approaches to measuring emotional intelligence reflect each model's differences in conceptualization (see Table 3.4). Mayer and Salovey (1997) emphasized emotional intelligence as a set of abilities related to IQ and involving cognitive-affective processes. Their tests, the MEIS and the MSCEIT, are performance based with tasks that require reasoning with emotions. Bar-On's (2000) emotional intelligence model encompasses both emotional and social intelligence and involves various personality traits (i.e., assertiveness, flexibility, social responsibility). The EQi, with its self-report format, closely resembles many of the existing well-established personality measures with which it correlates. Goleman's emotional intelligence model is rooted in effectiveness in the environment, particularly work settings (Boyatzis et al., 2000). The ECI involves a self-report with 360 degree assessment format that includes ratings from coworkers and supervisors.

Each format has its strengths. An abilities measure tests what a person can actually do and defines specific skills that may be transferable to various settings. A self-report format is relatively easy and quick to administer. A self-report with the 360 degree component has the strength of obtaining the perceptions of others in the social environment. There are, unfortunately, numerous limitations in each method, as described next.

An illustration of the discrepancies between emotional intelligence assessment methods can be found in a comparative study of the MSCEIT and the EQi that found them to be essentially uncorrelated (Pellitteri, 2001). Factor analytic techniques revealed no common factor structures between the two measures, which would be expected if they were measuring the same construct.

TABLE 3.4

Comparison of the Major Emotional Intelligence Models and Measures

Model	EI Conception	Structural Components	Measures	Assessment Method
Mayer and Salovey	Abilities	Emotional perception	MEIS and MSCEIT	Performance
		Facilitation of thinking		
		Emotional knowledge		
		Reflective regulation		
Goleman (Boyatzis, Goleman, & Rhee, 2000)	Mixed	Self-awareness	ECI	Self-report/360
		Self-management		
		Social awareness		
		Social skills		
Bar-On (2000)	Mixed	Intrapersonal	EQi	Self-report
		Interpersonal		
		Adaptability		
		Stress management		
		General mood		

Note.   EI = emotional intelligence; MEIS = Multifactorial Emotional Intelligence Scale; MSCEIT = Mayer–Salovey–Caruso Emotional Intelligence Test; ECI = Emotional Competence Inventory; EQi = Emotional Quotient Inventory.

Certain subcomponents of the two tests did have low correlations. The technical manuals of these tests report very low correlations between the overall scores of the MSCEIT and the EQi (Bar-On, 1997; Mayer et al., 2002). These findings not only reflect differences in measurement approaches but highlight the disparity in conceptualizations of emotional intelligence. Such studies suggest that the different emotional intelligence models and their respective tests are measuring different constructs and cannot be assumed to be equivalent.

Limitations in Emotional Intelligence Assessment

A major critique of the self-report measures of emotional intelligence are that skills, competencies, and abilities cannot actually be measured by one's self-report (Davies, Stankov, & Roberts, 1998; Mathews, Zeidner, & Roberts, 2002). This would be equivalent to obtaining an IQ score based on a student's Likert scale rating to the statement, "I know a lot a words." Clearly such a response would be influenced by social desirability, limitations of self-assessment, and other factors, and would have questionable validity at best. Bar-On's (2000) and Goleman's (1995) models have been criticized in that they include compe-tencies and skills as part of their definitions yet rely on self-report measures (Hedlund & Sternberg, 2000; Mathews et al., 2002; Mayer, Caruso, & Salovey, 2000). Another critique of the models based on self-reports is that they corre-late strongly with self-report personality tests, which opens the question of uniqueness and whether these emotional intelligence tests measure anything new that has not already been captured by existing, well-established personal-ity instruments. Mathews et al. (2002), in a comprehensive review of emo-tional intelligence theory and measurement, anticipated "that performance-based approaches to the assessment of EI [emotional intelligence] will outlive those based on self-report, which may be assimilated into existing personality theory" (p. 230).

The 360 degree format uses informants along with self-reports to provide an additional source of data about a person. With regard to the identification of traits, this method appears to increase validity of the self-report by confirming the target person's self-perception or drawing a contrast between the target's self-perception and others' perceptions of him or her. This is in line with Goleman's descriptive definition of emotional intelligence as the demonstra-tion of competencies (Boyatzis et al., 2000). However, given that informants vary in their capacities to assess their peers and may be influenced by their per-sonal relationships with the target person, data from informants have question-able validity. Another criticism of the 360 degree format is that reports from others merely measure reputation and not actual abilities or competencies (Mayer et al., 2000). Nonetheless, a measure of a target's reputation may be an important factor in the overall assessment of his or her functioning in an envi-ronment. "A person's reputation may even be more important than his or her actual abilities for some purposes (for example, running in an election), but reputation is also different from actual abilities ... [and] remains a step removed" (Mayer et al., 2000, p. 325).

One of the shortcomings of abilities-based measures, as mentioned previ-ously, is the difficulty in establishing a criteria for a "correct" or "better" re-sponse to test items. Mayer, Caruso, and Salovey (1999) attempted to address this problem by coordinating three scoring criteria: consensus, expert, and tar-get, as described earlier. The range of correlations among criteria, however, var-ies from high to low. Mathews et al. (2002) noted difficulties with reliabilities and interter correlations between the MEIS and two research versions of the MSCEIT. It is thus questionable whether current performance-based measures of emotional intelligence meet the standards of established cognitive intelligence tests. In addition, predictive validity of the MEIS and MSCEIT is still being established (Mathews et al., 2002), although structural (factorial) validity is supported by various analyses (Mayer et al., 2002). Although performance-based tests have inherent advantages over self-report measures, it clear that they are still in an early phase of evolution. It is important to note how currently well-established measures of cognitive intelligence arose out of various competing methods of measurement. It is anticipated that performance-based emotional intelligence assessment instruments will follow a similar developmental pathway and require several generations of instruments before they are firmly established and used.

A FRAMEWORK FOR COMPARING THE MAJOR MODELS

In defining the construct of emotional intelligence, it must inevitably be delineated and contrasted with existing psychological constructs. If emotional intelligence is actually a new concept and not a repackaging or redefinition of old concepts, it must show divergent validity from these concepts (i.e., personality, intelligence) and ideally be able to predict outcomes that could not be predicted by the existing constructs. Davies et al. (1998) described emotional intelligence as an "elusive construct," as such divergent validity is still inconclusive. The distinctions among the three major models presented here can be understood in terms of each model's conceptualizations and relationships to the previously established constructs of intelligence and personality. Mayer et al. (2000a) have already drawn this distinction in terms of personality traits and defined their model as an abilities-based model in contrast to the "mixed" models of Goleman (1995) and Bar-On (2000). This grouping of mixed models together in contrast to the abilities model also fits with regard to comparisons with intellectual functioning (IQ).

Comparison With Intellectual (Cognitive) Intelligence

Both Bar-On's and Goleman's definitions include descriptions of emotional intelligence as unrelated to intellectual functioning. Bar-On (1997) employed the term *noncognitive* and Boyatzis et al. (2000) stated that "this association [with cognitive capabilities] has not been substantiated when empirically studied" (p. 344). Mayer and Salovey (1997), by contrast, defined emotional intelligence as including the interaction between cognition and affect. Mayer and

Salovey claimed that emotional intelligence should be somewhat correlated with IQ (because they are both types of intelligences) but not too highly correlated because emotional intelligence is a distinct construct. Various studies confirm this moderate relation between the Mayer and Salovey emotional intelligence model and IQ (Mayer et al., 1999; O'Conner & Little, 2003; Pellitteri, 2002). Similarly, studies have found the mixed models to be uncorrelated or have low correlations with measures of IQ and cognitive reasoning (Bar-On, 1997; Pellitteri, 2001).

Comparison With Personality Traits

Davies et al. (1998) compared various emotional intelligence measures with personality tests. McCrae (2000) outlined the explicit associations between the mixed models and the five-factor model, which is a comprehensive taxonomy of personality traits. Goleman (1995) and Bar-On (2000) include personality as an element of emotional intelligence. "The dilemma of finding the best level of detail in defining constructs with which to build a personality theory maybe an issue of which focal point is chosen" (Boyatzis et al., 2000, p. 344). This difference in focal points is what distinguishes the three major emotional intelligence models.

Mayer et al. (2000b) also offer a focal point in their comparison of the components from the three emotional intelligence models in terms of their place within various subsystems of personality. The subsystems framework they used includes lower level biologically related mechanisms of motivational, emotional, cognitive factors; a middle level of the two types of interactions among these three factors; and a higher level of learned aspects of interpersonal and intrapersonal qualities. Mayer et al. placed their four emotional intelligence components exclusively within the middle level of the system in the area of "emotional and cognitive interactions" (p. 404). Three of Goleman's (1995) components (from his earlier model) are also within this interaction subsystem as well as the higher level, whereas Bar-On's (2000) five components are placed throughout the various levels of the personality model. This comparison illustrates the narrow focus of the Mayer and Salovey model in contrast to the broader conceptualizations of the mixed models. Such a narrow focus has allowed emotional intelligence to maintain the status of an intelligence that is distinct from IQ, which was difficult for the social intelligence construct to attain. By taking a broader focal point, Goleman's and Bar-On's models have become distinct from IQ and (as critics have claimed) redundant with existing construct of personality.

Bar-On (1997) made a significant point, however, in stating that "[emotional intelligence] is not just being aware of feelings and using that information to cope with life, but includes additional components that are no less important for determining one's success in dealing with environmental demands" (p. 3). To this extent the broader conceptualizations of the mixed models may have more relevance to various areas of adaptation and adjustment to the environment.

Zeidner and Mathews (2000) noted the distinction between personality and intelligence. These constructs are related as they describe functions of an individual's mental world. Yet they are distinct enough that they are rarely mistaken for each other. One can have severe deficits in his or her personality functions and yet have an extremely high IQ. Likewise, someone may have a low IQ and yet be free of psychiatric conditions or personality deficits. The comparison of the three models illustrated in Fig. 3.1 can be understood if one can conceptualize a continuum of mental functions with intellectual functions at one end and personality functions at the other. Within this continuum, related constructs such as IQ and the big five model of personality traits (McCrae & John, 1992) are placed at opposite ends. Social intelligence as a type of intelligence understandably falls close to IQ toward the intellectual end of the continuum but somewhat closer to personality than pure IQ. Emotional processes are dispersed to varying degrees throughout this mental functioning continuum because they influence personality formation and functioning but may also affect cognitive processes as well. The Salovey and Mayer (1990) model, in being distinguished from, and more focused on, emotions than social intelligence lies toward the middle of this continuum. Goleman's (1995) and

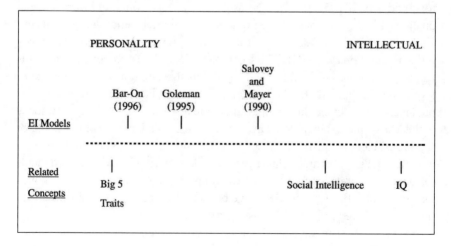

FIG. 3.1.   Emotional intelligence (EI) models on a continuum of mental functions.

Bar-On's (1996) models, being closely aligned with personality constructs and having been defined as noncognitive therefore lay closer to the personality end of the continuum. Even though Bar-On defined his measure as social intelligence, it does not represent the ability-based view of traditional researchers in social intelligence.

IMPLICATIONS FOR SCHOOL COUNSELORS AND SCHOOL-BASED PROGRAMS

A major implication of this chapter is that school counselors must be mindful of which emotional intelligence model they use because each model has a distinctly different conceptualization. One cannot assume that emotional intelligence means the same to everyone. This is particularly important if standard emotional intelligence measures are involved. For example, a counselor wants to gather data on emotional intelligence abilities as pre and post measures for an emotional intelligence program in school to establish the efficacy of the program. It would be a serious error if he or she chose the EQi self-report measure (because of the ease of administration time) but then implemented a program that involved the teaching of actual emotional intelligence abilities. The self-report measure on the posttests would not be a valid indicator of improvement because, as stated earlier, self-report measures do not test for actual abilities.

Likewise, if a counselor adopts Goleman's (1995) emotional intelligence model to structure a counseling intervention program, it would be essential to understand the abilities that might relate to the competencies and traits of his model. For example, what exactly is meant by self-awareness and what specific abilities or behaviors would need to change to indicate an improvement in this area? When an emotional intelligence model involves a personality trait, the counselor must question the relevance of the clinical goals. Traits are deeply rooted structures and patterns that are not easily altered and certainly not in a school setting.

On the other hand, if a counselor uses the Mayer and Salovey (1997) model, which is narrow in its focus, he or she must consider whether to incorporate social intelligence and other constructs that are related but different from the Mayer and Salovey model. The emotional intelligence abilities of this model, although circumscribed and delineated from other constructs, may not be the only or most pertinent area of concern for school counselors. Sometimes social responsibility, assertiveness, and achievement orientation are factors that counselors must address with students.

Another consideration is that the school counselor may want to use some of the many brief measures that assess the various subcomponents of emotional intelligence (Schutte & Malouff, 1999). Rather than measure the whole range of emotional intelligence components from a particular model, a counselor could test for only one area, perhaps emotional regulation. More focused attention to one set of skills or traits may be more manageable as well as more easily measurable. It is important that any data collection be accurate, valid, and consistent to support the intervention programs of the counselor. Administrators will more likely respond favorably in supporting a program or study that has solid empirical data. Counselors are increasingly required to be accountable, such that accurate data-collection methods may become necessary in justifying the clinical and psychoeducational work of the profession. A clear understanding of emotional intelligence theory, measurement instruments, and specific operationalized emotional intelligence skills would then be essential.

A distinction that can be drawn is between the *empirical application* of emotional intelligence, such as research programs that use existing psychometric measures to gather data, and *conceptual applications* of emotional intelligence that aim to increase the emotional orientation of the school. In the former, there must be a stringent adherence to the emotional intelligence model represented by the measures to ensure internal validity of the research study and relevance to the hypothesis. This type of application would most likely be a concern for academic scholars, those engaging in basic and applied research or program evaluation. In the latter there is less of a need for stringent adherence because there is no data collection involved but rather a consciousness raising to influence faculty, administrators, and students in becoming more emotionally aware. Most practicing school counselors will not be engaged in research but will likely make a conceptual application of emotional intelligence principles in their work. In this case, any of the emotional intelligence models can be used to serve this purpose. The faculty, students, and administrators that will be the target of the counselors emotional consciousness raising will not likely focus on such conceptual distinctions as are drawn in this chapter. At such an early stage of developing an emotional orientation in a school it is more important to be reflecting about emotional intelligence rather than debating the theoretical and conceptual distinctions among scholars. Creating an emotional orientation in a school setting will hopefully involve drawing attention to the unmet needs of students, improving the overall well-being of all individuals in the school, and creating a humanistic dimension to the education system that is sorely missing. It is in the historical nature of the school counseling profession to address these concerns. Emotional intelligence as a general concept can provide a starting point for such s transformation.

REFERENCES

Bar-On, R. (1996, August). *The era of the EQ: Defining and assessing emotional intelligence.* Paper presented at the annual convention of the American Psychological Association, Toronto, Canada.

Bar-On, R. (1997). *Emotional Quotient Inventory user's manual.* Toronto, Canada: Multi-Health Systems.

Bar-On, R. (2000). Emotional and social intelligence: Insights from the Emotional Quotient Inventory. In R. Bar-On & J. Parker (Eds.), *The handbook of emotional intelligence* (pp. 363–388). San Francisco: Jossey-Bass.

Boyatzis, R. E., & Goleman, D. (2001). *Emotional Competence Inventory manual.* Philadelphia: Hay Group.

Boyatzis, R. E., Goleman, D., & Rhee, K. S. (2000). Clustering competencies in emotional intelligence: Insights from the Emotional Competence Inventory. In R. Bar-On & J. Parker (Eds.), *The handbook of emotional intelligence* (pp. 343–362). San Francisco: Jossey-Bass.

Davies, M., Stankov, L., & Roberts, R. (1998). Emotional intelligence: In search of an elusive construct. *Journal of Personality and Social Psychology, 75,* 989–1015.

Goleman, D. (1995). *Emotional intelligence: Why it can matter more than IQ.* New York: Bantam.

Hedlund, J., & Sternberg, R. (2000). Too many intelligences? Integrating social, emotional, and practical intelligence. In R. Bar-On & J. Parker (Eds.), *The handbook of emotional intelligence* (pp. 136–168). San Francisco: Jossey-Bass.

Mathews, G., Zeidner, M., & Roberts, R. (2002). *Emotional intelligence: Science and myth.* Cambridge, MA: MIT Press.

Mayer, J., Caruso, D., & Salovey, P. (1999). Emotional intelligence meets traditional standards for an intelligence. *Intelligence, 27,* 267–298.

Mayer, J., Caruso, D., & Salovey, P. (2000). Selecting a measure of emotional intelligence: The case for abilities scales. In R. Bar-On & J. Parker (Eds.). *The handbook of emotional intelligence* (pp. 320–342). San Francisco: Jossey-Bass.

Mayer, J. D., DiPaolo, M., & Salovey, P. (1990). Perceiving affective content in ambiguous visual stimuli: A component of emotional intelligence. *Journal of Personality Assessment 54,* 772–781.

Mayer, J. D., & Salovey, P. (1997). What is emotional intelligence? In P. Salovey & D. J. Sluyter (Eds.), *Emotional development and emotional intelligence* (pp. 3–31). New York: HarperCollins.

Mayer, J., Salovey, P., & Caruso, D. (1999). *Test manual for the MSCEIT research version 1.1* (3rd ed.). Toronto, Canada: Multi-Health Systems.

Mayer, J., Salovey, P., & Caruso, D. (2000a). Emotional intelligence as zeitgeist, as personality, and as a mental ability. In R. Bar-On & J. Parker (Eds.), *The handbook of emotional intelligence* (pp. 92–117). San Francisco: Jossey-Bass.

Mayer, J., Salovey, P., & Caruso, D. (2000b). Models of emotional intelligence. In R. Sternberg (Ed.), *Handbook of intelligence* (pp. 396–420). New York: Cambridge University Press.

Mayer, J., Salovey, P., & Caruso, D. (2002). *Mayer–Salovey–Caruso Emotional Intelligence Test manual.* Toronto, Canada: Multi-Health Systems.

McCrae, R. R. (2000). Emotional intelligence from the perspective of the five-factor model of personality. In R. Bar-On & J. Parker (Eds.), *The handbook of emotional intelligence* (pp. 263–276). San Francisco: Jossey-Bass.

McCrae, R. R., & Costa, P. T., Jr. (1990). *Personality in adulthood.* New York: Guilford.

McCrae, R. R., & John, O. P. (1992). An introduction to the five-factor model and its applications. *Journal of Personality, 60,* 175–215.

O'Conner, R. M., & Little, I. S. (2003). Revisiting the predictive validity of emotional intelligence: Self report versus ability based measures. *Personality and Individual Differences, 35,* 1893–1902.

Pellitteri, J. (2001). *Which emotional intelligence: A comparison of the MSCEIT and the EQi.* Manuscript submitted for publication.

Pellitteri, J. (2002). The relationship between emotional intelligence and ego defense mechanisms. *Journal of Psychology, 136,* 182–194.

Salovey, P., & Mayer, J. (1990). Emotional intelligence. *Imagination, Cognition, and Personality, 9,* 185–211.

Schutte, N. S., & Malouff, J. M. (1999). *Measuring emotional intelligence and related constructs.* Lewiston, NY: Mellen.

Solomon, R. (1993). The philosophy of emotions. In M. Lewis & J. M. Haviland (Eds.), *Handbook of emotions* (pp. 3–15). New York: Guilford.

Sternberg, R. J. (1990). *Metaphors of mind: Conceptions of the nature of intelligence.* New York: Cambridge University Press.

Sternberg, R. (2000). The concept of intelligence. In R. Sternberg (Ed.), *Handbook of intelligence* (pp. 3–15). New York: Cambridge University Press.

Zeidner, M., & Mathews, G. (2000). Intelligence and personality. In R. Sternberg (Ed.), *Handbook of intelligence* (pp. 581–610). New York: Cambridge University Press.

4

The Importance
of Self-Awareness
for School Counselors

Robin Stern
Columbia University

Lauren Hyman
New York University

Courtney E. Martin
Brooklyn College

Counselor Rosemary LeBron is the kind of woman who walks in the room and people immediately feel safe. She stands tall, smiles generously, and has a no-nonsense air about everything she does. Students in her New York City public middle school see her as a "tough lady," but they also know they can count on her to follow through, to show up, to say it like it is.

Rosemary works hard, sometimes too hard—staying late into the night, especially near the end of the year. She truly takes on the emotional problems of her students and her community, feeling responsible for each and every problem that walks through her door (and some that just hover outside waiting for her to notice). She doesn't break promises, even to herself.

When Rosemary decided to work on developing her own self-awareness, she committed to journaling as much as she could about her thoughts, feelings, and behaviors throughout her day. She quickly discovered two beautiful and mirac-

49

ulous things. First, she realized that she really needed to let go when she got home. After a heart-to-heart with her husband, he began cooking dinner and cleaning up afterward each night when she got home from work. Not only did Rosemary feel more relaxed, rejuvenated, and ready to go to work each morning; her relationship with her husband improved.

The other thing she realized through conscientious journaling was that she truly was making a difference in the lives of children. For all of her journal entries where she was frustrated or angry there were two more where she recorded feeling inspired and fulfilled. When a student walked out of her office with a new perspective, recommitted to focusing on school and positive behaviors for the future, she was now self-aware enough to recognize the giant smile on her own face.

To seek self-awareness is to travel down an ancient path, beginning with Plato's declaration that "the unexamined life is not worth living" and Aristotle's claim that well-managed passion is a sign of great personal wisdom. For thousands of years, thinking men and women from all different cultures and classes have sought to understand, not only the world around them, but the world within them. Some have treated this journey as a spiritual one, as in the case of the Chinese philosopher Lao Tzu, who wrote as early as 600 BC, "Knowing others is wisdom, knowing yourself is Enlightenment."

Others have couched self-awareness in psychological terms, such as psychoanalyst Sigmund Freud (1933) in the late 19th and early 20th century, who sought to understand the formation of personality through the analysis of dreams and memories originating from the unconscious layers of the mind. Another major figure in psychology, William James (1890) studied the self extensively and the capacity of the self to become its own object of observation, a term he coined as "reflexivity."

Salovey and Mayer (1990) referred to the concept of self-awareness at the end of the 20th century through their research and theory of emotional intelligence. They attested to the primacy of self-awareness, which they described as "being aware of both our mood and our thoughts about that mood" (p. 40). Goleman, then a science writer for the *New York Times* and a psychologist, brought the framework of emotional intelligence into the public realm by popularizing the idea in his book *Emotional Intelligence* (1995). His pledge to the American people—that if they developed their emotional intelligence, including their self-awareness, they would be happier, more successful people—revolutionized the way the public viewed the importance of emotions in everyday life. Today's school counselor has a unique opportunity to use Goleman's work, and the work of other leaders in the field of emotional intelligence and education, to become self-aware leaders in their school environments and to teach and inspire those around them to be the same.

WHAT IS SELF-AWARENESS?

Self-awareness is the essential practice of looking inward and honestly assessing our feelings, behaviors, strengths, and challenges. "It involves a process of focusing attention on one's thoughts, feelings, and behaviors in order to understand what they are, where they come from, and what they mean" (Shelton & Stern, 2004, p. 1). Self-awareness is also referred to as self-focused attention and it influences what type of information in the environment is selected, remembered, and compared with one's personal standards (Wells & Mathews, 1994). In summarizing some of the research on self-focus, Carver (2003) noted, "Self-knowledge also lies behind the development of the self-concept.... People who spend a good deal of time engaged in that kind of selective processing [i.e., self-awareness] naturally develop a view of themselves that is more elaborate and more firmly anchored than do other people" (p. 183).

As we become more self-aware, we gain a clearer sense of ourselves. Learning to connect to ourselves allows us to connect better with others. This is a foundation of emotional intelligence competency. Each of the major models of emotional intelligence includes a form of self-awareness (Bar-On, 1997; Goleman, 1995; Mayer & Salovey, 1997). When we are able to recognize how we are feeling and how our behavior (both verbal and nonverbal) affects other people, we are able to make better decisions and solve problems, communicate more effectively, and be better, more effective counselors.

Some people believe this process happens automatically, but counselors and emotional intelligence practitioners attest that gaining self-awareness is conscious, deliberate, and challenging work. This is because there can be a tendency to resist self-focused attention when it might highlight emotionally painful self-discrepancies or personal flaws (Carver, 2003). It is evident that any inspirational leader today needs to devote ample time to self-reflection, whether through meditation, journaling, or dialogue devoted to uncovering his or her authentic self. Linda Lantieri, director of Project Renewal and a leader in the field of emotional intelligence, explained, "I find that my daily meditation practice and the time I take for reflection are essential in accessing the deep wisdom and the balance I need to live a life of compassionate service to the world. I find that the degree to which I am committed to this inner process is the degree to which my voice in the world can be of help" (personal communication, November 14, 2004).

Self-awareness is about authenticity and being present. It is about knowing "where you're at" in a given moment so you may then turn your attention toward others, truly listening to intuit "where they're at." This process is a central requirement for the counseling core condition of genuineness as described by Rogers (1961). Self-awareness is also the act of reflecting on your unique purpose in life and how this purpose is being diverted or fulfilled at the present moment.

Self-awareness is the stepping stone to vision. If you can interpret your feelings and thoughts about your state of being today, you can certainly dream of where you want to be tomorrow. You can also facilitate others' dreaming—one of the most important roles a counselor plays in the lives of their students. Counselors must repair, educate, reframe, reorient, and refocus the students they counsel, which requires challenging skills that demand a high level of self-awareness.

WHY IS SELF-AWARENESS AN ESSENTIAL SKILL FOR AN EFFECTIVE SCHOOL COUNSELOR?

School counselors are the emotional centers of their schools. As a result, it is imperative for them to model self-aware leadership on a day-to-day basis. This kind of modeling can affect an entire educational community, including students, staff, and administrators. As Mahatma Gandhi once said, "Be the change you wish to see in the world." School counselors have a unique opportunity to model the kind of self-aware behavior they would like to see reflected within their school environment. A self-aware community is one where conflict is easily de-escalated, change for the better is not only possible but probable, and each individual feels part of a healthy, happy, and eternally learning environment. A self-aware school is one in which the administration, faculty, and staff have reflected on philosophy, curriculum, management process, and culture, and have incorporated SEL into every aspect of the school environment (Shelton & Stern, 2004).

One school counselor, working in New York City District 2 for 3 years, recounted her own quest to model self-aware behavior for her students:

> As a third year school counselor I have very quickly become aware of how my thoughts, feelings and behaviors contribute to making me a better counselor. I have learned that the way I conduct myself is more influential than anything I intend to teach them. For example, I have an on going problem with students constantly and relentlessly knocking on my office door to come in when I am in session with other students. After several months of telling them to stop and eventually getting so frustrated I started raising my voice, a student pointed out to me that my angry behavior was atypical. Through journaling I realized that I was modeling for them that it was okay to yell when they get frustrated. I eventually started sharing with the students what I was doing and why they couldn't come in. Although part of me felt that I shouldn't have to explain myself to these children, I found that when I behaved respectfully, they did as well. I now keep a posted schedule with a sign on my door that asks the students to please be considerate when the door is closed because counseling is in progress. It's not perfect but it's a lot better.

It was through consistently reflecting and journaling for the first time that this counselor was able to step back and observe her own behavior objectively. In so doing, she not only eradicated toxic emotions in her day but began to model appropriate anger-management and constructive communication techniques for her students. "Negative affect appears to increase self-focused attention; perhaps such affect signals a discrepancy in self-regulation [i.e. inner balance] and self focus is an intermediate process aimed at facilitating appraisal and reduction of the discrepancy" (Wells & Mathews, 1994, p. 205). When counselors can not only be aware of their own emotions but see the message or information that the emotions provide, they can use their emotions in an intelligent way to form more effective responses within themselves and toward others. This in turn creates an emotionally intelligent environment.

Empathy is at the core of the school counselor's work in schools. If counselors spend time checking in with their own feelings, they will grow accustomed to doing it with others. Contrastingly, Goleman, Boyatzis, and McKee (2002) asserted in their book *Primal Leadership:* "Self-awareness plays a crucial role in empathy, or sensing how someone else sees a situation: If a person is perpetually oblivious to his own feelings, he will also be tuned out to how others feel" (p. 40). If counselors are not mindful about assessing their own emotional states, they will have a difficult time intuiting others.

Such views are supported by research on self-directed attention and attributions. "Using a variety of paradigms, this general finding has been replicated repeatedly, showing that self-aware persons ascribe greater responsibility to themselves for various kinds of events, including the plights of other people" (Carver, 2003, p. 182). When counselors are self-aware they can feel the needs of others and help them find solutions to their challenges.

Likewise, counselors are listeners; it is imperative that they listen to their own inner monologue before they can clearly and effectively listen to anyone else's. Counselors must take an inventory of their own triggers, biases, and stereotypes before unintentionally letting them affect their relationships with students. Goleman et al. (2002) went on to attest that:

> Without recognizing our own emotions, we will be poor at managing them, and less able to understand them in others. Self-aware leaders are attuned to their inner signals. They recognize, for instance, how their feelings affect themselves and their job performance. Instead of letting anger build into an outburst, they spot it as it crescendos and can see both what's causing it and how to do something constructive about it. Leaders who lack this emotional self-awareness, on the other hand, might lose their temper but have no understanding of why their emotions push them around. (p. 47)

School counselors are faced with high-pressure, intensely emotional, and volatile situations every day. When counselors are aware of their feelings, they have the advantage of being able to manage and adjust their own reactions during stressful times so as to stabilize the situation. In this sense, the self-aware counselor can set the tone in the room during crisis—be a calming presence in a storm of unregulated emotions. As intense emotions can be contagious to those around, self-aware school counselors not only shield themselves from being adversely affected but can be a critical force of calm during hard times.

On the other hand, if counselors are unaware of their own triggers, they run the risk of being, at best, ineffective at intervening in crisis. At the very worst, they could escalate conflict for reasons out of their awareness, thereby undermining their authority and effectiveness as mediators. Part of a counselor's challenge is to maintain composure during intense and difficult situations, work on the "problem" at hand, and begin the process of working with the people involved toward emotional repair.

Research studies on self-awareness and emotions suggest that self-awareness amplifies emotional experiences. "When participants [in a high state of self-focus] were then asked to report on their feelings, they reported feelings of greater intensity than did participants who were less self-aware" (Carver, 2003, p. 182). This can be an advantage for self-aware counselors in that they can more fully experience their own and others' emotions. However, it may at times be a disadvantage because too sharply focused attention can lead an undesirable degree of emotional intensity and to a loss of perspective (i.e., missing the forest for the trees). The cognitive basis of depression and other psychopathologies can result from excessive negative self-focus where the depressed person dwells on every mistake and personal weakness (Wells & Mathews, 1994). In counselors' own work on self-awareness and their work on developing others' self-awareness, it is important to achieve a balanced and "intelligent" degree of self-focus. One of Mayer and Salovey's (1997) emotional intelligence abilities is "to reflectively engage or detach from an emotion depending upon its judged informativeness or utility" (p. 11).

According to the ASCA's (1997) National Standards for school counselors, counselors must help their students to acquire specific personal and social development skills:

Standard A: Students will acquire the attitudes, knowledge and interpersonal skills to help them understand and respect self and others.

Standard B: Students will make decisions, set goals and take necessary action to achieve goals.

Standard C: Students will understand safety and survival skills.

Each of these standards requires the students to have developed a certain degree of self-awareness, particularly when it involves interpersonal relations and personal goal achievement. To maximize student development in these areas, counselors themselves must have developed a degree of self-awareness.

Furthermore, self-awareness helps counselors stay true to their original reason for getting involved in a helping profession—to help! Reflecting daily on the bigger picture of their work is an effective and inspiring way to remain aligned with counselors' original purpose. It can aid professional counselors in feeling more fulfilled by taking notice of the progress they are making in relationships and projects, and to be more in control of challenges as they arise.

If a school counselor's training only emphasizes the importance of self-awareness through readings and lectures, the only hands-on practice school counselors obtain, if any, is through their field work in schools. It can be daunting for some beginning counselors to integrate the practice of self-reflection into their daily lives and to be attentive to the impact of their own thoughts, feelings, and behaviors on their students. For example, if a high school student with an abusive boyfriend comes to speak with a counselor who is a past victim of domestic violence herself, it may be difficult for the counselor to be an active, supportive listener and advocate for the student. As the student tells her story, the counselor may experience feelings of anxiety and may begin to relate strongly to her student's abusive relationship. If the counselor is unable to identify these feelings she may mistakenly direct her student rather than truly helping her explore her options. In contrast, if the counselor had taken the time to explore her own issues with abusive relationships through a process of dedicated self-reflection, she may have the insight to refer her student to another counselor, or she may try to manage her own personal feelings while maintaining a nonjudgmental, empathic, caring role for her student. "Because change is predicated on the relationship that the therapist [or counselor] creates with clients, therapists [and counselors] must make a lifelong commitment to working on their own dynamics" (Teyber, 2000, p. 147).

Laurie Bernstein, a New York City school counselor, reflected on the importance of identifying these kinds of triggers:

> I have to be aware of my personal biases. Sometimes a student can remind me of someone I don't like or represent something I don't like about myself. I use self talk to separate my personal feelings from the mission of my work. I focus on my goal and remind myself that I really do believe there are no bad kids. I know they all need nurturing and guidance. It is those students that frustrate me the most that need me the most. By being aware of this I can support and care equally for all of my students.

WHAT ARE SOME STRATEGIES FOR ENHANCING SCHOOL COUNSELORS' SELF-AWARENESS?

Here are some possible reflection questions for counselors:

- I notice that I am reacting to this particular student in a way that is unusual for me. What is behind that? What feelings am I having as a result of interacting with this person? What memories does he or she invoke?
- Is this student pushing certain "buttons" in me? Is this student reacting to me in a way that suggests that I am pushing his or her buttons? If so, what buttons am I pushing?
- Is there a pattern in my reactions to certain types of students in ways that are not helpful to the client?
- Do I favor some students over others? Which ones and why? What feelings do these kinds of students evoke? What memories? What about the students I don't particularly like or feel drawn to? What feelings or memories do they evoke?
- Do some stories or topics affect me more than others?
- How do I deal with intense feelings, like anger, in my students? Am I comfortable allowing my students to show anger in their sessions with me? Why or why not?
- Am I comfortable with my students expressing very positive feelings or feelings of being very needy?
- When I feel tension in the room, am I able to identify where it is coming from? Do I feel comfortable addressing this with my students?
- What are my emotional triggers? Which topics cause me to tense up or get angry?
- Identify and acknowledge my feelings during sessions. What physical signs tell me I am upset (i.e., racing heartbeat, sweaty palms, tense jaw)?

It is important for counselors to take time to reflect on their reactions and feelings about students and teachers in school. One helpful way to accomplish this is by keeping a *journal*. This activity allows counselors to reflect on their day and describe particular clients or situations that may have affected them in a profound or unusual way. The process of writing about thoughts and feelings will help counselors to figure out which situations are challenging and how they might deal with certain issues more productively in the future. One school counselor explained her own process:

I can not imagine counseling without incorporating self reflection into my very busy day. After each counseling session I think about the way that student (or group of students) left the session. I ask myself if they were happy, sad, empowered, excited, bored or indifferent. I think about how much was learned and how my behaviors and feelings contributed to that outcome. I contemplate what I could do different in our next session to affect change.

By making reflection an integral and consistent part of her daily routine, this counselor is able to watch the relationship with each of her students grow and, in turn, her own efficacy. *Be mindful always to practice active listening.* Pay attention to what you are feeling as clients are talking to you. Pay attention to how your body is reacting. These are important cues for learning more about how our inner self is reacting. *Understand how you react to people who are different from you.* When a child of a different race or ethnicity or religion is sharing a story with you, do you relate to what he or she is saying? Do you find yourself judging his or her family or cultural values? These are difficult and critical questions that require honest, sometimes uncomfortable, conversations with yourself. It is important not to place your own personal values on the student. Self-awareness is essential to be a culturally sensitive counselor, as ethnocentricity and personal bias are natural for any human being (Ivey, Ivey, & Simek-Morgan, 1997).

DOES SELF-REFLECTION REALLY WORK IN A BUSY SCHOOL ENVIRONMENT?

The answer is a definitive YES!, but it is important to consider first the challenges that exist in a school community. First of all, the process of being self-aware is inherently difficult because it requires an individual to be honest and forthright about his or her strengths *and* challenges. In an environment where each school leader is expected to be the best, to have a range of strengths and talents, to be organized and expert communicators, and to be empathic and ambitious, acknowledging challenges in one or more of these areas might be difficult. Patti and Tobin (2003) tackled just this issue in *Smart School Leaders* when they wrote:

> This process of appraising one's own efficacy beliefs is not easy because it touches upon our concept of self. A basic human need is to feel competent and achieving. For school leaders, this process becomes even more difficult because the expectations placed upon them is that they have to be competent in all areas. After all, they are the "LEADER." As a result, developing an accurate picture of our efficacy beliefs is challenging and leaders will benefit if they can use their feelings as guide markers to self-understanding. (p. 17)

Ideally, the school administration and the school environment will support each professional's self-awareness development. When honesty and personal growth is celebrated, not avoided, each individual can feel safe to explore the truth about his or her own limitations. Without this support, school counselors may feel stifled—unable to share their reflections or observations with others. A school counselor in an unsupportive environment, however, can and should attempt to gain self-awareness through personal reflection, although the work will be made much more difficult (and, consequently, much more necessary)!

There are many examples of school counselors who have dedicated themselves to a process of self-reflection and gained great benefits from it—even those working in overloaded, stressful school situations. Jan Hynda, a school counselor in a busy New York City public school district, started down the path to self-awareness reluctantly. She didn't like journaling and felt overloaded as it was. After discussing the obstructions in her own life that were keeping her from self-reflecting, she realized that she preferred to write letters and talk out loud as opposed to journaling. After a semester of dedicated self-reflection in the methods that felt most comfortable for her, Jan felt more effective, relaxed, and healthy. She took a day off when she realized she was too stressed out to do good work. By the end of the school year she had even decided to go back to school to get a higher degree in administration.

Peggy Chung, another school counselor in an overloaded New York City public school, largely populated by new immigrants and non-English speakers, was also transformed by self-reflection. As a new counselor, Peggy found the demands of the job overwhelming and draining. She was reaching a point where she didn't know if she could continue. She was tired of spending all of her time, energy, and emotion on her work. Through a process of dedicated journaling each lunch hour, she realized that she hadn't developed an awareness of when she had reached her limit, when she needed to say "no," or take a walk. Peggy embodied Goleman's warning in his landmark book *Emotional Intelligence* (1995): "Emotions that simmer beneath the threshold of awareness can have a powerful impact on how we perceive and react, even though we have no idea they are at work" (p. 49). She began to identify these moments through careful observation of her own internal cues and body sensations, and she practiced protecting herself.

Peggy has decided to stay with the profession and dedicate herself, not only to helping young immigrants get the education they deserve, but to continuing to develop her own ability to self-protect and balance. Without the tool of self-reflection, Peggy may have burned out long ago and her students would have lost her inspiring influence.

HOW DO I GET STARTED ON THE PROCESS
OF SELF-REFLECTION?

Just do it—you are worth every minute of attention to yourself! Reflective process takes a real commitment of spirit, time, and attention. Seeking self-awareness is, not surprisingly, a self-directed process, one to which you need to be dedicated for your own reasons and motivations. There are no overt penalties for not practicing self-awareness in your work or life, but benefits abound from choosing to follow through. Such benefits may include more satisfaction on your job, better relationships with coworkers, friends, and family, and a greater sense of accomplishment. Committing yourself to a regime of self-reflection can be the first stepping stone on your way to inspirational leadership. As Patti and Tobin (2003) wrote:

> The star or outstanding leader is the person who is self aware and who consciously works at improving his or her competencies. She knows her strengths and limitations, seeks out feedback, and learns from her mistakes. As she directs her own learning, she capitalizes on her strength areas in her performance while she continuously works on strengthening her limitations. Her goal is to bridge the gap between her ideal self, the leader she wants to be and her real self, the leader she is now. (p. 1)

But how do you bridge that gap? The practical side of self-awareness building can be difficult. How can you realistically work journaling into your busy day? Most school counselors wish there were more hours in the day already. Many feel as if the administrative demands of filling out paperwork and attending meetings distracts them from their real purpose: to spend quality time transforming their students' lives. It is difficult to work time for self-reflection into this already strained schedule, but it is also essential. Many school counselors have had great success journaling during the last 15 minutes of each day.

In Table 4.1 is a framework developed by Star Factor, a consulting firm whose mission is to enhance emotional intelligence competence in leaders. It was used by New York City school counselors and was part of Project EXcellence in Social Emotional Learning (EXSEL), to great success. The framework provides a structure for examining your emotional reactions to gain greater clarity and control of your feelings.

The most compelling reason for the school counselor to commit to the process of gaining self-awareness, ultimately, is that being self-aware can enhance the whole person—not just at work, but at home, with friends and family. A self-aware individual has the unparalleled opportunity to experience the world in an authentic way and to avoid what Palmer (1997) coined "divided lives" in

TABLE 4.1
Project EXSEL Counseling Journal Model

Trigger

- Usually a condition, comment, or succinct situation. Sometimes a person can be a trigger or a specific interaction.
- Example: bad headache.

Event

- The situation that proceeds the trigger.
- Example: forgot meeting.

Thoughts/Feelings

- How did you feel during the event? What was your inner monologue/self-talk telling you?
- Example: I'm in trouble. She's so strict. I'm embarrassed.

Internal Action

- How did you react internally to the event and your resultant thoughts/feelings?
- Example: deep breathing.

Actions

- What did other see? What were your outward, visible actions and reactions?
- Example: e-mail apology.

Ideal Action

- What do you wish you had done? What would have been more effective, honest, constructive?
- Example: phone call.

Gap Analysis

- Why didn't you do the ideal action?
- Example: I didn't want to deal with her reaction.

Competency

- What competency or competencies did this event ask me to utilize?
- Example: self-awareness, self-management.

© Star Factor

his book *Courage to Teach*. Those who don't take on the challenge of learning about their own thoughts, feelings, and behaviors often suffer from a sense of fracture in their lives—they are moving constantly and unconsciously, unable to unify their many selves, haphazard and unfair in their relationships with others. By contrast, those who take on the difficult project of lifelong self-awareness commit themselves to honesty and vulnerability and the possibility of personal growth. One school counselor summed it up:

> I find that it is especially important for school counselors to be aware of our roles in the students' lives. One of the biggest challenges I and many of my colleagues face is accepting the limitations of our empowerment to help children and allowing ourselves to become too emotionally involved. I see myself as an educator of social and emotional growth. Some students learn goals and values at their religious schools, others at home, but many just don't. As counselors, I believe we have a moral obligation to educate students with the knowledge and tools to help them lead successful, productive and well rounded lives. I find that I must remind myself to be aware of my role so that I create lessons and feel satisfaction at my job. Through self-aware counseling I know that students are actually learning life skills while sharing their feelings and getting the rare opportunity to have their voices heard.

The process of self-awareness is a journey that we are on together—counselors, students, and colleagues alike. As we work toward deepening our own awareness, we influence others to do the same. The insights of one person on this quest will increase the visions for us all.

REFERENCES

American School Counselor Association. (1997). *Sharing Counseling Programs*. Alexandria, VA: Author.

Bar-On, R. (1997). *Emotional Quotient Inventory user's manual*. Toronto, Canada: Multi-Health Systems.

Carver, C. (2003). Self awareness. In M. R. Leary & J. P. Tangney (Eds.), *Handbook of self and identity* (pp. 179–196). New York: Guilford.

Freud, S. (1933). *New introductory lectures on psychoanalysis*. New York: Norton.

Goleman, D. (1995). *Emotional intelligence: Why it can matter more than IQ*. New York: Bantam.

Goleman, D., Boyatzis, R., & McKee, A. (2002). *Primal leadership: Realizing the power of emotional intelligence*. Boston: Harvard Business School Press.

Ivey, A., Ivey, M. B., & Simek-Morgan, L. (1997). *Counseling and psychotherapy: A multicultural perspective* (4th ed.). Boston: Allyn & Bacon.

James, W. (1890). *The principles of psychology*. New York: Holt.

Mayer, J. D., & Salovey, P. (1997). What is emotional intelligence? In P. Salovey & D. J. Sluyter (Eds.), *Emotional development and emotional intelligence* (pp. 3–31). New York: HarperCollins.

Palmer, P. (1997). *Courage to teach: Exploring the inner landscape of a teacher's life*. San Francisco: Jossey-Bass.

Patti, J., & Tobin, J. (2003). *Smart school leaders: Leading with emotional intelligence.* Dubuque, IA: Kendall Hunt.

Rogers, C. (1961). *On becoming a person.* Boston: Houghton Mifflin.

Salovey, P., & Mayer, J. (1990). Emotional intelligence. *Imagination, Cognition, and Personality, 9,* 185–211.

Shelton, C., & Stern, R. (2004). *Understanding emotions in the classroom.* Port Chester, NY: Dude Publishing.

Teyber, E. (2000). *Interpersonal process in psychotherapy: A relational approach* (4th ed.). Belmont, CA: Wadsworth/Thomson.

Wells, A., & Mathews, G. (1994). *Attention and emotion: A clinical perspective.* Hove, England: Lawrence Erlbaum Associates.

III

APPLICATIONS IN SCHOOL SETTINGS

In this section we focus on the emotionally intelligent school counselor and a range of applications for grades K–12. While the relational demands on the counselor's mastery of emotionally intelligence are independent of the age, the context calls for delivering SEL differently from grade to grade. Chapter 5 first considers the overall school environment and offers particular methods that have been "field-tested" and shown to increase emotional awareness and positive tone in a school's ecology. Chapter 6 looks at the many roles of the elementary school counselor in forming a foundation for students through comprehensive developmental counseling programs. Chapter 7 focuses on the middle school challenges and provides the language of emotional literacy necessary for students' dialogue, self awareness, and identity development. Chapter 8 introduces the concepts of *emotional networks* within the school ecology, and *emotional anchors* within individual's life space which serve as potential resources for guiding the adolescent through the high school years. It becomes evident in this section how the individual student and the school environment are linked and how the emotionally intelligent school counselor must work at both levels.

5

Infusing Emotional Learning Into the School Environment

Charles Fasano
Bay Ridge Preparatory School

John Pellitteri
Queens College, CUNY

Every school has significant opportunities to develop the emotional intelligence of children through the management of the school's environment. There are a variety of factors that constitute the milieu or school ecology and exert an influence, directly or indirectly, on all students from kindergarten through high school. Such factors include teachers and peer models, curriculum and learning experiences, and the social dynamics of group interactions. These factors, as well as other influences, contribute to the emotional tone in the school and can directly moderate student behavior. The players that are involved in, and responsible for, developing and maintaining this milieu include teachers, administrators, school counselors, and even the students themselves. When school personnel focus attention and effort at controlling the emotional dimensions of the school environment, the conditions are set to develop students' emotional intelligence. Opportunities to provide emotional learning experiences naturally occur during any school day. An emotionally intelligent school professional is anyone who recognizes these windows of opportunities and uses these teachable moments to advance the emotional awareness of the students and staff.

For such an approach to have an impact, it is ideal for the whole school to be involved in a commitment to emotional learning. School administrators are critical in providing the support and guidance for such systemic infusion of emotional learning into the school environment. Infusing emotional learning into a school goes beyond distinct "add on" programs that teach social-emotional skills but are often disconnected from other aspects of the school. The approach described in this chapter consists of informal as well as formal interventions that involve staff and students. It requires a systemic-ecological perspective that considers the impact that each member of the school environment has on each other. The methods described in this chapter have been used effectively at Bay Ridge Preparatory School in Brooklyn, New York. We have found that these methods not only create emotional learning opportunities but have influenced a variety of other academic-related issues, such as student motivation, scholastic achievement, and positive peer interactions.

This chapter focuses on three areas of intervention that can increase emotional learning and have a significant impact on the school environment. They include: (a) the role of the teacher in modeling and reinforcing emotionally intelligent behaviors, (b) the role of the administrator in implementing *productive discipline* that will result in higher levels of emotional intelligence, and (c) classroom instruction of psychological concepts designed to facilitate students' contributions to emotionally healthy school environments. The role of the school counselor in facilitating and coordinating these interventions and structures is emphasized in this chapter. At Bay Ridge Prep, emotional awareness is embedded as part of the philosophy. A unique aspect of the school is that the administrators are psychologists and have designed the methods of interventions. In educational settings that do not intentionally focus on emotional learning, the school counselor or other concerned professional may need to propose such ideas and present the relevance and importance of adopting an emotional orientation toward students. One approach that counselors can use in persuading the use of emotional intelligence is to emphasize (and hopefully demonstrate) the relationship emotional factors have with achievement, motivation, and positive social functioning.

THE ROLE OF THE TEACHER IN DEVELOPING EMOTIONAL INTELLIGENCE

Teachers as Models

Teachers provide powerful models of behavior that affect individual students and the entire classroom environment. This basic principle is central not only for teaching emotional intelligence skills but for the overall processes of learning and interpersonal interactions in the classroom. Students will learn what they observe whether the teacher intends to demonstrate the behaviors or not. Therefore, it is critical that the teacher has a high degree of self-awareness and is perceptive to the verbal and nonverbal cues that he or she exhibits. Bandura (1986/1995) has identified several attributes that increase the likelihood that an observer will copy a model's behavior—these include the model's prestige, trustworthiness, and competence. Teachers are in a natural position of power as adults and as the leaders of the classroom.

The relationship between the teacher and child is important, as this influences the power the teacher has in the eyes of the students. The school counselor or administrator can assist in enhancing the teacher's power as a model by complimenting the teacher in front of students, speaking with respect and high regard for the teacher when in the presence of students, and creating conditions where the teacher's competences can be demonstrated. The respect that the students have toward the counselor or administrator will be transferred to the classroom teacher. In this way, the therapeutic relationships the counselor establishes with the students give the counselor power in building up the image of another staff member or peer as a desirable model. It is essential, of course, that the counselor has determined that a teacher or peer actually exhibits desirable behaviors before his or her status as a role model is built up.

Modeling can be used in various aspects of teaching. Teachers often model the correct sequence of solving mathematic problems, or reading decoding skills, or methods of studying. An emotionally intelligent teacher is also cognizant of modeling emotional reactions. When the teacher demonstrates appropriate emotional restraint in an upsetting situation, the students observing the teacher are learning about emotional regulation. If a teacher verbalizes his or her feelings, students witness emotional expression. Teachers can also model persistence, optimism, and effective problem-solving approaches by verbalizing their thinking processes while addressing barriers and dealing constructively with their own failures. "Rather than being exposed only to 'success models' who handle tasks with ease, students are exposed to 'coping models' who struggle to overcome mistakes before finally succeeding" (Brophy, 2004, p. 131). When a teacher inevitably makes a mistake or encounters a barrier, his or her capacity to tolerate frustration and verbalize constructive thinking processes provides students with examples of how to deal with problems.

Any social interaction involving the teacher is an opportunity to demonstrate emotional intelligence. Appropriate social interaction at a basic level includes treating people with respect, kindness, patience, and fairness. When a teacher exhibits these positive qualities, students in the presence of that teacher are more likely to act in a consistent manner (thus copying the behaviors associated with the positive qualities). The same students in the company of a less emotionally advanced teacher (one who exhibits anger or low frustration tolerance with his or her students) will be more likely to exhibit behavior problems and have difficulties interacting with their peers. The negative emotions that can be generated by a teacher with low emotional intelligence can have a detrimental effect on the group dynamics of the students. We have observed how the variability of student behavior is modified by the presence of a particular teacher (or other school personnel). Stuhlman and Pianta (2002) found a correspondence between teacher's emotional responses and student's behavior, noting that teachers' negative descriptors of their students lead to more instances of behavior problems.

Teachers as Reinforcers

Modeling can explain how some students acquire particular behaviors. However, it is the subsequent reinforcement that provides the motivation to enact the behaviors that are learned. The teacher's behaviors therefore can encourage or discourage particular behaviors in students. These basic social learning principles can be systematically used to increase the students' behaviors that are associated with high emotional intelligence. Through direct compliments and praise, teachers can intentionally reinforce any desirable student behaviors or behavioral tendencies. The powerful role of the teacher adds to the weight or strength of the praise. Increasing positive behaviors will not only improve social interactions between peers but will influence the student's self-concept and self-efficacy. Children's self-perception can often be affected by the teachers' perception of them. If children think that the teacher believes they are mature and caring, it is more likely that they will become more mature and caring.

One example is of a middle school student who showed undeveloped potential in her social skills. She was consistently praised by her teacher for being an excellent role model to other students. The teacher praised her for the concern she showed others and for her attentiveness to interpersonal nuances in the social environment. As a result, this girl developed more concern for others and developed a stronger awareness of the social dynamics in the classroom. Her behavior was exemplary and she became well respected by other teachers and students. The first author of this chapter, on meeting this girl's relative, described her as a great student and a role model to her peers. The relative interjected that sometimes she behaves in an inconsistent and negative manner. He jokingly told the relative that he could not hear anything bad about her because he wanted to maintain his positive view of her. It was believed that this positive unconditional view of the student was a major factor in her self-perception and self-concept. In addition, her pattern of positive prosocial behaviors was due in part to the positive beliefs that the teachers and administrators conveyed to her. The goal is that the student's positive behaviors will eventually generalize to other environments and become consistent attributes of this student's personality. This takes time, however, and can be affected by conditioned stimuli within these other environments.

An emotionally intelligent environment is more than the modeling and acquisition of particular social skills. It involves the interpersonal relationships among all members of the school ecology. In counseling, the core conditions of empathy, unconditional positive regard, and genuineness established by Rogers (1961) provide a basis for any therapeutic relationship. The essence of student-teacher relationships is the same. When the teacher communicates empathy to the students, they feel understood and supported. When the teacher acts with beliefs of unconditional positive regard about the students, they come to develop positive self-concepts and increased self-esteem. When the teacher is authentic and genuine in his or her relationship with the students, the teacher is more credible and influential.

Consultation and Teacher Development

The key, then, in using teachers to infuse emotional learning into the school is to develop the emotional intelligence of the teachers. In a manner parallel to student development, the teacher's emotional development will not occur through mere in-service training in theory or skills but through the supportive relationships with colleagues and supervisors in the school. The professional school counselor can be instrumental in building the self-efficacy and self-esteem of teachers. Alderman (2004) noted how the self-efficacy of teachers is important in that it can have an impact on the self-efficacy of students. Counselors, in the consultation process with teachers, can create the Rogerian core conditions and express understanding of the difficulties and challenges that teachers face. It is the counselor's role in the school to provide support services to teachers (Davis, 2005). This support most often needs to be of an emotional nature and not merely a problem-solving approach. When teachers feel supported, appreciated, and successful about what they are doing, they are less likely to generate negative emotions in the classroom and more likely to bring positive feelings into their work and create a productive environment.

The emotional intelligence of the counselor is critical when consulting with teachers. The counselor must be perceptive to the overt as well as subtle emotions of the teachers. It is important, to convey accurate empathy, to be reflectively attuned to the teacher's tone of voice, body language, and any unexpressed needs or tensions. The counselor must consider the teacher's temperament (i.e., highly reactive, tendency toward negativity, openness) as well as the teacher's capacity to tolerate frustration. An understanding of the teacher's emotional functioning will assist in determining his or her zone of proximal development (Vygotsky, 1935/1978) with regard to emotional learning. In other words, the counselor must assess the teacher's capacity and degree of willingness to develop his or her own emotional intelligence. The counselor can then begin to influence the teacher's emotions in a productive manner that leads to an effective response to the students' situation. The counselor should draw on knowledge of emotion research, cognitive-emotional processes, and cognitive-behavioral counseling techniques to shift the thinking of teachers to increase their optimism and motivation to effect classroom change.

Teachers' expectations, attributions, and beliefs about students have been shown to have a direct influence on student's behaviors and performance (Alderman, 2004; Brophy, 2004; Gredler, 1997). For example, the *"sustaining expectation effect* occurs when a teacher has an existing expectation about a student and continues to respond to the student in the same way although the student's behavior has changed. This response maintains the [originally undesirable] behavior" (Alderman, 2004, p. 171). This is especially pertinent when a counselor has worked with a struggling or disruptive student and has motivated the student to improve his or her approach to school work or to decrease disruptive behaviors. At this critical period in the change process the student needs immediate reinforcement for any new and positive behaviors that he or she exhibits in the classroom (or any setting outside of the counselor's office). If the teacher holds onto the negative emotions and negative impressions that may have originally formed in response to the student (i.e., "I'm disappointed in his low achievement"; "He's a problem child"; "He'll never change"), the sustaining expectation effect will undermine the therapeutic impact of the counselor. It is at this point that the counselor must increase the emotional intelligence of the teacher so he or she can disengage from negative emotions, become flexible and open-minded to see the student in a new light, and be optimistic about the student's potential to improve.

In sum, teachers are powerful role models and can provide emotional learning for students by exhibiting the behaviors and traits associated with high emotional intelligence. Equally important, teachers can administer systematic reinforcement of desired behaviors and shape students' attempts at behavioral improvements. The student-teacher relationship and the teacher's expectations regarding the students are significant variables in moderating students' performance, students' self-perception, and academic motivation. The counselor serves as a psychological consultant and an emotional support for the teachers and can, based on the quality of the teacher-counselor relationship, increase the teacher's emotional intelligence. We now focus on the administrator's use of emotional intelligence regarding disciplinary issues.

THE ADMINISTRATOR AND EMOTIONALLY INTELLIGENT DISCIPLINE

Productive Discipline

Administrators are often faced with scenarios where students are sent to their office by a teacher or other school official because of some problematic behavior. A traditional approach to discipline would focus on what the child has done wrong and possibly implement a negative consequence (i.e., detention, call to parents). When children are punished for inappropriate behavior, the result is that they usually feel angry or misunderstood or that they have been treated unfairly. A student is most likely to improve for a short time and then resume the problem behavior. This usually does not lead to any type of emotional development; in fact, it probably has a negative impact on the child's self-esteem. In addition, one of the numerous disadvantages of punishment (Gredler, 1997) is that imposed consequences often lead the child to feel angry at the punisher, which causes a strain in that relationship.

When children have misbehaved in class and are sent to the office, this can be a golden opportunity to help them increase their self-awareness and become more mature in thinking. It is a special opportunity because the children are often upset about being in trouble and are motivated to reduce their anxiety. They come with high emotional energy, which can be used for a productive discussion. (This is similar to a counselor who uses a client's emotional intensity in a crisis as an opportunity to activate coping potential.) At these moments, the student may be more willing to share his or her feelings and be open to feedback. It is also a critical time to strengthen the relationship between the student and the administrator. Once a child senses that the administrator is looking out for his or her benefit, it helps him or her to develop a sense of trust and respect. This in turn allows the administrator to have a more significant influence on the student's thinking and feelings.

If an administrator does not have a relationship with the "problematic" student, the first step is to develop a relationship. This can take the form of a statements such as, "I do want to talk to you about what happened today; however, first I want to learn more about you," or "How has your school expe-

Hence been going? What is going well? What is not?" This type of questioning quickly conveys to the child that he or she is not going to be judged immediately but rather there is an effort on the part of the administrator to understand more about *who* he or she is. This often decreases the guardedness of the student. Once rapport has been established and the student is less defensive, the administrator can then inquire about the specific situation by saying, "Tell me what happened today." After careful and reflective listening, the administrator can take the opportunity to help the child understand the situation from the perspectives of all people involved. A critical component for success is the genuine and centered emotional tone of the administrator. If he or she conveys anger, judgment, or criticism through vocal quality or facial expressions, then even if the correct words are used the message of support for the student will not be fully communicated. Such a centeredness on the part of the administrator requires emotional regulation, including the abilities to detach from negative emotions, to suspend judgment, and to remain open to understanding different perspectives.

An example of this approach to productive discipline comes from the work of the first author of this chapter with an eighth-grade girl who has learning difficulties and was placed in a special group with other children to receive support. The teacher running the group reported that the girl was difficult to manage, saying to her classmates, "This group is for the dumb kids. I won't take part in it." When the class was over, the teacher asked if the principal would speak to her. She came into the room crying, partially feeling that she was about to get in trouble. Already having a relationship with this student, the principal asked her to describe what she was feeling and why. She explained that she really wanted to be with another homeroom teacher and did not feel that she needed this advisory support group. There are many factors to be considered and several levels on which one can approach this situation. First, the student is mostly likely insecure about her learning abilities and does not want to feel different by being in a support group. Second, the way she expressed herself hurt the feelings of others (i.e., referring to the group as one for "dumb" kids). Finally, her negative emotional expression interrupted the flow of the group and made it difficult for the teacher to accomplish what she needed. It was also perceived by others as disrespectful. Discussing her insecurity at this point did not make sense but might be addressed in a future counseling session. The principal decided that it was relevant to address how her comments might affect the feelings of the others in the group. He did this by breaking down the situation and asking her, "When you said, this is the dumb group, what affect do you think this had on the others?" She was able to identify that it must have made them "feel bad." When asked how she thought it affected the goals of the teacher, she was initially unsure and unaware that the teacher had specific goals. Once she was able to realize the teacher's perspective, she further understood the impact of her behavior. She asked if he would consider moving her to a different group. The principal asked her how the group would interpret such a move (after her negative outbursts) and helped her understand that it would set a bad precedent. He informed her that if she had come to him without causing such a scene, he might have been able to move her, but that would be difficult now. They agreed to revisit the issue in a week providing that she had perfect behavior in that group for that time. She left the office feeling like she was heard and hopeful that there was a chance she might be able to be moved. She also left with an increased understanding of how her actions affected both her classmates and the teacher.

Contrast this with a disciplinary meeting where a student is punished for acting the way she did. The final result would be a girl who might improve for a short time but would still be angry. If she were punished, her feelings would most likely override her ability to comprehend truly the impact of her behavior. An angry student will often have a negative impact on the environment, causing other students to become negative. Instead, this student left motivated to improve her behavior and feeling good, which can only lead to improved self-esteem and increased social awareness.

A productive discipline approach was used in another school where there was a history of significant behavioral problems. In the 1st year as a principal at this school, many of the students were disrespectful, cutting classes, and bullying other children. The productive discipline approach was used to work with these students and help develop alliances and increased social awareness. The impact of this strategy was significant. The environment improved considerably and the number of problem behaviors decreased rapidly in the first few months. The best compliment came from the custodian after 3 months when he stated that he knew the school was on its way to turning around. He based this on the fact that there was no graffiti in the bathrooms for several months. This was the result of students becoming connected to the school through their relationships with the administrators and not feeling angry over being disciplined.

The result with productive discipline, if everything is executed correctly, is a student who feels understood, is closer to the administrator, has an increased level of emotional maturity, and has an increased awareness of social situations that might occur in the future. If the student has leadership potential, this can be a great opportunity to cultivate a positive leader within the classroom. A student who has a trusting and communicative relationship with an administrator can be the eyes and ears for that administrator (or counselor) in the student groups and classrooms. Through the student, important information about potential problems among the children can be communicated. Discussions with that student and other potential leaders in the class can help increase the cohesion and positive tone of the student groups and the overall classroom environment.

Imposed Versus Natural Consequences

In some situations however, negative consequences may be unavoidable and perhaps necessary. Depending on the child's level of moral development (see the following section on Kohlberg, 1978), some children do not interpret their behavior as wrong unless they believe there is a negative consequence. An important distinction to make when considering consequences for negative behaviors is the difference between imposed and natural consequences. An administrator calling parents or giving detention is considered an imposed consequence. The student does not see it as a natural extension of his or her behavior but rather one arbitrarily implemented by the administrator. A natural consequence is one that happens purely as a result of the child's behavior. For example, detention would be an imposed consequence for a student who talks constantly in class. If this student fails a test, however, it would be more of a natural consequence, providing that the student understands that talking in class can lead to missing important information. If the child clearly attributes failing the test to talking and not to intelligence, this can be effective. Attribution of failure to ability would have detrimental effects on motivation and self-efficacy and would not be desirable.

An administrator or counselor can help coach a teacher to make consequences more natural, or at least appear more natural. If the student gets upset about failing, the teacher can help him or her to discover what leads to failure. Discovery and insights are more effective than simply saying, "If you stopped talking, maybe you wouldn't fail." Understanding cause-and-effect relationships and making accurate attributions for one's failures (and successes) are important. Determining what causes are under a student's control (i.e., more effort at studying, better organization of materials, etc.) can increase student motivation (Brophy, 2004). Natural consequences that are valued by the student can be highly powerful motivations. For example, if a student's actions will disappoint a highly respected teacher or lead to rejection from a desired group of friends, the student will be less likely to engage in such actions. Similarly, the positive relationships that students develop with teachers, administrators, counselors, and peers can be used as motivations to increase on-task behaviors and reduce discipline problems.

In summary, productive discipline is an approach that can be used to turn a situation that arises as a problem into an opportunity to develop social and emotional intelligence in a student. It can help a child analyze his or her behavior and the behavior of others, resulting in a more emotionally intelligent environment. If done correctly, it reinforces a positive relationship with the administrator and enables the student and administrator to handle future situations more effectively.

PSYCHOLOGY INSTRUCTION AS A MEANS OF DEVELOPING STUDENT AWARENESS

Counselor as Psychoeducator

One of the defining roles of counselors is to use psychoeducational interventions as a means of preventing future problems and enhancing well-being (Gelso & Fretz, 2001; Ivey, Ivey, & Simek-Downing, 1987). Teaching principles of psychology to middle school and high school students relates to this preventive role in that it provides a resource for individual students to understand themselves and their environments. Learning about the science of human behavior can help students to become more self-aware, increase their capacities to cope, discover their potential, and enhance their well-being. Miller (1969) used the notion of "giving psychology away," which refers to the importance of disseminating knowledge of psychology to nonprofessionals.

One of the practices at Bay Ridge Prep is to teach psychology to develop an awareness of the self and others. Students can benefit from developing knowledge of psychology at a young age. Self-awareness, an important component of emotional intelligence, is increased when there is an understanding of what makes us act the way we do. Knowledge of psychological principles can be applied to understanding the behavior and motives of others as well. When all the students in a grade develop *psychological mindedness,* the collective understanding of each other's behaviors in itself prevents or diminishes a range of conflicts. The psychological terms (described later) provide a language by which teachers and parents can communicate with students when discussing behavior and motivation. In formal psychology instruction, students enjoy learning about the basic concepts and relating those concepts to themselves. This enhances the relevance and meaning of the subject matter for the student. The acquisition of psychological knowledge may also increase a students' sense of self-efficacy in that it provides a greater sense that one can control his or her environment.

The psychology instruction can be directly provided by the counselor, who ideally should be a psychological specialist well versed in behavior modification

and group dynamics as well as developmental, social, and personality psychology. School psychologists, of course, would naturally be qualified to teach the
subject as well. If necessary, classroom teachers can be coached on what and
how to teach. The important ingredient in the psychology lessons is to make
the connection to the student's personal and interpersonal behaviors to
increase self-awareness.

Basic Principles of Psychology

One area of psychology that is taught involves basic principles of behavior-
ism. In one lesson for a group of eighth-grade students, they were asked,
"Why did you get up for school this morning? Why are you going to do the
homework and study for that test next week (or not)?" Students responded by
listing various reinforcements and punishments they would receive based on
their behaviors. Once the behaviors were listed, they were categorized according to internal versus external motivations. For example, "I get video
games when I get above an 80 on a test," would be an external motivation,
whereas "It makes me feel good when I do well" is an internal motivation. A
light often goes off in the students' heads when they realize just how controlled they are by external forces. A discussion of B. F. Skinner's (1971) book
Beyond Freedom and Dignity is appropriate during these discussions. An understanding of what motivates people can help them control more of these
factors and learn to use them to their advantage. The basic principle that positive reinforcement needs to come after a behavior, as opposed to before, is
very important. In applying this principle, students are taught to withhold reinforcement (going out to play, playing a video game, etc.) until they finish a
certain amount of homework. They learn to use these reinforcers to keep
themselves motivated. The benefit is also that students learn how to self-re-
inforce in other goal-oriented tasks.

    With regard to the group dynamics of a class, an understanding of behavior-
ism enables students to support each other. For example, if a student is acting
out in class, his or her psychologically minded classmates may recognize that
this stems from a need for social attention. If a teacher is intentionally reinforcing this student to improve his concentration on the school work, the other
students will know not to laugh when this student acts out because laughter
will reinforce disruptive behaviors. The teacher may speak privately with some
of the other students and encourage them to support his efforts to get the act-
ing-out student back on task. The removal of reinforcement for inappropriate
behaviors enhances the teacher's rewards for on-task behaviors. This type of
group effort is also based on the students' development of genuine concern for

each other. Once students engage in intentional behaviors to help their classmates succeed, they begin to value their classmates and their well-being.

Another psychology lesson that is valuable is teaching about the conscious and unconscious mind. Hall's (1954) book, A Primer of Freudian Psychology, is useful for spelling out basic principles in simple terms. An effective focus for this principle is through teaching basic defense mechanisms. The concept of projection, for example, helps students understand why other students act the way they do and helps them understand themselves better. Teasing and criticizing another often involve projection and are aimed at protecting one's self-esteem (Crocker & Park, 2003). Students who have poor self-esteem often put other children down. If they are self-conscious about their intelligence, they will often tell other children that they are "stupid." This is the most basic form of projection, where a student's unconscious (and unacceptable) feelings are being projected onto classmates where the unacceptable attributes can be verbally attacked. When other students understand this defense mechanism, they are not as personally affected by the derogatory comments. More insightful and emotionally intelligent students may even feel sympathy for the defensive child. Knowledge of projection therefore shifts the emotional reactions of students from being insulted, hurt, or angry toward being empathic or at least tolerant.

A third lesson that can be incorporated is the teaching of Kohlberg's (1978) levels of moral development. In brief, people generally function on three levels of moral reasoning. Level 1 consists of avoiding punishment and gaining reward. Level 2 consists of following rules set out by society. Level 3 consists of more internalized controls and motivations that are independent of the first two levels. In other words, doing the right thing because it is the right thing (Level 3) is different from acting this way because it is the law (Level 2) or because you will be rewarded for doing so (Level 1). A great exercise to start out with is the one that Kohlberg used to determine the levels of the participants he studied. He gave a scenario where a man's wife is dying and he cannot afford the medication that will save her life. He decides to steal the medication. The question is: Was this the right thing to do? Why or why not? The level of moral development is more tied to the explanation than to the answer. Stealing the medication because he was confident he could get away with it is the lowest level, whereas stealing it because human life is more important than the law is the highest level. Gender differences also emerge in examining the reasons behind these answers (Gilligan, 1982) and can be a fruitful focus of discussion.

This lesson gives a context for students to understand better their behaviors and the behaviors of those around them. For example, when students are unsupervised, do they do things they would not do in front of the teacher? Would they cheat on a test if they felt they could get away with it? It sets up a *cognitive dissonance* (i.e., internal conflict) in students where they must ask themselves: If I cheat on this test, does it mean I am at a low level of moral development? The moral development concept sets up a framework for talking to students if they are not living up to expectations. This exercise can be taken one step further by discussing that most people develop a sense of others in terms of their moral development. In other words, people learn if someone is trustworthy. Part of the exercise is having students rate how trustworthy they are. This is a personal examination and students can keep it to themselves. The goal, however, is for students to reflect on how people perceive them and how they want to be perceived.

CONCLUSION

If a school is to become emotionally intelligent, the affective dimensions of the social environment must be moderated. Interventions that consistently target a particular aspect of the environment will improve the emotional intelligence of a person or a group, which in turn will effect others in the system. This chapter presented three methods—teacher modeling and reinforcement, productive discipline, and psychology instruction—that can be used to develop awareness in self and others. Through these channels school personnel can infuse emotional learning into the environment. This in turn can decrease problematic behavior, increase motivation, and improve the overall quality of students' interpersonal interactions.

REFERENCES

Alderman, M. K. (2004). *Motivation for achievement*. Mahwah, NJ: Lawrence Erlbaum Associates.

Bandura, A. (1995). Reciprocal determinism: The triadic model. In W. Frick (Ed.), *Personality: Selected reading in theory* (pp. 200–214). Itasca, IL: Peacock. (Original work published in 1986)

Brophy, J. (2004). *Motivating students to learn*. Mahwah, NJ: Lawrence Erlbaum Associates.

Crocker, J., & Park, L. M. (2003). Seeking self esteem: Construction, maintenance, and protection of self-worth. In M. R. Leary & J. P. Tangney (Eds.), *Handbook of self and identity* (pp. 291–313). New York: Guilford.

Davis, T. (2005). *Exploring school counseling: Professional practices and perspectives*. Boston: Houghton Mifflin.

Gelso, C., & Fretz, B. (2001). *Counseling psychology*. Belmont, CA: Thomson/Wadsworth.

Gilligan, C. (1982). *In a different voice*. Cambridge, MA: Harvard University Press.

Gredler, M. E. (1997). *Learning and instruction: Theory into practice*. Englewood Cliffs, NJ: Prentice Hall.

Hall, C. S. (1954). *A primer of Freudian psychology*. New York: New American Library.

Ivey, A. E., Ivey, M. B., & Simek-Downing, L. (1987). *Counseling and psychotherapy: Integrating skills, theory, and practice* (2nd ed.). Boston: Allyn & Bacon.

Kohlberg, L. (1978). The child as a moral philosopher. In J. K. Gardner (Ed.), *Readings in developmental psychology* (pp. 349–357). Boston: Little, Brown.

Miller, G. A. (1969). Psychology s a means of promoting human welfare. *American Psychologist, 24,* 1063–1075.

Rogers, C. (1961). *On becoming a person.* Boston: Houghton Mifflin.

Skinner, B. F. (1971). *Beyond freedom and dignity.* Toronto, Canada: Bantam/Vintage.

Stuhlman, M. W., & Pianta, R. C. (2002). Teachers' narratives about their relationships with children: Associations with behavior in classrooms. *School Psychology Review, 31*(20), 148–163.

Vygotsky, L. (1978). Interaction between learning and development. In M. Cole, V. John-Steiner, S. Scribner, & E. Souberman (Eds.), *Mind in society: The development of higher psychological processes* (pp. 79–91). Cambridge, MA: Harvard University Press. (Original work published in 1935)

6

An Elementary Counseling Program: Nurturing Social and Emotional Learning for Life

Barbara Muller-Ackerman
Parsippany Counseling Center

Susan Stillman
Bolton Center Schools

THE ELEMENTARY SCHOOL COUNSELOR—
A TYPICAL DAY

An elementary school counselor stands on the playground animatedly greeting students. Although she isn't assigned playground duty, she feels that being visible and available, for students and parents alike, is an important part of her position. Before she is inside the door, a parent may have pulled her aside to discuss a concern over her son being bullied, the principal may have flagged her to quickly suggest implementing a peer mediation program to assist with playground conflicts, and a child may come to her upset about forgetting her homework. As she travels to her office, the counselor may be stopped by a fourth-grade teacher who wants to refer a student to the Cool Kids (anger management) group, and a second-grade teacher mentions that the class needs a lesson on listening skills as she leads them noisily through the hallway on the way to their room. Arriving at her office, the phone is already ringing; a counseling colleague needs ideas on running a school-wide career day. She quickly hangs up and runs to get to the Character Education Committee meeting, which she chairs. The first bell rings for homeroom.

If this is the first 30 minutes of an elementary counselor's day, what is typical? What do we talk about and work toward with students? Who is the school counselor? W, hat skills do they need to develop? What tools and structures do they use? And what is his or her role within an elementary school counseling program?

PERSONAL COMPETENCIES AND LEADERSHIP SKILLS

What personal competencies and leadership skills do elementary counselors need to implement effective school counseling programs? The ASCA National Model (2003) calls for counselors to take leadership roles in their schools. We believe this requires school counselors to strengthen their own social-emotional skills, to enable accomplishment of both the school counseling mission and to infuse SEL throughout the school community. Henderson and Gysbers (1998) identified the skills school counselors need: genuineness, the recognition of power, optimism, courage, a sense of time as a gift, a sense of humor, the capacity for intimacy, openness to fantasy and imagery, respect, and consideration for others. These skills seem particularly appropriate given the nature of an elementary school counselor's role.

Elementary school counselors develop effective relationships to facilitate authentic growth in their students, in those with whom they consult, and in themselves. The skills elementary counselors bring each day include active listening, being a team member, being able to facilitate a group process, solving interpersonal conflicts, using effective decision making, and being flexible and adaptable. School counselors draw on their own strong communication, organizational, consultation, and political skills as they play a multitude of roles with different stakeholders from teachers, parents, and community members, to first graders. Counselors must develop several important skills of emotional awareness and autonomy to fulfill these roles. Some of these SEL skills required are acceptance and mature control of their emotions, confidence in their own choices and decisions, and optimism and perseverance in the face of often difficult life challenges for their students and the school community.

Finally, SEL for elementary counselors means a self-awareness of their own life stages and needs, a desire for professional and personal growth, a motivation for lifelong learning, the willingness to take on new responsibilities as a school leader, and a commitment to enhance collaboratively the elementary school counseling program with SEL concepts.

SEL CONCEPTS

What are the SEL concepts that students need to integrate with the components of a school counseling delivery model? Psychologist and author Goleman (1995), renowned for his groundbreaking book on emotional intelligence, asked a straightforward question: "What do children need to learn in order to flourish in life?" (p. xiii). The Collaborative for Academic, Social, and Emotional Learning (CASEL; 2004) has devised a useful set of personal competencies that help elementary school counselors and others answer this question. This set of skills is familiar to elementary school counselors who work each day with children, their teachers, their families, and the school community. The skills—knowledge of self, regulating emotions, caring for others, responsible decision making and social effectiveness, detailed in Fig. 6.1—helps elementary school counselors determine learner outcomes in their classroom lessons and provide more effective interventions in their counseling and consultative activities.

Elementary counselors working in model school counseling programs help students and the school community address the skills and competencies vital for *all* children to grow and be successful as students, and to accomplish their goals in life as friends, family members, successful workers, and knowledgeable and responsible citizens. Goleman (1995) reminded us, "It's not just kids with problems, but all kids who can benefit from these skills; these are an inoculation for life" (p. 285).

The ASCA National Model (2003) includes National Standards (ASCA, 1997) that address these same social-emotional competencies through the structure of a comprehensive school counseling program. Focusing on these standards, advancing the personal-social, career and academic development of all students, elementary school counselors are natural leaders in the effort to foster a healthy, caring, and inclusive school environment where students can learn the skills they need for academic achievement and success in life.

It makes sense to merge the critical skills of SEL for students with the premises and structure of a model school counseling program. In doing so, counselors can make an even stronger contribution to the vital mission of an elementary school—to ensure success for all students in a nurturing, inclusive, challenging, and motivating learning environment.

PROGRAM STRUCTURES

What structures do school counselors use to advance their program and SEL? This chapter explains one major component of a comprehensive school coun-

Self-Awareness
- Identifying emotions: Identifying and labeling one's feelings
- Recognizing strengths: Identifying and cultivating one's strengths and positive qualities

Social Awareness
- Perspective taking: Identifying and understanding the thoughts and feelings of others
- Appreciating diversity: Understanding that individual and group differences complement each other and make the world more interesting

Self-Management
- Managing emotions: Monitoring and regulating feelings so they aid rather than impede the handling of situations
- Goal setting: Establishing and working toward the achievement of short— and long-term pro-social goals

Responsible Decision Making
- Analyzing situations: Accurately perceiving situations in which a decision is to be made and assessing factors that might influence one's response
- Assuming personal responsibility: Recognizing and understanding one's obligation to engage in ethical, safe, and legal behaviors
- Respecting others: Believing that others deserve to be treated with kindness and compassion and feeling motivated to contribute to the common good
- Problem solving: Generating, implementing, and evaluating positive and informed solutions to problems

Relationship Skills
- Communication: Using verbal and nonverbal skills to express oneself and promote positive and effective exchanges with others
- Building relationships: Establishing and maintaining healthy and rewarding connections with individuals and groups
- Negotiation: Achieving mutually satisfactory resolutions to conflict by addressing the needs of all concerned
- Refusal: Effectively conveying and following through with one's decision not to engage in unwanted, unsafe, unethical, or unlawful conduct

FIG. 6.1. Social-Emotional Skills for Counseling. Source: Collaborative for Academic, Social, and Emotional Learning (2004).

seling program. The delivery system, as found in the ASCA National Model, (2003) includes: (a) responsive services, (b) individual student planning, (c) curriculum, and (d) system support. We show how elementary counselors armed with an understanding of SEL can integrate these concepts and activities into the four major areas of the delivery system and develop a truly excellent elementary counseling program that supports student achievement and academic, personal-social, and career development and contributes to a caring community within the school.

Responsive Services: Individual, Small Group, and Crisis Counseling

Counseling is the process of helping people by assisting them in making decisions and changing behaviors. Elementary school counselors work with all students, setting counseling goals based on student needs, the competencies in the ASCA National Standards, and SEL skills. Elementary counseling goals for students are skill based and developmentally appropriate.

Contrary to popular opinion, the elementary counselor doesn't do "therapy" with students. What they do is listen to students, respond to their needs for caring and concern, connect them with appropriate resources within and outside of school, and teach them the SEL skills that will enable them to thrive and grow, academically and personally. Elementary school counselors regularly attend to the social-emotional, academic, and career awareness needs of students.

These needs may best be conceptualized by categorizing them according to a model designed by Elias et al. (1997). In the model, they have suggested that the four components of social emotional learning comprise: (a) life skills and social competencies, (b) health promotion and problem prevention, (c) support for transitions and crises, and (d) positive contributory service.

Counseling, whether individually or in a small group, is one method to personalize both the comprehensive developmental counseling goals and the SEL competencies. How does this work in a counseling session? In essence, counselors help students be more aware of their own thoughts, feelings, actions, and behaviors and use this information to enable stronger relationships with other people. In an individual, small-group, or crisis counseling session, counselors may work to empower students by teaching the following skills (for a more complete list of some of the skills, attitudes, and behaviors, see Fig. 6.2):

- Learning to reflect on their behavior and choices—what will be the consequences of this behavior for themselves or others? Is it a good choice?
- Learning to regulate emotions and use self-control—learning to deal with anger and stress, normal developmental concerns that may spiral out of control.

The social emotional skills, taught in counseling sessions, which help children flourish are:

- Learning to reflect on their behavior and choices—what will be the consequences of this behavior for themselves or others? Is it a good choice?
- Developing a sense of responsibility for each other; learning to care about others—recognizing their interdependence and need to work together, learning to include others and recognize the value of diversity.
- Learning to regulate emotions and use self-control—learning to deal with anger and stress, normal developmental concerns that may spiral out of control.
- Learning a feelings vocabulary and what to do with emotions, being able to recognize and reflect on them—self-awareness is also a key social emotional learning goal. Many wonderful charts, posters, and activities elicit emotional awareness. "I-messages" are popular teaching tools for helping children express their feelings.
- Learning to participation in groups—understanding how to share thoughts, time, materials, and space; learning to use a "speaker power" tool to facilitate communication, learning to ask follow-up questions; learning to show appreciation.
- Developing empathy and awareness of others' perspectives—empathy is a skill learned over time and school counselors can be instrumental in modeling and teaching this skill.
- Learning how to solve social problems by using a social decision-making process, as illustrated in Chapters 9 and 15.
- Learning to ask for help.
- Learning to be assertive when being bullied or harassed.
- Learning to recognize and address bullying, victim, and bystander behaviors.
- Learning to share thoughts, materials, and needs.
- Learning the best way to communicate needs and ideas, and handle differences of opinion.
- Learning how to cope with setbacks and disappointments.
- Learning how to handle and work through change—from personal-social crises such as family divorces, deaths, and moves to the daily changes we tend to resist.
- Learning how to handle difficult situations effectively.
- Learning about peer relationships—how to make and keep friends, and to move away from friends as they outgrow them.
- Learning how to develop optimism and perseverance— a wonderful activity reminds students "how to turn lemons into lemonade."
- Developing an awareness of their own strengths and needs for growth, developing an awareness of future interests, setting goals.
- Developing an awareness of organizational and study skills.

FIG. 6.2.   Social Emotional Learning for Children

- Learning to participate in groups—understanding how to share thoughts, time, materials, and space; learning to use a speaker power tool to facilitate communication; learning to ask follow-up questions; learning to show appreciation.
- Learning how to handle and work through change, from personal-social crisis such as family divorces, deaths, and moves to the daily changes we tend to resist.
- Learning to be assertive when being bullied or harassed.

Elementary counselors work with many students each day, individually and in groups, on these common developmental skills that also teach SEL competencies. At the same time, elementary students are learning and overlearning the same social emotional learning skills, in not only in counseling settings but, in the classroom with peers, in their relationships with adults in the school, and ideally at home with their parents. Elementary counselors play a major leadership role in advocating for these essential SEL skills to be taught and practiced consistently. All adults working with children participate in reinforcing these skills, using a common language and nurturing the overall climate of caring.

Individual Student Planning

The individual student planning component of a comprehensive developmental school counseling program addresses the SEL skills of self-awareness, perseverance, motivation, and goal setting. The elementary counselor might meet with parents, teachers, and students to develop goals and behavior plans, design necessary modifications of programs, and address needed skill sets for particular students. Elementary counselors may help students and their parents choose appropriate extracurricular opportunities or suggest ways students might become involved in service learning or leadership opportunities. In addition to classroom instruction, particular interventions might be useful for students in transition—those new to school or those moving into middle school. This individual student planning component of the school counseling program is useful in delivering all three domains of personal-social, career, and academic development and helps all students in partnership with their parents and teachers create personalized strategies for success.

Curriculum

A school counseling curriculum is planned, organized, sequential, and consistently taught to all students at every grade level. It enhances students' learning process and achievement outcomes in the three areas of development. In short, it teaches students to communicate, cooperate, respect self and others, set goals, make decisions, be aware of self and others and plan for the future. It is the anchor of an SEL program (Elias et al., 1997) as well as the educational mission of the school.

Although responsive services may offer individual or small-group practice in SEL, it is through large-group classroom lessons that *all* students have an opportunity to experience, and benefit from, an elementary school counseling program. Within that program's design, the curriculum is where SEL becomes the basis of lessons in all three domains: personal-social, career and academic. The skills listed in the individual, group, and crisis counseling section earlier, and presented in greater detail in Fig. 6.2, are the skills that are taught in the large-group lesson as well.

If one objective of a school counseling program is to enlist all stakeholders in taking responsibility for delivering its competencies, the elementary campus is the ideal level for making this happen. Infusing lessons that cover the skills of personal-social, academic, and career development is made easy through the use of literature, whether it is in a language arts, math, history, science, social studies, art, or music class. Chapters 10 and 16 of this volume describe Project EXSEL in New York City, which is a wonderful example of how teachers and counselors collaborate to teach SEL skills during the literacy block in elementary classes. The Project EXSEL Web site offers lessons that were developed using books to deliver SEL skills (see Appendix C).

Although literature is a natural way to integrate curriculum competencies, commercial programs used in all classes are another. *Don't Laugh At Me*, by Operation Respect, directly tackles the issues of bullying and ridicule. *Steps to Respect*, by the Committee for Children, is a particularly effective program for teaching the skills of character education, and *Second Step* offers key skills for violence prevention. Many other research-validated programs are provided through their Web sites in Appendix C.

Empowering students to solve problems, through conflict-resolution and decision-making models, provides another effective unit of classroom lessons from the curriculum, first modeled by the counselor, then continued by the teacher who may be in many different content areas. Class meetings are another perfect vehicle for SEL. Here, too, the school counselor goes into classroom and works with both teacher and class to learn class meeting structure and meanings. In meetings, the students learn hear differing perspectives and experiences, learn to give compliments instead of put-downs, practice problem solving, and goal set for future activities.

The time one commits to morning meeting is an investment that is repaid many times over. The sense of group belonging and the skills of attention, listening, expression, and cooperative interaction developed are a foundation for every lesson, every transition time, every lining up, every upset and conflict, all day and all year long. Morning meeting is a microcosm of the way we wish our schools to be—communities full of learning, safe and respectful and challenging for all (Kriete, 1999). Similarly, Nelson's model is quickly converted to family meetings and gives parents a way to reinforce the concepts taught through the curriculum, now applied at home (Nelson, Lott, Glenn, 2000).

System Support

Although the ASCA National Standards (1997) set forth the curriculum competencies detailed in the previous section, The ASCA National Model (2003), a framework for school counseling programs, emphasized that counselors need to develop specific competencies in themselves to ensure effective programs. To weave the themes of leadership, advocacy, system change, and collaboration into the fabric of one's program also requires the counselor to know and practice SEL skills. The abilities of self-awareness, conflict resolution, motivation, empathy, decision making, perseverance, and other social skills that counselors hope to instill in their youngest students need to be a part of who they are and how they act in the role of elementary counselor. In actively maintaining school counseling program support, the elementary counselor must perform the following duties.

Advocate With Teachers for Students

Elementary school counselors work with teachers to develop a classroom climate that respects students, encourages their best work, and enhances their emotional and social growth. Elementary counselors might introduce the skills of SEL in class meetings, consult with teachers on classroom management, assist with individual behavior plans, and work on early intervention committees, case partnering with teachers to support individual student needs with attention to social-emotional and behavioral concerns.

Interact With Parents and Families

In advocating for their students, elementary counselors take the lead in creating opportunities to interact with parents. This interaction can take the form of working with PTA and PTO, organizing breakfast clubs; facilitating parent book discussions; running groups for parenting and family management issues; establishing parent book, tape, and CD lending libraries; and presenting educational workshops on a range of topics from child development to specific parenting concerns, both academic and behavioral.

A comprehensive developmental school counseling program is prevention oriented and collaborative in nature. Parent-family-school partnerships are vital for students' success, and elementary counselors are in an excellent position to help parents understand and build their children's SEL.

Collaborate With Administrators

The collaboration of elementary school counselors with administrators takes many forms. Many elementary school counselors work closely with administrators but strongly preserve their presence as a counselor rather than as disciplinarian. Counselors need to advocate for their programs with administrators by negotiating away the quasi-administrative tasks that take them away from time for student contact. At its ideal, the relationship-building ability of the elementary counselor creates a role where, through consulting, planning, cooperating, communicating, and advising, the administrator is educated to the potential of the school counseling program and its benefits to all its stakeholders. Functioning in this capacity, all stakeholders are best served.

Lead Committees

An elementary counselor needs to be seen as involved in the vital working of the school. One way of accomplishing this is by taking a leadership role on committees. The names of these committees may vary from school to school and district to district but can include those on site-based management, diversity, character education, sensitivity, SEL, behavior management, principal's advisory, PTA, crisis management, early intervention, and student support. The school counselor's presence on committees brings their unique perspective, ensuring that the whole child's development is taken into account, and brings their unique talents to problem solve and create consensus from disparate points of view. It is no wonder, then, that school counselors are responsible for creating and chairing many of the committees and the resulting programs and policies that follow, as they keenly understand the needs of children and of those who function, and who function less than optimally, in the buildings in which they work.

Create a Safe School, Inclusive, Caring Climate

Although school counselors are now charged with being tied to the academic mission of the schools, the words within those missions are changing.

Words such as *nurturing* and *safe* stand side by side with those that describe high standards of learning. Whole-school initiatives, based on SEL philosophy, help schools create a positive climate throughout the school community. These initiatives might have elementary counselors lead or collaborate on schoolwide antibullying programs, promoting an awareness of multiculturalism and an appreciation and sensitivity to diversity issues, introducing a peer-mediation and conflict-resolution program, and developing service learning and leadership potential for students. Additionally, in faculty meetings, and in behavior management and SEL committees, counselors are working with staff, parents, and students to create mission statements and behavior management plans that help schools develop a nonpunitive discipline system based on rights and responsibilities. It is in these committees and in these dialogues that "emotionally safe schools" (Bluestein, 2001) can be created (see Fig. 6.3). "In the end, I would hope that what comes through is a sense of optimism, rooted in a firm belief in our ability to create the kind of school environments and relationships that will support learning, achievement and cognitive growth as well as compassion, creativity, resiliency, commitment, productivity, self-understanding and self-actualization. (Bluestein, 2001, p. xviii). Positioned as coordinator of the program and facilitator of ongoing dialogue about its implementation and progress, the elementary counselor has a direct impact on systemic change.

Be Visible

A school counselor, and the school counseling program, is designed to be central, integral to school and the facilitation of its mission. Bulletin boards,

---

This was developed by school counselor and Social Emotional Learning committee in conjunction with students, parents, administration, and staff of Bolton Center School, Bolton, CT.

Rights		*Responsibilities*
	Go hand in hand	
Be respected		Respect others
Be accepted		Accept others
Be safe		Exercise self-control
To learn		Do our best
Make choices		Make wise decisions

FIG. 6.3.   Rights and Responsibilities Statement

Web sites, articles in the monthly newsletters, brochures, and presentations to the PTA, the board of education, and the larger community keep both the school counselor and the school counseling program visible. If students are able to overlearn SEL skills from multiple interventions at school, these other public relations efforts make overlearning possible in the greater school community. It is in reaching out to all stakeholders that counselors can best reinforce the competencies they are working on for their students and the systems they are influenced by.

A SYNERGY

A synergy is created when SEL is combined with a comprehensive developmental school counseling program. An model elementary counseling program achieves the followimng:

- Builds SEL skills into the three domains of personal-social, career, and academic development through the delivery system of responsive services, individual student planning, a curriculum, and system support.
- Builds SEL skills in students, parents, staff, community, and themselves.
- Emphasizes the importance of connecting the school counseling program and SEL to the academic mission of the school.

Elementary school counseling is foundational—it relies on early intervention and prevention. This is the hallmark and hope of elementary school counseling programs. In crafting the ASCA role statement for the position, ASCA (2003) defined elementary school counselors as:

> Professional educators with a mental health perspective who understand and respond to the challenges presented by today's diverse student population. Elementary school counselors don't work in isolation; rather they are integral to the total educational program. They provide proactive leadership that engages all stakeholders in the delivery of programs and services to help students achieve school success. Professional school counselors align with the school's mission to support the academic achievement of all students as they prepare for the ever-changing world of the 21st century. This mission is accomplished through the design, development, implementation and evaluation of a comprehensive, developmental and systematic school counseling program. ASCA's National Standards in the academic, career, and personal/social domains are the foundation for this work. The ASCA National Model: A Framework For School Counseling Programs (ASCA, 2003), with its data-driven and results-based focus, serves as a guide for today's school counselor who is uniquely trained to implement this program.

Armed with this training in a comprehensive school counseling program model; adept in the model's integral skills of leadership, advocacy, collaboration, and system change; and fortified with SEL competencies, the elementary counselor can affect the school climate for student learning and long-term life success. On this foundational level, elementary counselors teach the skills of friendship and conflict resolution, and of what is necessary to show respect, caring, responsibility, fairness, and citizenship. The school counseling "classroom" may be the office used for a one-on-one counseling session or for a small-group counseling experience. It may be the classroom where a large-group lesson is presented or the faculty room where a staff in-service is provided. The classroom may be the larger school house or the community where a service learning project may be undertaken. As school systems grapple with how to put peacemaking and conflict resolution skills into practice, as they try to create schools that are safe havens for children, as they try to build children of character who respect one another, and as they try to foster the concept of lifelong learners, these challenges may be most seamlessly implemented at the elementary level by using the counselor in this mission's critical role not only as facilitator of the school counseling program but also coordinator and visionary in promoting SEL.

REFERENCES

American School Counselor Association. (1997). *Sharing the vision: The National Standards for School Counseling Programs*. Alexandria, VA: Author. Retrieved from www.schoolcounselor.org/content.asp?contentid=178

American School Counselor Association. (2003). *The ASCA National Model: A Framework for school counseling programs*. Alexandria, VA: Author.

Bluestein, J. (2001). *Creating emotionally safe schools: A guide for educators and parents*. Deerfield Beach, FL: Health Communications.

Collaborative for Academic, Social, and Emotional Learning. (2004). Retrieved September 19, 2004 from http://www.casel.org/about_sel/SELskills.php

Elias, M. J., Zins, J. E., Weissberg, R. P., Frey, K. S., Greenberg, M. T., Haynes, N. M., Kessler, R., Schwab-Stone, M. E., & Shriver T. P. (1997). *Promoting social and emotional learning: Guidelines for educators*. Alexandria, VA: ASCD.

Goleman, D. (1995). *Emotional Intelligence: Why it can matter more than IQ*. New York: Bantam.

Henderson, P., & Gysbers, N. C. (1998). *Leading and managing your school guidance program staff*. Alexandria, VA: American School Counselor Association.

Kreite, R. (1999). *The morning meeting book*. Greenfield, MA: Northeast Foundation for Children.

Nelson, J., Lott, L., & Glenn, H. S. (2000). *Positive discipline in the classroom: developing mutual respect, cooperation, and responsibility in your classroom* (Rev. ed.). Roseville, CA: Prima.

7

Middle School Challenges: Reflection, Relationships, and Responsibility

Claudia Shelton
The Hopewell Group

Jennifer Allen
Learning Environments

Middle school is an exciting time, but also a time of confounding adventures. Where elementary school children begin to develop a sense of self, adolescents are suddenly facing the realization that they have choices for who they are and whom they may become. The favor of peers may become more important than the admiration of parents and teachers. Emotions swing from joy to emptiness in the whisk of an interaction with classmates. Indeed, adolescents face the overwhelming task of realizing the potential they hold within themselves—and this, we believe, is central to the educational goals of middle school development.

We recognize the middle school years as a time for adolescents to face the specific social and development challenges of integrating emotional awareness and defining identity, as well as recognizing social boundaries and owning one's responsibilities. Every middle school counselor and teacher has watched students wrestle with these issues. From our experiences as a school counselor and a middle school principal, we offer perspective on these fundamental developmental priorities and specific programs for school counselors to implement.

DEFINING IDENTITY

Adolescence is a major turning point in developing the capacity for self-awareness. Of the seven profound biological changes that occur during the human life
(including birth and death), three occur from ages 10 to 14 (Sylwester, 1999):

1. growth of reproductive capabilities,
2. maturation of the brain's structure to support social and ethical judgment, and
3. development of personal and social identities.

It is this period of middle school, therefore, when children need to adjust not
only to physical changes in their bodies but also to the sometimes overwhelming changes in self-knowledge and emotional awareness. As they adjust to new
capacities in their brain and perception, they often daydream and tune out, or
spend time alone and more time sleeping. Listening to music also provides a
backdrop to their changing sense of themselves.

Counselors and teachers can help adolescents to cultivate self-awareness as
a means to understand their changing thoughts and feelings about themselves
that form their emerging identity. We can help them engage in a reflective process that is constructive and disciplined. We can encourage them to build their
self-awareness in ways they can understand and feel confident about. We can
help them integrate their new thoughts and feelings into self-knowledge,
which reinforces healthy academic and social performance.

Hinebauch (2002) pointed out the importance of middle school teachers
as role models for their students: "By bringing oneself—one's genuine self,
full of questions, flaws, and insecurities, but also full of confidence, humor,
and compassion—teachers show students what it means to be genuine, to be
true to oneself" (p. 21).

Kessler (2000) offered ways that teachers can build on this authenticity to
facilitate discussions that are not only meaningful academically but also teach
listening, speaking directly, and respecting others. These techniques also help
students feel safe and confident in their class discussions.

In addition to role modeling, the school counselor can integrate useful
concepts and opportunities for skill building in developmental guidance
lessons. These lessons can also provide a comfortable arena for students in
which to share perspectives on their emerging identities in mutually supportive ways.

IDENTITY BUILDING
IN DEVELOPMENTAL GUIDANCE LESSONS

The school counselor can introduce concepts and skills that students can use to explore and discuss their identity-building adventures. For example, one way of exploring personal identity is for students to focus on self-awareness and other awareness—the different ways individuals experience the world and engage other people. The source of each student's awareness of their way of perceiving and experiencing the world can be taught through reference to the concept of *innersense*—a way of sensing the world that allows an individual to understand certain situations from a unique perspective (Shelton, 1999).

Innersense is simply a word that gives adolescents an opportunity to explore individual differences and discuss them with one another in a way that is both safe and reassuring. Exploring innersense can include discussion of a range of qualities that contribute to building one's self-awareness —communication style, learning style, values, intuition, stress factors particular to the individual, what gives life meaning, and emerging sense of life purpose—to name a few. What is important is that this concept provides students a focus for guided exploration of important characteristics that can broaden their sense of personal identity—beyond the way they are dressed and their popularity.

In one developmental guidance session, students discussed their understanding of their innersense in many different ways. One seventh-grade boy wrote, "I am naturally good at facing and resolving conflicts—whether it is at home with my mom and sister or on the ball field with friends." A seventh-grade girl stated, "I like quiet and peace and alone space, which shows in almost everything I do. I like to think about my answers in class before I express them.... I enjoy dancing alone and listening to music alone." In contrast, a more outgoing seventh grader explained, "I think that your innersense is linked to your outersense closely. I like the interaction with people whether it comes from social activities or competition in class to have the best answer."

As students share their different points of view, others in the class often appear mystified by the range of different experiences. With consistent discussion of different aspects of innersense over the middle school years, students gain both empathy and appreciation of their own strengths in contrast to the strengths of their peers.

The concept of innersense can be easily interwoven into the English class writing curriculum, where students have a chance to develop essays about aspects of their emerging selves. It can also be interwoven into the history curric-

ulum, where students can debate the possible factors of innersense that influenced leaders and other historical figures.

CORE SKILLS

In the lower grades it is important to focus on attention to feelings and physical
sensations that enable students to be self-aware in the moment. For Grades 6 to
9, skills can be developed to enable students to move the development of
self-awareness to the next level. Skill building can be easily introduced by the
counselor and from there can be carried into other academic classes.

Three core skills are fundamental (Shelton & Stern, 2004):

1. *Relax* is an approach helps student to get in touch with their inner
   thoughts and feelings so they can separate what they think and feel from
   what others think and feel. It can help students focus on slowing down to
   process and interpret their increasingly complex adolescent feelings.
2. *Temperament watch* is a framework for helping students focus on the pattern of natural inner strengths they bring to relationships with themselves,
   their schoolwork, their families, their friends and their eventual careers.
3. *Reflective feedback* gives students a way to compare their own thoughts
   and feelings about themselves with feedback from others including
   peers, teachers, parents, and friends.

Relax

As adolescents move throughout their classes and social groups during the day,
they can experience a whole range of physical sensations, which are often related to their feelings—stomach or head pain, tight muscles, irritability, and a
whole range of distracting qualities. With busy schedules and demanding academic work, they learn to tune out this information and tune in to the task at
hand. Unfortunately, by tuning out, adolescents can ignore the important emotional information so necessary to their emerging sense of emotional awareness
and personal identity.

The relax exercise is a high-performance visualization technique often used
by athletes. By visualizing something in your imagination, your mind believes
you are actually doing the activity. Your body will respond accordingly.

The relax technique has three steps:

1. Have students sit relaxed in a comfortable position focusing on breathing. Slowly, have them follow your voice to focus and relax each part of

their body as they slowly breathe in and out—feet, legs, stomach, shoulders, arms, fingers, head, face. (The sequence and words used to instruct students should be repeated to make the exercise most effective.)

2. When the students have completed Step 1, have them, in their imaginations, go to a special place they can create. They can bring anything into this place that will help them relax more effectively.

3. When they have finished creating their imaginary places, tell them they can stay there for a moment and then return to the room.

When this exercise is practiced at least once a week with the entire class, students learn to relax and get in touch with their emotional information in a moment or two. The exercise can then be combined with other work. For example, the class can be asked when in their relaxed state to imagine a situation in which they might be vulnerable to using drugs or alcohol, an eating disorder, or becoming a victim. Whatever the question, their answers are much more realistic and serious after relax. Together with journaling, the exercise can help students to get to the feelings behind the issues.

This exercise can be used effectively in other academic classes: for helping students in math class to overcome math anxiety, to understand the emotional issues understanding historic events, or to develop new ideas for art or drama class.

Temperament Watch

This skill helps students understand their temperament and how their temperament plays a role in many aspects of their life. Temperament is an innate emotional pattern of behavior, which is another important aspect of personal identity and emotional awareness. It includes the behavior one is inclined to express, such as aggression or withdrawal under pressure, the degree to which one favors social interaction, and so forth. Temperament is a natural behavior preference, which can be looked at somewhat like left- or right-handedness: Some people have a dominant preference for one hand; others are more ambidextrous. It is important that temperament preference does not necessarily indicate skill. An individual with a strong right-handed preference can have poor handwriting with the right hand, just as someone who is naturally introverted can still have excellent skills in social interaction. Environment, social pressure, practice, and many other factors influence skills.

There are a number of methods for defining and recognizing temperament that can be used with adolescents, including Human Dynamics, Myers Briggs, and the enneagram. These three are explored in more detail in *Understanding Emotions in the Classroom* (Shelton & Stern, 2004).

Once students have a method for recognizing temperament differences, they can use it to understand themselves and others in group situations. They can also use it to understand the character of historic and literary figures. For example, one eighth-grade class used the Myers Briggs model in the study of the American presidents. Students compared and contrasted the leadership of Thomas Jefferson and Andrew Jackson using the temperament models they used to understand themselves. The students collected data about each president from their reading and then debated which Myers Briggs preference they believed each president represents.

With practice, students learn to examine consistently the character and temperament of individuals and groups as well as the issues that most classes address. However, with temperament watch, students often are far more interested and animated in their discussions.

Reflective Feedback

The process of reflective feedback helps students give and receive reactions from peers about their emotional-social contributions. It is usually used with group work, but it can be used to provide feedback related to any subject a student wishes to explore. Students are asked to select five people to provide feedback to them on the subject under consideration, for example, "What kind of a contribution do you think I am making to the class?" The designated students provide the feedback. For middle schoolers, this exercise often takes training and clear direction. Students should be reminded that it is important to give feedback in the way they would like to receive it—with both positive and negative comments in a way they would like to hear them.

Reflective feedback is a three-step process:

1. Peers prepare feedback for the designated student.
2. The teacher reviews the feedback, and perhaps grades its depth and usefulness, before it is given to the designated student. This step encourages thoughtfulness, gathering evidence for one's comments, and greatest sensitivity to others' feelings.
3. The student prepares a response for peers and the teacher about the usefulness and results of the feedback, and how the student plans to use it to change his or her behavior.

The goal of the process is to help students become comfortable with providing objective, candid information to one another, as well as giving students additional data they can compare and contrast with their own ideas. It can be an important confidence builder for students who feel they are unpopular or over-looked. Students who assumed they were nonexistent can suddenly feel no-ticed by their peers for the first time in their middle school career. Remarkable changes can occur.

One interesting benefit of the method is the opportunity for the students to hear the opinions of the "popular kids." They express the same concerns that other students have about who they are. Such frank discussion begins to break down some of the myths about what it takes to be popular. It also enables stu-dents to be more comfortable with how they are different. Difference does not have to mean "weird" or "socially unacceptable."

PERSONAL BOUNDARIES AND RESPONSIBILITIES

Relax, temperament watch, and reflective feedback are three tools the coun-selor can use to help students gain greater emotional awareness and knowledge about their emerging personal identities. In addition to increasing students' self-awareness, helping middle school students focus on their relationships and responsibilities to others is critical as they face growing independence. There are a number of ways for schools to address these social-emotional skills, one of which is in dealing with matters of student discipline.

Moving to middle school often represents a shift to more complex social cir-cumstances as students change classes more frequently and interact with in-creasingly more people with markedly less supervision. With this added complexity comes more opportunity for independent choice and, in turn, a greater opportunity to make mistakes. How adults respond when children make questionable choices sends an important message to students: Do school personnel believe that mistakes should be a source of isolation, or do they ac-cept the notion that it is not only human to make a mistake but also a valuable opportunity for personal growth?

Contrary to the message we send to students with strictly punitive disci-pline programs, learning can begin when things don't go right (Chelsom-Gossen, 1997; Raider & Coleman, 1992). Counselors can work with students to develop skills to engage in meaningful dialogue to reflect on what has taken place and develop strategies for future decision making. Given a com-mon vocabulary and set of key questions, adults and students can turn poten-tially difficult circumstances into teachable moments—opportunities to help students expand their reflective capacities as well as their empathic capabili-ties and problem-solving strategies regarding students' personal boundaries and responsibilities to others.

DEVELOPING A NEEDS VOCABULARY

We all make choices for a reason. When a student makes a mistake, he or she does so with a particular purpose. If a student becomes disruptive in class, it is an important exercise to help the student reflect on why he or she has chosen to be disorderly. What was the student needing at that time? Was the child bored? Feeling alienated? Overwhelmed at not understanding the course content? There are many reasons students act out, but children cannot express their reasons without a vocabulary to do so. That is why the vocabulary of basic needs (Chelsom-Gossen, 1997) provides them with an invaluable tool to use as they learn to reflect on their actions:

1. *Survival,* the most basic need, comes into play when a student feels physically or emotionally at risk. If the student feels unsafe, he or she is likely either to retreat or to act out. Many factors can contribute to a sense of both physical safety and social-emotional safety (Allen, Sandy, Chen, & Cohen, 2004). When these basic needs are not met, a child may act out in an effort to gain attention from an adult.
2. *Power and freedom* needs are essential to many of us and involve the desire to have control over one's actions and decisions. Some students, given a sense that they have little or no choice in the school setting, will act out in an effort to gain a feeling of control or to address their need for looser boundaries.
3. *Fun*—sometimes seen as lacking to a student in his or her school day—can generate a need to lighten up the circumstance. At times, this can prove to be disruptive to others in the class, particularly the teacher.
4. *Belonging,* the need for connection to peers and to adults, can often interfere with the constraints of the conventional classroom. Acting out can be a means of gaining approval of peers.

Developing a common needs vocabulary can help students in three important ways. First, students can begin to reflect on their own actions, to understand why they do what they do (reflection). Second, this vocabulary gives students the tools to understand not only their own needs but also the needs of others (empathy). Finally, the language associated with basic human needs, after helping develop a sense of self and others, creates the opportunity for dialogue about how better to deal with circumstances when the needs of two individuals are in conflict (problem solving and conflict resolution).

OPENING UP A DIALOGUE

Once students and counselors have established a common needs vocabulary, there is increased opportunity to explore what may have gone wrong in an interaction and how the student can rethink his or her choices. To accomplish this, there are four steps in the subsequent dialogue: (a) clarifying what the current circumstance appears to be, (b) determining why the student made the choice(s) that he or she did—what his or her needs were at the time, (c) identifying how the student's action interfered with the needs of others, and (d) brainstorming alternative courses of actions that would allow all parties to have their needs met. Following are examples of ways to begin each step in the dialogue:

1. *Clarifying the circumstance:* "What are we facing right now? We don't need to know who started the problem. Let's just focus on what's going on at this moment."
2. *Determining student needs (reflection):* "You didn't do this without a reason. What were you needing at the time?"
3. *Considering the needs of others (empathy):* "How did meeting your needs interfere with the needs of someone else? (i.e., the teacher, another student, other students in the class)?
4. *Naming alternative courses of action (problem solving and conflict resolution):* "What can you do next time to get what you need and, at the same time, not interfere with the needs of others?"

When students make mistakes, there is an opportunity for important social and emotional growth. For this to happen, adults in the building—ideally not just counselors but, in time, every adult who works directly with students—must embrace the notion that discipline problems can lead to important lessons. By establishing a common needs vocabulary and opening up a needs-based dialogue, educators can help middle school students as they face the increasing need to recognize social boundaries and to meet their growing responsibilities as early adolescents.

CONCLUSION

Anyone who works with middle school students recognizes that the middle school years are dynamic times during which children go through enormous physical and social- emotional changes. Thus, it is essential for the school counselor, and in fact all adults who work with middle school children, to make an explicit commitment to helping students develop critical skills that should not be left to chance. We submit that schools can and should think purposefully and systematically about how they teach students to become more socially and personally aware, how to recognize social boundaries, and how to take personal responsibility. It is not surprising that current research supports the notion that increased focus in schools on these and related social-emotional skills results in an increase in student achievement (Zins, Weissberg, Wang, & Walberg, 2004). There are a number of ways that this can be accomplished. Developmental guidance lessons and the school discipline program offer two concrete examples.

REFERENCES

Allen, J., Sandy, S., Chen, J., & Cohen, J. (2004). *ASSESS: Assessment of social and emotional school safety.* Manuscript in preparation. Center for Social and Emotional Education.
Chelsom-Gossen, D. (1997). *Restitution: Restructuring school discipline.* Chapel Hill, NC: New View.
Hinebauch, S. (2002). Nurturing the emerging adolescent identity. *Independent School,* 61(4), 18–24.
Kessler, R. (2000). *The soul of education: Helping students find connection, compassion, and character at school.* Alexandria, VA: Association for Supervision and Curriculum Development.
Raider, E., & Coleman, S. W. (1992). *Conflict resolution: Strategies for collaborative problem solving.* Garrison, NY: Coleman Raider International.
Shelton, C. M. (1999). How innersense builds commonsense. *Educational Leadership, 57,* 61–64.
Shelton, C. M., & Stern, R. (2004). *Understanding emotions in the classroom: Differentiating teaching strategies for optimal learning.* New York: Dude Publishing.
Sylwester, R. (1999). In search of the roots of adolescent aggression. *Educational Leadership, 57,* 65–69.
Zins, J. E., Weissberg, R. P., Wang, M. C., & Walberg, H. J. (2004). *Building academic success on social and emotional learning.* New York: Teachers College Press.

8

Emotional Networks and Counseling the High School Student

Michael T. Dealy
Bay Ridge Preparatory School

John Pellitteri
Queens College, CUNY

High school counselors can be critically important members within the school environment and serve as catalysts in the creation of emotionally intelligent schools. Unlike teachers who have specific subject specialties, counselors tend to take an ecological (whole system) view of the school. From this perspective counselors work directly with administrators, teachers, and students from all grade levels and can moderate the relationships among them. If a counselor makes a commitment to work from an emotional intelligence base, all aspects of his or her work become opportunities to influence the emotional dimensions of the school environment. Emotions are the dynamic substance of relationships and interpersonal interactions. In this view, the creation of emotionally intelligent schools is accomplished through the channels of human relationships. Professional counselors, by training, are equipped to understand and facilitate interpersonal interactions. Whether the counselor is in a guidance role with a student's schedule change, in a consultation role with a concerned teacher, or in a clinical role during a crisis intervention, there is an opportunity to facilitate emotional learning and awareness. For such efforts to be effective, the counselor must first under-stand the terrain of each school's unique environment and how the needs of the developing adolescent interact with the environment.

The ecological perspective in counseling is often noted as important be-cause a focus on the person–environment interaction is a defining aspect of the profession (Conyne, 1988; Gelso & Fretz, 2001). However, it can take a signifi-cant degree of effort for counselors to shift their mindset consistently into such a systems way of thinking. This chapter provides a framework to guide counsel-ors toward an emphasis on dynamic emotional systems in the school ecology. The first section outlines the process of constructing an understanding of the psychological field (Lewin, 1944/1997b) within which the counselor must op-erate. Once the topology of the field is outlined, the emotional networks of that field can be moderated and affective potentials in the environment can be acti-vated to facilitate a positive, emotional tone in the school. The second section provides examples of emotional prescriptions and finding emotional anchors, which are interventions that influence the emotional network. The third sec-tion focuses on the students and their emotional journey from freshman to se-nior year. It examines how the emotionally sensitive environment can foster healthy and positive movements through the different challenges of each year and optimize the high school student's development.

MAPPING EMOTIONAL NETWORKS
WITHIN THE SCHOOL ECOLOGY

Emotional Networks in the Psychological Field

The first step for the emotionally intelligent high school counselor is to decons-truct the traditional divisions of schools (i.e., academic departments, educa-tional functions, or professional roles). Rather than consider the hierarchical delineation of principal and assistants, or to understand the particular organi-zation of the scheduling guidance systems, or to examine student records, the emotionally intelligent school counselor views the school as an *emotional net-work*. An emotional network is the system of emotions and emotional poten-tials in any group of individuals. The behaviors and motivations of each individual are influenced by the varying emotional needs and the affective di-mensions of the interpersonal interactions. In considering the emotional net-work of the ecology, the counselor views the school as pure energy that flows and changes within a system. The dynamic flow of emotions can be viewed as different colors of intensity, much like the color distinctions of MRI pictures.

The emotional colors can wax and wane like the shifting satellite images of weather systems. A change in one color of the system can influence the neighboring colors and alter the overall configuration of the whole gestalt.

The emotional network perspective focuses on dynamics and potential emotional expressions of each person in the system. The emotionally intelligent counselor does not only see particular people (i.e., student, teacher, or principal) in their social roles but looks beyond the surface to the undercurrent of the emotional world. In perceiving this emotional layer of the human psyche, the counselor can understand the reciprocal dynamic connections among individuals as they move through space and time and interact with each other.

Emotional networks are conceptually similar to Kurt Lewin's (1936) construct of *psychological field,* which has been influential in ecological psychology, systems theory, and group dynamics. Psychological field is also referred to as *life space* and considers human needs, perceptual configurations, cognitive structure, and emotional forces that form vectors and determine the direction and strength of a person's behaviors and motivations at any given time (Lewin, 1943/1997a). Field theory in school counseling, by nature is an integrative approach in that it requires the counselor to consider the interaction of multiple intrapersonal and interpersonal determinants of human behaviors (Pellitteri, 2000). In viewing the school as a large psychological field, the counselor has created a systems-ecological perspective (Conyne, 1988) that provides a particular advantage over more conventional individualistic approaches. In focusing on the emotional networks within the field, the counselor creates a perspective that can facilitate emotional intelligence.

To understand the dynamics of the psychological field and the emotional networks that are one dimension of it, the counselor needs to identify what structures the field. *Cognitive maps,* a term used by early behaviorist researchers, refers to one's mental representation of the environment and the use of that information to solve problems (see Tolman, 1932). The cognitive map of the school becomes one of the structures of the psychological field. In addition, other social and cognitive factors, discussed later, create psychological structures that influence the field. Before a cohesive map of such a psychological system can be constructed, the counselor, like any good cartographer, must first note the significant markers in the terrain.

The counselor in a school setting will mentally (and physically) walk through the territory to prepare the map of the psychological field. The counselor need not actually draw the physical maze of the building but must have a mental representation of the physical spaces, as these can have an influence on behavior. The physical space of the school contains the flow of emotional energy. It limits or facilitates interpersonal interactions and thus influences the emotional elements that arise from such interactions. Classroom interactions may be different depending on the seating arrangements. The energy dynamics of a few students may change depending on whether they are sitting in a small office space or in a large auditorium. There are stationary landmarks of the building layout, room size, school yard, hallways, stairwells, desks, and so forth that divide the landscape. Most people, upon entering a new environment, develop a mental representation of the physical layout that enables them to move efficiently between the necessary locations of the building.

In addition to the structures created by the physical boundaries of the school, cognitive structures are created by the social roles and collective beliefs of students and faculty. These structures include the implicit and explicit rules of behavior, such as role expectations of students, teachers, and office workers. In a classroom, the teachers are expected to teach and the students are expected to learn. The faculty and administrators, too, have expectations placed on them by others as well as by themselves that eventually filter into the emotional elements of the field. For example, the secretary is expected to respond to the requests of the assistant principal. The assistant principal, in turn, may expect to have a more collegial relationship with the principal, and therefore interactions between them carry a different emotional tone. The culture of a particular school is composed of the unwritten rules and expectations in the collective consciousness of the school personnel. It is necessary for the counselor to understand these social and political forces in the field to assess accurately the resulting emotional variables.

School is a concept so familiar to all that it has gained many enduring connotations. It is associated with study, career, discipline, and advancement, as well as restriction, challenge, frustration, anger, conflict, pain, fear of failure, homework, evaluation, self-efficacy, and so forth. These cognitive associations are activated merely by being in the school environment and influence behavioral potential in the field. Even though many of these beliefs may be automatic thoughts and operate at nonconscious levels (Wells & Mathews, 1994), they can still have a pull in the current situation. Different locations in the school also come to be associated with different behaviors, such as a math classroom for performing calculations, a science lab for conducting experiments, or the cafeteria for eating and socializing.

The school culture is determined by the principal's leadership style, the history of the school evolution, and the collective personalities of the school personnel and student body. However, macro-level forces in the larger ecological system (Bronfenbrenner, 1979) such as district policy, state curriculum, and community groups can exert an influence on the semipermeable system of each school. It may not be feasible for the counselor to map these larger ecological spheres; however, it is important to note their potential influence on the contained system within the school. For example, numerous external forces can include gang and drug-related activities in the community, parent group opinions, or pressures from district superintendents, as well as state and national policy on curriculum and testing.

As all the elements exert their gravitational forces, the concentrations of energy change and the potential for homeostasis within the school ecology is modified. The whole school covers such an incredible territorial expanse that it can never really be in balance. There is a constant movement of the school's dynamic ecological system. To achieve change in such a complex psychological system, the emotional network of the school ecology must be considered along with the physical and cognitive structures.

Emotional Associations and Emotional Networks

In addition to the space restrictions that channel human activity, the physical stimuli in the school become imbued with associational meaning. A particular classroom can be a cue that activates emotionally charged memories of past experiences there or memories of similar places in the person's past. An embarrassing situation, a depressing failure, or an exciting moment of insightful learning create emotions that are the "glue" of behavioral conditioning. Because the past learning of each individual affects the present situation, every physical place in the school can potentially influence the emotional states of students and in turn be a vector for their immediate behavior. The emotional associations with physical space help create the cognitive structures related to the school environment.

Emotional reactions can be generalized not only to real experiences in the school but also to imagined experiences. Increasing fear of what might happen or could happen can lead a student to develop school phobia and avoidant conditioning (Silverman & Kurtines, 2001), which actually is an escape from the painful emotions associated with the school. Continued associations of negative emotions in the school environment create the risk of the student having a systematic sensitization to certain stimuli in the school. (This would be the opposite and precluding process of the behavioral therapy of systematic desensitization [see Wolpe, 1958].) The emotional history of each student is present in his or her life space. Each life space contributes to the forces that influence the psychological field of the whole school.

The counselor has now mentally created an elementary schema of the basic physical constraints as well as a schema of the collective beliefs and the sociopolitical forces that constitute the school culture. On top of this cognitive map, the counselor must lay the multicolored transparency of the *emotional network*. Each basic emotion can correspond to various colors and the intensity of each emotion can be represented by the depth of each hue. The movement of the colors can represent the potential to influence, disperse, transform, or blend other colors. The color metaphor directly translates to the emotional dimensions of each individual in the system. For example, a friendly and enthusiastic teacher may convey a certain bright emotional energy to her class whereas a negative and disgruntled secretary may project a dark and unpleasant emotion to be avoided. A blended color may represent a concerned but overstressed administrator who may be an asset to one's cause but must also be approached cautiously.

The emotional energy that each individual conveys creates an emotional tone in the immediate environment. These emotions are resultants from previously described forces in addition to each individual's personality and history. Emotion research suggests that emotions communicate information about the safety level in the environment (Schwarz, 2002). When the counselor becomes attuned to the emotional dynamics of each person in the system, he or she is positioned to orchestrate forces that aim to create a harmonious metamorphosis for a productive educational environment. Counseling interventions based on emotional intelligence abilities can be used to influence the emotions not only of students but of teachers, office staff, administrators, and parents. When the counselor works from an ecological perspective, he or she can see how a change in one person's emotions can influence all those around. For example, easing a new teacher's anxiety about controlling the class by offering concrete strategies can help her convey a sense of confidence to the students, which in turn will give the students the feeling that the class is well managed. When a counselor works with a student who is a group leader and instills a sense of maturity and focus, the other students who follow the student may increase their focus on learning.

The emotionally aware counselor realizes that he or she is a participant-observer and that his or her own emotions influence his or her perception of the environment as well as play a role in shaping the environment. The emotional intelligence trait of self-awareness is a critical component in making an accurate assessment and map of the psychological field. The counselor therefore must maintain a sense of equilibrium in himself or herself (through the reflective regulation of emotions). When the counselor is emotionally centered, the likelihood of accurate perceptions of environmental cues without distortion is maximized. Before emotional prescriptions can be devised and implemented, the counselor must ask, "Should the emotional energy be changed in a particular area of the school?" If so, the question becomes, "How can this best be accomplished?"

DEVELOPING AN EMOTIONAL MILIEU

"Hot Zones" and Emotional Prescriptions

Emotions are embedded in interpersonal relationships. It is through the collective energy of relationships that the emotional dimensions of the environment are established. The milieu, or environment, is a significant influence on students' immediate behaviors as well as on their long-term development. The emotional energies of the teachers, staff, and administrators are also part of the milieu. Given the power differential and role responsibility of a teacher, his or her mood will have a more influential pull in the psychological field of the classroom than any one student. It is for this reason that emotionally intelligent school counselors focus their clinical acuity on school personnel as well as on students. If a counselor is to develop an emotionally intelligent environment, every player in that system (students and teachers alike) must fall under the counselor's umbrella of emotional sensitivity and safety. The core conditions that are the basis of the counselor–client relationship (Rogers, 1961), of course, must be applied outside of the clinical encounter. Unconditional positive regard, empathy, and genuineness must structure the counselor's relationships with everyone whom he or she encounters in the school. It is through an emotional awareness of the interpersonal environment that the counselor can devise interventions that alter the dynamics of the situation and move the life space of a group toward productive development.

The emotionally intelligent counselor is aware of emotional *hot zones* of energy. These are configurations where several individuals converge to create particularly intense emotions. Examples can be a resistant, unmotivated student whose anger can be poisonous to his immediate peers, a group of students who have passion and enthusiasm for sports, or a pair of teachers who mutually reinforce each other's negative feelings toward the school administration. The counselor at this point can draw on knowledge of emotional intelligence to devise *emotional prescriptions* (D. Wiedis, personal communication, September 1999) that will remedy the emotional unrest or direct the positive intensities in a productive manner. For example, a clique of loud and disruptive students may not have any ill intent but are merely exhibiting immaturity in their emotional regulation. The prescription for these students may be a friendly, informal conversation with the counselor that redirects their energies toward a more serious topic or gentle feedback on the consequences of their disruptive behaviors. A teacher's negativity toward the administration can signify the personally unmet needs of the teacher such as a need for respect and appreciation. The counselor's prescription for this teacher may be to comment in a genuine manner on his or her talents and draw attention to the positive influence that he or she has on certain students.

An example of directing positive hot zones is a student who had a spirit for debating controversial topics. She was loud and vocal in class and was always questioning the validity of the teacher's points. The teacher was bothered by this and found the criticisms disruptive. The emotional prescription of the counselor was to enlist the student to lead a study group in his office that focused on complex issues in history. All of the students involved debated the topics vociferously. Although the group was noisy at times, they were focused on learning, and the particular student's emotions were directed toward a more productive purpose. Other students and teachers were impressed with the study group's investment in arguing such germane topics. What had previously been a burden for the teacher became a facilitative force both inside and outside the classroom.

Personal Histories and Emotional Anchors

Beyond the empathy of the immediate encounter, however, a counselor must have empathy for elements of the person's emotional history. Emotionally charged events can transform an individual for better or worse, and the residual of such life occurrences can exert a force in the person's current life space. The emotionally intelligent counselor develops relationships with each person in the milieu and in doing so can come to understand what structures each person's inner world. The counselor's developed emotional awareness allows him or her to tune into emotional needs of people. When the counselor can read the terrain of a person's life space, he or she can identify the past traumas that may have created vulnerabilities as well as the *emotional anchors* in that person's history that give stability (Dealy, 1994). Such anchors provide a means for the counselor to connect with the person and to provide assistance toward personal growth.

When a staff member or a student share a significant historical event in his or her life, there is a window of opportunity to deepen one's relationship with that person. A school counselor, for example, through casual but mindful conversations, discovered various important emotional events about different individuals. For instance, there was a teacher who had a skiing accident at the age of 13 that significantly changed her life. The counselor also knew that a particular student lost his brother to cancer and had to watch him die. There was an administrator who struggled his whole life because of his mother's mental illness that included paranoid delusions. When emotionally charged memories are disclosed to a counselor and met with careful sensitivity, an emotional bond has been established with the counselor who now understands something about the person that is personal, deeply meaningful, and perhaps painful.

The intervention at this point is to find what emotional anchors have kept this person going despite the difficulties of the life event. Emotional anchors stem from early childhood and from positive, protective, and nurturing emotional experiences. The emotions from these grounding experiences form stable structures within the individual's personality and have a ripple effect that blends into the affective hues of positive self-worth. It is not only the memory but the energy of these positive emotions that evolves with the developing person and becomes a lasting residual in the person's current life space. Emotional anchors represent the potential strength within the person that can be actualized in crises or in other emotionally intense states. They are often unconscious, yet once they are discovered they can be used by a psychotherapist to facilitate healing, coping, and life enhancement.

In the case of the student whose brother died of cancer, the counselor found an emotional anchor in how he made sense of the loss. He saw in his grief that a hopeful emotion had progressed out of the tragedy and out of the student's awareness of the fragility of life. The student had stripped away the superficial concerns that occupy most people and had thought about how he could live a more meaningful life. Through discussions with the counselor, the student explored the meaning of his brother's life as well as the purpose of his own life. In discussing the positive memories of his relationship with his brother he found in himself an increased desire to help people. He considered how understanding others could become part of his career choice and lived each day in a more mindful and reflective manner. This deeper meaning was possible because of the positive emotional connection that he had with his brother. He actualized the potential to live life in a meaningful (rather than a depressed) manner as a result of the discussions with the counselor. The counselor's emotional perception and search for his emotional anchor allowed him to see the hopefulness that was underneath his painful affect and to focus him on its potential.

Interventions in the Emotional Network

An understanding of an individual's emotional sensitivities is important not only to support the person but to facilitate connections with others and to influence the larger emotional system of the school. One example involved the custodial staff of a school that had a particularly negative attitude toward the teaching staff. They thought that teachers had exceptionally easy jobs that involved merely passing out papers and sitting around until 3:00 p.m. dismissal. The teachers did not understand the custodians' cynicism and resistance to help. The delays in custodial help made life difficult for teachers and lead to the detriment of the physical and psychological environment. As the counselor had established positive connections with both the teachers and custodians, he was in a position as a trusted party for a meeting of the minds. The counselor arranged for the head custodian to be in the classroom at the beginning of the day, to hand out papers, and to observe firsthand the students' rowdy, resistant, and challenging behaviors. This experience had a strong impact on the custodian, who felt the stress of the classroom environment and realized the difficulty of keeping the class in line and actually getting students to learn. The emotional learning experience for the head custodian led to a different emotional tone between the two groups based on mutual professional respect.

Another example of influencing an emotional network involved the stubbornness within a principal's life space. The principal was resistant to a particular family program in the school that the teachers wanted very much, and this in turn created disappointment and resentment in the teachers as a group. The counselor had a pleasant relationship with the principal and happened to know that he loved football. In the discussion about the program the counselor created a positive mood in the principal by interjecting associations to the game. He very skillfully phrased the initiation of the program as the "bomb" (the big pass) that might be a risk but could also win the Superbowl. With that metaphor, that principal's perception of the program was more positive to the degree that he was willing to approve it on a trial basis.

In summary, the counselor can develop an emotionally positive milieu through his or her relationships with students and staff and an understanding of each person's emotional sensitivities. The counselor's emotional intelligence is a significant factor in accomplishing the challenging task of infusing positive emotions into the school's milieu. The next section describes the emotional challenges that can face high school students at each year and how the school ecology can support each student's development and emotional well-being.

THE EMOTIONAL ODYSSEY
OF THE HIGH SCHOOL STUDENT

The Journey to the Self

The journey that begins as an entering freshman and culminates as a graduating senior is one of many odysseys that forms the threads of a person's life. Although this 4-year journey may not be the most profound of one's life, given the important psychosocial developments of adolescence, it is certainly formative. The hero Odysseus, in Homer's epic poem, struggles with many challenges on his archetypal trip back to his homeland. The high school student, in essence, is challenged to create and discover a psychological home within the self. The journey home is one of self-discovery. Another theme within the Odyssey is that of Odysseus' son who is searching for his father. This search is archetypal and symbolic in that relationships with parents are an emotionally charged aspect of one's identity development.

The emotional struggles associated with social groups, family, physiological changes, and academic demands during this time are opportunities for growth and they spur the emergence of identity. Erikson (1968/1987) formed a type of road map for counselors in outlining the stages of psychosocial changes through the lifespan. The adolescent crisis of identity versus identity diffusion in many ways is the crux of our existential being (thus the question, "Who am I?"). Identity development lays the foundation for the whole span of adult development. Adolescence has sometimes been described as a storm of distress. However, the journey to the self need not be distressing or steeped in conflict. Adolescence, however, is a period of tremendous emotional transformations of the magnitude that may not occur again until the changes that eventually accompany midlife transitions (Howell, 2001).

It is interesting to note that the Chinese symbol for crisis is a combination of the symbols for danger and opportunity. As the counseling profession works from a developmental model (Blocher, 1988), the counselor views developmental crises as challenges that are part of normal transitions, filled with great potential, and requiring guidance and support. When the counselor also incorporates the concept of person–environment fit (Swartz & Martin, 1997), it is clear how an emotionally positive school environment is critical in supporting the identity development and well-being of the adolescent. It requires the emotionally intelligent qualities of flexibility, optimism, and positivity to separate the opportunity from the danger and find creative solutions to the adolescent's personal life challenges.

Ontogeny recapitulates phylogeny; that is, the development of an individual parallels and reflects the development of the whole species. In this way, the stages of change from freshman through senior can be seen as a microcosm of the social evolution periods of human civilization. One can view freshman as ancient times, sophomores as the medieval times, juniors as the enlightenment era, and seniors as modern times. Freshman can be characterized as ancient times, when civilization was in its infancy, because of the unformed nature of their emotions. Human potential is just emerging, and the whole path of society's evolution lies ahead as freshmen enter the huge new world of high school. Sophomores enter the medieval times, the Dark Ages, with sullen and oppositional emotions. There is a quality of dark magic, displacement of negativity, and they can be boisterous and complaining as they push their way through difficult transformations. When high school students reach junior year, they enter the Age of Enlightenment. They tend to feel more confident, task oriented, and, based on their 2 years of experience, have a greater sense of mastery and direction. In senior year, students must face the crushing reality of moving on into an even larger world. It relates to the current modern era and the Information Age that is highly complicated, uncertain, and potentially threatening. This powerful transition, though welcomed by some, signals the loss of a comfort zone and can lead to emotional regression. Seniors no longer have the solace of the "separate peace" of Knowles' (1959) famous novel on coming of age.

The emotionally intelligent high school counselor, after mapping the emotional networks and creating a positive emotional milieu, must try to harness the potential in the school environment to address these general emotional tendencies in each of the four high school age groups. The following sections describe some general emotional characteristics of each high school year. Individual students of course, may not adhere exactly to these descriptions. The metaphors used earlier can be used to understand each year in a developmental context.

Freshmen—The Journey Begins

One of the major steps in psychosocial development is entering high school where the adolescent has more freedom, the social circles are wider, and the responsibilities and expectations are greater. This period, as described earlier, is marked by the process of identity development. Entering freshmen are in a developmental transition between two school structures and require the observation of professional counselors to ensure that they can adjust to the changes of this transition.

The school environment for freshmen has to be controlled, more so than for the other years. Freshmen, in general, are the least self-directed and are more influenced by their surroundings. They are under greater stimulus control; therefore, the school personnel should carefully modulate the stimuli to which freshmen are exposed. The environment for freshman must be structured and learning experiences must be designed to create success under any circumstances. Contrary to popular belief that students should learn the lesson, "If you don't do the work you will fail," the emotionally intelligent environment provides the message, "If you do, you succeed." This sets a positive emotional tone of success rather than the negative feelings associated with failure. A learning structure should be established where freshmen believe they are doing the work and getting rewarded for their efforts, even if the efforts are minimal. These efforts are approximations of learning strategies that will develop by senior year as opposed to failed attempts at learning. If freshmen are meeting minimum requirements (without knowing they are only at the minimum) and receiving reinforcement for their efforts at studying, they will begin to develop a mastery orientation toward learning (Brophy, 2004) and an increase in academic self-efficacy (Alderman, 2004).

The high school counselor can accomplish these goals through collaboration and consultation with freshmen teachers. Educating teachers on freshmen's social-emotional needs and potential vulnerabilities as well as providing support for successful learning opportunities will set a tone of success for the new high school students. Group counseling for new students can dispel some of their initial anxieties, create peer connections, and position the counselor as a support for their journey. The counselor can use his or her knowledge of the emotional networks in the school environment to steer freshmen clear of potentially negative social groups and detrimental influences. The environment for freshmen should be nurturing as they are still in the "infancy" of their high school development.

Sophomores—The Great Transition

Sophomore year is a transition period between incipience and accomplishment. It is the road between aptitude and achievement. Whereas freshmen are learning how to learn, sophomores are building a long-term memory storehouse to network the increasing academic information. They are further into puberty, as can be seen in growth spurts, and can appear significantly older than freshmen. Social life becomes more prominent than the video games and skateboards of childhood. Emotions are more intense (i.e., sadness may be a deeper sadness), yet they can still have the "shallow panic" of young adolescents toward unimportant topics. Sophomores are more vulnerable than other years to ostracism, isolation, ridicule, insults, and embarrassment.

As much as structure helps, it merely keeps sophomores contained. Being more feeling oriented, the academic tasks become secondary to their emotional-interpersonal needs. In general, they undervalue parental advice and look more to peers for emotional support. In response to these interpersonal needs, the emotionally intelligent counselor works to develop a stronger network of peer supports. Psychoeducational workshops can be used not only to educate students about psychosocial issues but to create these peer networks among participants.

The use of peer mediators and peer reporters can be powerful. The counselor can recruit certain students as "emotion reporters" that monitor and relay information about the emotional milieu back to the counselor. Such a system can be critical in the preventive role of the counselor in that it can alert him or her to the presence of suicidal or depressed students, peer conflicts, and potential violence. Peer reporting can be used to assess the emotional dynamics in a classroom and prevent polarizations between students and the teacher.

In one example a peer reporter in a sophomore class assisted the counselor in assessing and intervening in a student–teacher conflict. The teacher was upset by how little the students seemed to have learned for the most recent exam. The students' complaints were based on their perceived attitude that the teacher was negative. Emotional reactions in a class tend to spread to many of the students and in this case there was a larger, more intense response than was warranted. Through a peer reporter, the counselor discovered that only a few students had negative reactions to the teacher, yet these students were facilitating and intensifying the whole class upheaval. The counselor intervened with one of the group leaders, who appeared to have the most emotional flexibility and therefore the potential to be a positive facilitator of this conflict. The emotional prescription was for the girl to bring in croissants for the teacher and the whole class to eat (it was a French language class). This action began a healing process for various reasons. It created a positive mood in the class, particularly for the French teacher who appreciated the connection of the croissants to her subject matter, and food is symbolically a form of nurturance that suggests a regression to a more secure, infantile time of life. Another reason was that the girl who brought the food now had cognitive dissonance (Strauman & Higgins, 1993). She did a favor for the teacher (bringing her food) which is inconsistent (in dissonance) with her previously negative attitudes toward the teacher. This led her to alter her negative attitudes to have more self-consistency, resulting in the attitudes matching the kind and generous action.

As a result of this intervention, the excessive negativity of the student–teacher conflict was regulated. Although this did not completely remove the differences, it reduced the emotional intensity of the group to a manageable level where more open and productive discussions could take place between the teacher and the particular students. The emotional prescription had influenced the group dynamics and shifted the ecology of the classroom. The emotional resources in the psychological field (i.e., the flexibility of the girl to carry out the prescription) had been used. The tendencies of the sophomores to be oppositional, to exhibit more intense emotions, and to be more highly sensitive were considered in devising the emotional prescription that would meet their needs.

Juniors—The Age of Enlightenment

Juniors find that the bridge from youth to young adulthood has been crossed. Both the cognitive and emotional developmental leaps of this year are notable. There is a focus on achievement, as academic and career goals share a larger piece of the emotional storehouse of expression. Students are able to hold emotional needs in abeyance or sublimate them into academic and philosophical tasks. There can be an increase in altruism (i.e., food drives) and positive steps to change the world. Social affiliation tends to be more mature. Ridicule and insults toward others can decrease and when it does occur, other students will be less apathetic and intervene to stop it. The student's sense of society, historical issues, and literary opinions have more emotional "heat," as there is an emerging young adult that seeks to assert his or her identity. Juniors have come a long way but still have a long way to go. They work harder than before on college issues knowing that their career choices may be most influenced by the grades of this year. Emotionally, however, it is an optimal time for student investment in subject matter and for discussions about philosophy of life. Juniors have a greater sense of mastery that is built on the experience of 2 years in high school.

It is particularly beneficial when counselors relate to every junior as an individual because the student may need to feel unique. Knowing juniors by name can contribute to this feeling that they are special individuals. The emotional climate for juniors depends more on their affiliations with teachers who serve as parents, extended family, and authority figures. It is important that teachers work together because students can perceive friction between teachers. Such perceived conflict can be detrimental to the emotional security of juniors, who are, for the first real time, taking steps toward being successful. As the teaching faculty may serve symbolically as a family, conflicts among the staff can create a sense of being children of divorce. Juniors need to see unity among the teachers as a support for them as they venture out into the world.

The self-exploration of career development enters a more serious level as juniors prepare for the SATs, may take interest inventories, and begin to think about college and career pathways. Their increased emotional and cognitive maturity allows them to assess their value systems and to elaborate their developing identities. It is an opportunity to advance emotional awareness of the self and others.

Seniors—A Brave New World

Seniors have gone from the make-believe world of childhood and now face the huge and threatening world of adulthood. They may be very willing to leave but can still be afraid to go out there. In this *senior crisis* there may appear to be a natural depression at the impending loss of earlier life structures. This depression may parallel the natural depression found in middle adulthood (Howell, 2001) and should be considered part of a developmental transition rather than a clinical syndrome. Educationally, they are at the top of high school but at the bottom of college, life, and work worlds. Seniors are paper tigers and contain a false confidence that can mask their underlying anxieties about growing up.

Seniors can be more reflective as they approach the natural end of their high school career. Looking back can make them feel anxious and regretful of their failures, frustrations, and lack of knowing. Counselors need to get seniors talking about feelings, ambitions, and their life philosophies. Such topics are tied to identities and can integrate their intellectual capacities with their emotional worlds. Even though seniors' life experiences are limited to 18 years, counselors can use the power of nostalgia to help them process and make sense of their personal development to this point. Reflective processes help seniors identify and solidify the positive emotions of their last 4 years that might otherwise be overlooked and forgotten. Positive nostalgia can become an emotional anchor for them in their lives. An effective small-group activity for seniors is for each member to make positive statements about what they have learned about each other over the past 4 years. They can discuss what they have learned about each particular student, and in doing so they affirm the positive experience for that student.

As the upperclassmen of the school, seniors have an opportunity to be examples and role models for the freshmen and sophomores. Counselors can creatively address varying needs of different student groups by setting up mentoring programs between seniors and freshmen. The latter will benefit from the support and the former will benefit from helping others. It is an opportunity for the counselor to focus the seniors' attention away from themselves and in doing so create a social consciousness and an emotional awareness of others. By discussing the needs of freshmen, the levels of challenges to be addressed, and the coping skills they will require, seniors can gain a deeper understanding of themselves and the process of growth that they have come through in the last 4 years. Senior year is working if the seniors are motivated to make the pathway healthy for freshmen. Hazing, ridicule, or insults toward freshmen is a sign that the emotional educational process of the whole school has failed miserably. The continuity of emotional learning from freshmen to senior should ideally permeate the school ecology and strengthen the positive emotional networks of all those involved.

CONCLUSION

The journey of each high school student is one of an evolving life space moving through a larger psychological field in a reciprocally influencing process. The affective dimensions of each person's life space have been shaped by personal histories, emotional memories, associational meanings, needs, and potentialities. The emotional networks of the school consist of the collective life spaces of each participant and the group dynamics that unfold from their interactions. The emotionally intelligent school counselor is a social ecologist (Conyne, 1988) and a cartographer that has mapped out the terrain of the psychological field by identifying the physical, cognitive, and social structures along with the emotional energies that flow within these structures. Metaphorical views along with empirically grounded knowledge of adolescent development provide a framework for the counselor to understand the pathways of the high school student. The school counselor's creativity, flexibility, and emotional awareness are necessary to determine how each developing individual will fit with the particular psychological environment that has been mapped out. In this sense school counselors are providing *guidance*—through a rugged terrain with changing climates, hot zones, and pitfalls. The counselor is the indigenous local native who knows the land and has the pressing responsibility to guide safely the scientific explorers on their adventure of discovery to the mountain top. The wisdom of being in tune with the terrain results in the adaptive advice of emotional prescriptions. The counselor's perceptive emotional acuity allows him or her to find the emotional anchors that keep the mountaineers in place until the day when the students are looking over the great expanse from the peak and may not even realize how they got there.

REFERENCES

Alderman, M. K. (2004). *Motivation for achievement*. Mahwah, NJ: Lawrence Erlbaum Associates.

Blocher, D. (1988). Developmental counseling revisited. In R. Hayes & R. Aubrey (Eds.), *New directions for counseling and human development* (pp. 13–21). Denver, CO: Love Publishers.

Bronfenbrenner, U. (1979). *The ecology of human development*. Cambridge, MA: Harvard University Press.

Brophy, J. (2004). *Motivating students to learn*. Mahwah, NJ: Lawrence Erlbaum Associates.

Conyne, R. (1988). The counseling ecologist: Helping people and environments. In R. Haynes & R. Aubrey (Eds.), *New directions for counseling and human development* (pp. 304–324). Denver, CO: Love Publishers.

Dealy, M. (1994). *Emotional anchors in crisis intervention and psychotherapy*. Unpublished manuscript.

Erikson, E. (1987). The human life cycle. In S. Schlein (Ed.), *A way of looking at things: Selected papers from 1930 to 1980* (pp. 595–610). New York: Norton. (Original work published 1968)

Gelso, C., & Fretz, B. (2001). *Counseling psychology*. Belmont, CA: Wadsworth/Thomson.

Howell, L. (2001). Values and women's midlife development. *Journal for Counseling & Values, 46*, 54–65.

Knowles, J. (1959). *A separate peace*. New York: Scribner.

Lewin, K. (1936). *Principles of topological psychology* (F. Heider & G. M. Heider, Trans.). New York: McGraw-Hill.

Lewin, K. (1997a). Defining the field at a given time. In D. Cartwright (Ed.), *Field theory in social science: Selected theoretical papers* (pp. 200–211). Washington, DC: American Psychological Association. (Original work published 1943)

Lewin, K. (1997b). Constructs in field theory. In D. Cartwright (Ed.), *Field theory in social science: Selected theoretical papers* (pp. 191–199). Washington, DC: American Psychological Association. (Original work published 1944)

Pellitteri, J. (2000). *Lewin's field theory as an integrative framework for psychological counseling.* Manuscript submitted for publication.

Rogers, C. R. (1961). *On becoming a person.* Boston: Houghton Mifflin.

Silverman, W., & Kurtines, W. (2001). Anxiety disorders. In J. Hughes, A. M. LaGreca, & J. S. Conoley (Eds.), *Handbook of psychological services for children and adolescents* (pp. 225–244). New York: Oxford University Press.

Schwarz, N. (2002). Situated cognition and the wisdom in feelings: Cognitive tuning. In L. F. Barrett & P. Salovey (Eds.), *The wisdom in feeling: Psychological processes in emotional intelligence* (pp. 144–166). New York: Guilford.

Strauman, T. J., & Higgins, E. T. (1993). The self construct in social cognition: Past, present, and future. In Z. Segal & S. Blatt (Eds.). *The self in emotional distress: Cognitive and psychodynamic perspectives* (pp. 3–40). New York: Guilford.

Swartz, J. L., & Martin, W. E., Jr. (1997). Ecological psychology theory: Historical overview and application to educational ecosystems. In J. L. Swartz & W. E. Martin (Eds.), *Applied ecological psychology for schools within communities* (pp. 3–27). Mahwah, NJ: Lawrence Erlbaum Associates.

Tolman, E. (1932). *Purposive behavior in animals and men.* New York: Apple-Century-Crofts.

Wells, A., & Mathews, G. (1994). *Attention and emotion.* Hillsdale, NJ: Lawrence Erlbaum Associates.

Wolpe, J. (1958). *Psychotherapy by reciprocal inhibition.* Stanford, CA: Stanford University Press.

IV

APPLICATIONS WITH SPECIFIC GROUPS

There are many stakeholders in every school that may simultaneously require attention from the counselor. The emotionally intelligent qualities of flexibility and empathy, along with the ability to take multiple perspectives and to adjust communication styles, are only a few of the skills that counselors need to meet the various demands of different groups. In chapter 9, there is an emphasis on the social-emotional skill building for children with special needs. In chapter 10, there are examples of how counselors can collaborate with teachers on implementing SEL programming. Chapter 11 presents the emotional intelligence of various leadership styles that give a perspective for counselors when collaborating with administrators. In chapter 12, the emotional intelligence of family systems is described to assist counselors in facilitating emotional intelligence development when consulting with parents. We believe the counselor needs to understand the different perspectives of special needs students, teachers, administrators, and parents to better apply interventions based on emotional intelligence.

9

Promoting Social and Emotional Intelligence for Students With Special Needs

Victoria A. Poedubicky
Highland Park Public Schools

Linda Bruene Butler
*The University of Medicine and Dentistry of New Jersey,
University Behavioral HealthCare*

Joseph Sperlazza
Faileigh Dickenson University

Bringing emotional literacy into schools makes emotional and social life themselves topics, rather than treating these most compelling facets of a child's day as irrelevant intrusions or, when they lead to eruptions, relegating them to the occasional disciplinary trips to the guidance counselor or the principal's office ... the common thread is the goal of reaching the level of social and emotional competence in children as a part of their regular education—not just something taught remedially to children who are faltering and identified as "trouble."

—Goleman (1995a, p. 263)

"Andrew, you really look angry. Have you tried using *keep calm*? Remember what we learned about how it will help you slow down so that you can think better? Let's try it together, breathe in for the count of five, hold for two, and breathe out for another five. Good, let's try it again."

"Carlos, I understand that you had a problem communicating with your teacher this morning. I am wondering if you remembered to use your *active listening* skills." I remember that you and several other students said that sometimes it is hard to remember to use these skills when feelings are strong. I'm also interested in knowing what you were saying to yourself at the time."

"Keisha, I'm interested in knowing what you were thinking when you said that to Julie? How were you feeling before you said what you said? On a scale from 1 to 10 everything appears to be a 10. We need to keep working on your skills to *regulate your emotions* when something triggers you, so that you can stay in control. Which social decision-making skill might have helped you? Let's see if we can think of something else you could have said instead and a better way to say it."

Ask any group of students what tool is used to put a nail in a piece of wood and they will all say a hammer. They will also know what tool is used to cut the wood in half or to measure the wood. However, if you ask the same group of students what tool or tools they might use to manage their emotions, to appropriately confront a peer, or to make sure they heard a message accurately, they might not be able to identify one. Knowing what tool a carpenter might use in a given situation is something that comes from observing, overlearning and experiencing skill usage, and so is the case in social and emotional situations.

As difficult as this concept is for some children, it is even more difficult for children with special needs. Some common skill deficits of students with special needs include: a short attention span; a need for concrete examples; an inability to focus, organize, and read social and emotional cues of others; poor communication skills; and learning difficulties, to name a few. Additional deficits that impede effective negotiation of social interactions and social problem solving include deficits in: identification and expression of feelings of self and others; the ability to identify problems and put them into words; and the impulse control needed to stop, keep calm, and think when faced with a situation that triggers strong emotion. Students with high levels of aggressive behavior also often have a hostile attribution bias and interpret a situation that most other children would interpret as neutral or solvable as hostile and respond aggressively rather than reading the situation accurately and reacting more appropriately (Crick & Dodge, 1994; Dodge, 1986; Dodge, Pettit, & Bates, 1994).

These challenges and others create the need for counselors to take a central role in developing wrap-around programming that supports the social and emotional education for students with special needs. A comprehensive school counseling model places a school counselor in an ideal position to coordinate the provision of instruction and practice of social-emotional skills for all students. Such instruction can provide a fundamental and powerful adjunct component of an individualized educational plan (IEP) for intervention. As Goleman (1995a) stated in our opening quote, social and emotional competence skills are a valuable part of students' regular education, not just something done as remediation when children have trouble. What we describe in this chapter is how students with special needs can benefit from the combination of building social and emotional competencies as a part of their regular education. This focus on competencies is integrated with remediation and intervention services for identified problems. School counselors, though faced with multiple responsibilities, can accomplish these goals of promoting SEL.

Chapter 15 (this volume) focuses on Bartle School in Highland Park, New Jersey. This school has systematically institutionalized a research-validated SEL model—social decision making/problem solving (SDM/PS; Bruene Butler, Hampson, Elias, Clabby, & Schuyler, 1997) within the everyday routines and lessons of a normal school day for all students. The skills are embedded so cleanly, in fact, that sometimes students do not realize they are actually acquiring the skills necessary to help them become socially and emotionally intelligent because the practice of these skills is so much a part of everyday.

This chapter focuses on what happens when a counselor applies the skills, language, and decision-making framework of the SDM/PS model as counseling tools. This model is grounded in theoretical approaches while providing the ongoing support and skill practice needed for special needs populations to internalize and overlearn skills that are needed.

The SDM/PS model is a skill-based curriculum with an instructional design that can be compared to teaching athletic skills in any sport. This chapter introduces three children (Andrew, Carlos, and Keisha) with special needs and emphasizes the counselor's role. The objective is to illustrate how SDM/PS methods can be infused within counseling sessions and applied to affect directly the individualized needs of these students.

Whether schools have institutionalized school-based SEL programs as they have at Bartle School or not, school counselors will find many applications for the teaching and coaching of skills, language skill prompts, and the decision-making framework of the SDM/PS model within their counseling sessions with students. Let us examine the connections.

SOCIAL DECISION MAKING
AND TIES TO COUNSELING THEORIES

School counselors will find that an important strength of the SDM/PS model is its compatibility with clinical intervention approaches, such as cognitive behavioral therapy (Meichenbaum, 1977), Ellis' (2001) rational emotive behavioral theory (REBT), and Glasser's (2001) reality or choice therapy.

Meichenbaum's (1977) theory, like SDM/PS, supports the use of *self-talk*, or inner speech, and helps individuals recognize how they think, feel and act as well as to recognize one's impact on others. Many of the strategies and skills taught through the SDM/SPS program (i.e., Keep Calm, BEST, and Active Listening) provide students with concrete skills that can be accessed by students through self-talk. For example, they are taught to say aloud, "I need to stop, use keep calm, and think." Students can then be taught to reflect on their unique physical signs of feelings and way of thinking that can lead to negative behavior. Once that self-awareness occurs, students can begin to identify and develop skills and more positive self-talk to replace negative thoughts and behaviors.

The SDM/PS eight-step decision-making framework can be used as the basis for reflective questions that counselors can use. These questions help students become aware of the irrational thoughts that may drive negative or irrational emotions and behaviors. Once students are aware of thinking patterns, SDM/PS helps replace negative thoughts with more positive and concrete skills. Glasser's (2001) reality or choice theory requires individuals to reflect on goals and to notice if solutions selected are effectively helping individuals reach those goals. Again, using the eight-step decision-making framework of the SDM/PS model, counselors have a language that will be familiar to students and achieve the same outcome Glasser suggested.

The SDM/PS decision-making framework is also compatible with methods used to develop other clinical interventions. For example, Knoff (1995) described a framework that involves four sequential stages: problem identification, problem analysis, intervention design, and evaluation of effectiveness. A school counselor can directly link the steps students are learning to what goes on in the counseling process. This provides students with adult modeling of how these skills can be used in real life to solve problems while increasing their active involvement in treatment. This active involvement also aids the long-term objective of getting students to internalize the skills.

CHILD STUDY TEAM PARTNERSHIP

As a counselor, it is imperative to build a strong connection with the members of the Child Study Team. The counselor can provide a pivotal role in supplying information about the day-to-day operations of the school and student performance to members of the Child Study Team.

Often, IEPs include participation in small-group sessions (i.e., social skills, anger management, loss, etc.) or at Bartle School the Social Decision Making

Lab may be enlisted. Child Study Team members often have their time split between school buildings, so it is the school counselor who is the constant within the building who is available to assist students when an emotional meltdown occurs or when a poor choice is made that needs reflection. Student performance within a problem-solving session using the eight-step problem-solving process can provide valuable diagnostic information. A student might present with a limited feelings vocabulary or an inability to put problems into words, or generate a list of possible solutions that all fall into the range of "fight or flight" or "beat 'em up or run like a chicken" (a student's words). This information can then be fed into the design of interventions to build skills to improve these abilities. For example, interventions can be aimed at increasing a student's awareness and vocabulary for feelings, providing additional practice in identifying and clearly stating problems in words, or using the keep calm and BEST skills for responding to situations that are causing them trouble.

Consultation is also essential. For example, when the school counselor works with a special needs child in the Social Decision Making Lab, providing feedback to Child Study Team members can result in additional input and insight from the Child Study Team members that can be invaluable to the counselor. It can also provide direct input from the child into intervention design and communication with parents.

At Bartle School, the Child Study Team is fully educated and informed regarding all aspects of the SDM/PS model and the program components that may be valuable in designing IEPs for specific student needs.

THE SDM/PS TOOLBOX OF SKILLS

The SDM/PS model contains a number of concrete skills that can increase students' ability to develop productive and mutually acceptable relationships with their peers. This ability has been found to be predictive of many later life outcomes (Asher & Parker, 1989; Goleman, 1995a; Parker, Rubin, Price, & De Rosier, 1995; Putallaz & Gottman, 1982). These same skills can also be used in a wide range of counseling situations as a set of central tools. For example, one of the first skills students are taught is *speaker power*. Speaker power fosters the character trait of respect by teaching students to take turns taking and to listen without interrupting. The person speaking holds an object labeled with the language cue of speaker power. The person holding the speaker power object has the power to speak. A school counselor can model this skill by waiting to speak until the student has finished speaking. During counseling sessions they can develop a plan for what the student can do if respecting speaker power is a problem behavior. The referred negative behavior (i.e., calling out) is replaced with a positive one (speaker power). A student with special needs may need additional support through a tailored intervention to help increase the use of skills, but skill instruction, practice, and feedback occurs within the academic curriculum shared with peers. The school counselors can then work with language and skill sets that are a part of the existing mainstream curriculum by infusing the language, modeling, and prompting of these social skills. The combination of classroom instruction and additional support through counseling efforts provides a solid foundation for ongoing and systematic skill building that occurs within and beyond counseling sessions. As with most cognitive behavioral approaches, the counselor's role is that of a teacher and a coach who works with the student to reteach this skill and provide additional opportunities for special needs students to practice and apply skills to specific target areas in a safe environment.

The following is a list of some of the skills that serve as tools found in the SDM/PS toolbox. Other chapters (chaps. 14 and 15, this volume) also describe the SDM/PS model. Some examples of how these skills can be incorporated within counseling efforts follows.

Share Circle

This skill builds community within the class and develops respect, good listening, and speaking skills. When used in counseling, it takes the form in small-group or one-on-one counseling sessions. Using share circle topics helps build a strong cohesive group or build a relationship with the counselor. This activity helps to create a learning environment that is safe and establishes interactivity that helps students participate successfully.

Speaker Power

This technique involves a visual prompt that helps students identify the person speaking and guidelines for respectfully attending to the person holding the speaker power object. It encourages one-at-a-time speaking because only the person holding the prompt is allowed to speak. When used in counseling, this skill typically is modeled and practiced during counseling sessions.

Listening Position

Listening position is a skill that helps students be attentive and focused listeners. This skill cuts down on misunderstandings and miscommunications. When used in counseling, this skill is typically modeled and practiced. It is easily infused into the counseling approach entitled SOLER (Sitting, Open, Leaning, Eyes, Relaxed).

Keep Calm

This is a skill that teaches the student to regulate physical signs of feelings. Student breathes in for 5 seconds, holds for 2 seconds, and breathes out for 5 seconds. Repeat until calm. When used in counseling, this skill helps reduce impulsive behaviors such as calling out or making quick decisions without thinking through the consequences of behaviors. Prompting and coaching students to use this skill in a crisis helps diffuse a highly emotional state, which is a prerequisite for clear thinking.

Hassle Log

This tool is a worksheet that provides a structured framework for problem solving and decision making. It includes steps such as: identifying feelings, identifying the problem, setting the goal, thinking, and listing as many solutions as possible. When used in counseling, this tool gives the counselor a framework of questions (also known as facilitative questioning) to help students reflect on decisions. Using the same framework that students learn in their classrooms and apply within their academic subjects also helps students overlearn and internalize the process.

BEST

BEST stands for body posture, eye contact, say appropriate words, and tone of voice. It helps students present themselves in a positive way in times of conflict or during presentations. When used in counseling, it gives the counselor and student a framework to guide students in coming up with plans to address social problems with other students or others. Counselors typically model and coach students to use this skill during counseling sessions and within role-play practice of plans to solve social problems. It reinforces a nonjudgmental approach with students.

Active Listening

This is a set of skills that teaches students to be active listeners through repeating back, paraphrasing, and asking questions to clarify. This skill helps prevent miscommunications and misunderstandings. When used in counseling, this skill is a cornerstone to good counseling technique. This skill strengthens good listening skills and helps the counselor gain a clear understanding of the student's problem. This skill also helps when reviewing what a student may have wanted and the decisions they made that resulted in a problem.

Footsteps

This is a skill that develops empathy and helps students see another point of view through a combination of active listening and FIG (feelings, identify the problem, and goal). Students have an opportunity to put their feelings, a problem, and their goal into words and to listen to the feelings, problem, and goal of another person to ensure that two points of view are considered before moving into conflict resolution and problem solving. When used in counseling, it could also be called role reversal. Students are actually placed in the other person's seat for them to see, feel, and hear what the other person is seeing, feeling, and hearing.

Choosing Friends

This is a method for helping children to identify social skill that helps students in making and keeping friends. During counseling sessions, this method can be used to help students consider how different behaviors affect others. Students consider what behaviors are most likely to lead to mutually acceptable and productive relationships with others.

Giving and Receiving Praise and Criticism

Students are taught to give and receive praise and examine the impact of these skills on class climate and productively working as a team. They are also taught to provide constructive criticism in an objective, helpful way and explore the impact of harsh criticism on class climate and productivity. In counseling sessions these skills are modeled; they often provide helpful tools when developing plans for improving student's social interactions.

APPLICATION OF SDM/PS TOOLS
IN COUNSELING SITUATIONS

Have you ever observed the action in an emergency room in a hospital? The attending doctors and nurses all respond rationally and methodically. They seem to click into a mode that appears to be instinctive or to be on automatic pilot. By reacting in this manner, the emergency team is able to act in an effective way that will best support the patient. This is similar to the way many counselors react when a child is in crisis. The emotionally intelligent counselor is able to use skills such as keep calm in crisis or stressful situations when rational thinking is paramount.

Counselors use social and emotional intelligence when working with children with special needs by modeling these skills and using the same skills as a counseling teaching strategy to help the child develop and use these skills in situations that are causing them life difficulties. Perhaps the most important time for a counselor to model appropriate skills is when approaching a student in crisis or having an emotional meltdown. Many of the students in this population have disabilities ranging from learning and physical disabilities to autistic or emotional disturbances. The active focus on keeping calm also helps promote clear thinking.

Case Study 1: Andrew Learns Self-Talk to Monitor His Emotions

As the school counselor, you've just received a call from a special education teacher in a collaborative class (a class that combines both special needs students and regular education students, with both teachers teaching together). The teacher has informed you that one of her students, Andrew, classified as emotionally disturbed, is hitting himself in the head and saying things like, "I'm stupid, I'm stupid, I'm stupid." He has become frustrated because the teacher won't come over to help him and has completely worked himself up into an emotional state.

It is very important that, as the counselor, you remain calm so you can think rationally and assess and guide the child through his emotion. As you approach the classroom, you are breathing in for a count of 5 seconds, holding for 2 seconds, and breathing out for 5 seconds, repeating this several times as you get closer and closer to the classroom. While breathing this way, you are thinking what you might want for this child and how you are going to reach that goal.

The two skills from the SDM/PS model are keep calm and FIG TESPN, the decision-making framework. Keep calm helps regulate emotions as you begin to bring FIG TESPN to mind. FIG TESPN stands for: Feelings; then Identify the problem; Goals to guide yourself; Think of many possible alternatives to reaching your goal; Envision consequences; Select the best solution that will help you reach the goal; Plan, practice, and prepare for anticipated obstacles before acting; and Notice what happens and use this information for future problem solving. By applying these two skills, you will be better able to think rationally for yourself to assist the child effectively. You are also modeling for the child in a stressful situation how he should respond when stressed or frustrated.

The second way in which a counselor uses the social and emotional skills of the SDM/PS model is by using the skills as counseling tools, teaching and reinforcing skills with each student. Let us continue to examine Andrew's situation once you have made contact with him. The tools focused on in this case study are keep calm to help him manage his feelings and a change in his self-talk to turn negative thoughts to positive.

"*Andrew, you really look angry. Have you tried using keep calm to slow down your heart and breathing rate so that you can think better? Let's try it together, breathe in for the count of five, hold for two, and breathe out for another five. Good, let's try it again. Now tell me what the problem was.*"

Although classified as emotionally disabled, Andrew is able to put the problem into words because he's been taught through prompts and cues. After listening to Andrew identify the problem, the counselor determines that the irrational belief in his head is initiating the emotional outburst and destructive behaviors. His belief is that he alone is stupid and that nobody will help him. The counselor disputes the irrational belief by pointing out that he is NOT stupid if he can't answer a question or two and, if he would wait with his hand up, his teacher would have come around to help him as she has in the past.

By encouraging Andrew to notice when he becomes annoyed while waiting and to use keep calm during wait time moves Andrew into a more positive problem-solving mode. Andrew practices how to change his self-talk from "I'm stupid" to "I need to stop, keep calm, and think." The ability to self-monitor and self-regulate emotions is a critical component in becoming socially and emotionally intelligent and a major component of the SDM/PS model. If Andrew's irrational belief returns, he needs to be reminded or coached to say to himself that he just needs a little help as do the others in his class and that by doing Keep Calm he will not appear different from any other students in his class. Using the familiar prompts and cues Andrew has learned in health class and reinforced in other school settings makes this conversation and counseling session easier.

Case Study 2: Carlos Learns to Apply Good Listening Skills

Carlos is a sixth-grade student with attention deficit disorder (ADD). He attends regular education classes; however, his inability to focus, be organized and maneuver socially with her peers cause him problems on a daily basis. Often, Carlos finds it necessary to get up and walk around the classroom, which draws attention to himself.

Recently, Carlos became distracted and missed the assignment for homework. The next day, he was unprepared and the teacher deducted points from his grade and told him she was going to call home to alert his parents. When Carlos argued with his teacher, he received a lunch detention and a referral to meet with the counselor to reflect on his decision making. The following is the dialogue between Carlos and the counselor.

Counselor: "Carlos, I understand you had a problem communicating with your teacher this morning. Let's think about what happened. I am wondering if you remembered to use your active listening skills.

Carlos: I forgot to. Okay.

Counselor: I want you to think back to the trouble. Okay? So, how were you feeling BEFORE the trouble started?

Carlos: I think I was feeling really, really annoyed and angry.

Counselor: Okay. It is important that you identify how you were feeling. What social decision-making skills might you use to help you control that feeling?

Carlos: Keep Calm!

Counselor: Great! Now, tell me about how it went.

Carlos: Well, I forgot to use it. I just got angry and said some really bad things.

Counselor: So, you were feeling annoyed and angry (reflection of feelings). Where in your body did you feel the anger and annoyance?

Carlos: Mostly in my stomach.

Counselor: Okay. It is important that you are able to notice where in your body angry feelings are triggered. You are getting much better at this skill than when we first started working on it. Can you remember how difficult this was for you at first? You have come a long way. You also learned today that this situation is a trigger for you, and whenever it happens, you will get that funny feeling in your stomach. That is the signal to use keep calm. Let's practice it together (counselor and Carlos begin the skill of Keep Calm).

Counselor: Okay, so you said that you missed the assignment the day before, right? If you're not sure of something someone has said, what social decision-making skill or tool might you need to use?

Carlos: Listening Position?

Counselor: That skill would have helped you hear the assignment in the first place. It's a skill that would specifically help you to keep yourself on task. Did you know that you were unfocused at that time?

Carlos: Kind of.

Counselor: Do you remember Active Listening?

Carlos: Oh yeah, that's the one when you repeat back what someone has said. You say things like "so, what you're saying is …" or "do you mean?" and then repeat back what they said or say it in my own words.

Counselor: Excellent Carlos! You do remember!

Carlos: Yes.

Counselor: So let's rewind the tape and replay it, but this time we're going to do something different instead of what you really did. When you first realized that you had missed the assignment, tell what skill you could have used.

Carlos: Okay, I should have used Active Listening and raised my hand and asked "do you want us to ..." saying what I thought she had said and wait for her response to either say yes that's right or no it's not. This way I would have heard the assignment and been prepared for class.

Counselor: Great! What if a teacher confronts you again? Which social decision-making skill/tool should you be using?

Carlos: Keep Calm definitely!

Counselor: Excellent Carlos! Is it hard to remember to use Keep Calm in the situation?

Carlos: Sometimes.

Counselor: Just keep practicing and planning ways to use your skills in problem situations and your skills will continue to get stronger. How would you feel if I ask your teacher if we can come up with some strategies to help you remember to practice your active listening skills? We can let her know that this is your goal and come up with some ways to help cue you to use the skill during trigger situations.

In this dialogue, the counselor used the familiar eight-step decision-making framework in the form of questions, and through this the counselor was able to reflect on feelings, paraphrase, clarify statements, and use open-ended questions that provided fruitful answers. Had Carlos not remembered what active listening was, it would have made for a wonderful teachable moment. By using concrete examples that he can relate to (i.e., a teacher giving him a series of class assignments to do, his parent giving him chores to complete, or a friend telling him about what he was going to do at the end of the school day), the school counselor can provide opportunities for role-play practice of ways Carlos can use active listening skills applied to situations that cause him difficulties to rehearse and prepare new behavioral responses before facing the situation again. Other skill prompts, such as Keep Calm and BEST, can also be used to help Carlos develop a plan that is socially competent.

At the conclusion of the session with Carlos, it is important to meet with his teacher to fill her in regarding the outcome. This way she can help facilitate or coach him when he needs to use Active Listening or Keep Calm. Carlos is also referred to the Social Decision Making Lab so that he can meet on a weekly basis and work on other active listening skills (i.e., paraphrasing, repeating back, and asking questions to clarify). He will be put in role-play scenarios to give him practice with his peers and teachers. This will cut down on the amount of miscommunications Carlos has with other people.

Case Study 3: Keisha Learns to Regulate Her Emotions

"Keisha, I'm interested in knowing what you were thinking when you said that to Julie? How were you feeling before you said what you said? On a scale from 1 to 10 everything appears to be a 10. Let's see if we can work on your ability to use keep calm. If you learn to regulate your emotions you will have more control and will be able to solve problems with other people in a better way. What social decision-making skill might have helped you? Let's see if we can think of something else you could've said instead and a better way to say it."

In this case study, Keisha is a fourth-grade student with a specific learning disability. She's a sensitive child who internalizes everything that happens as an affront against her. Therefore, if she thinks someone does not like her or an idea she has offered, she will have a meltdown. She will either go into a crying episode or withdraw completely from the situation. Either way, her peers alienate her. As the counselor, the goal is to help her to identify her signs of feelings, use Keep Calm, to place each particular situation on a scale from 1 to 10, and to respond accordingly.

Keisha reveals that she wanted to be included in on her friend Julie's conversation with other girls. She was feeling left out because she goes to resource room during language arts time and misses out on group work with the others. She accused her friend of not liking her and leaving her out, and said that maybe they shouldn't be friends anymore. This upset Julie very much.

At this point, the counselor asked Keisha what she really wanted to have happen (her goal). Keisha said that she wanted to be included. The counselor then asked her if what she chose to do helped her reach her goal. Keisha shook her head. Drawing the connection to choices that are made and the desired goal is very important.

The counselor's strategy of drawing a continuum with the numbers 1 to 10 will help create the visual that most students with special needs require. The counselor asks Keisha where on the line she might place the situation of someone hitting her. She responds with "10." Next, the counselor asks Keisha where on the line she might place losing her place on line. She responds with "10." The counselor asks her to look at both of those situations; having her explain how both those situations warrant the same response will get her to recognize that not everything that happens is a 10 on the scale. What about her situation with Julie? Keisha now places it at a 5 and in this case decides that keeping calm and then using the skill of BEST might have helped clear up this misunderstanding. The counselor then asks Keisha if she'd like to meet with Julie in a peer mediation setting so that she and Julie can have an opportunity to tell each other how each felt, what the problem was, and what they now want, and to brainstorm solutions to reach their goal. Keisha says she'll agree if Julie agrees. After talking to Julie, she also agrees to go to peer mediation to clear the air with Keisha.

Keisha takes the scale back with her to class so she can reflect on situations as they happen and decide where on the line each situation falls.

DISCUSSION

Given the strong predictive nature of social and emotional competencies, it is imperative that students with special needs are targeted for assistance socially and emotionally so that the playing field becomes leveled.

For students such as Andrew, Carlos, and Keisha, learning social and emotional skills in a preventative setting with their peers, in combination with counseling and other additional interventions (to support the development of their social and emotional skills), provides a "safety net" to enhance their chances of success.

We end as we began with some words from Goleman (1995a):

> In a time when too many children lack the capacity to handle their upsets, to listen or focus, to rein in impulse, to feel responsible for their work or care about their learning, anything that will buttress these skills will help in their education.... Emotional literacy enhances schools' ability to teach.... Beyond these education advantages, the courses [in SEL] seem to help children better fulfill their roles in life, becoming better friends, students, sons and daughters—and in the future are more likely to be better husbands and wives, workers and bosses, parents and citizens. While not every boy and girl will acquire these skills with equal sureness, to the degree they do we are all the better for it. (p. 285)

Isn't this the primary mission of a school counselor? The promise of SEL as a central component of comprehensive school counseling is that it broadens the potency of counseling efforts to prepare students for the inevitable challenges they face now and will continue to face in their personal, professional, and community lives.

REFERENCES

Asher, S. R., & Parker, J. G. (1989). Significance of peer relationship problems in childhood. In B. H. Schneider, G. Attili, J. Nadel, & R. P. Weissberg (Eds.), *Social competence in developmental perspective* (pp. 5–23). Dordrecht, Germany: Kluwer.

Bruene Butler, L., Hampson, J., Elias, M. J., Clabby, J. F., & Schuyler, T. (1997). The Improving Social Awareness-Social Problem Solving Project. In G. A. Albee & T. Gullotta (Eds.), *Primary prevention works: Issues in children's and families lives* (Vol. 6, pp. 239–267). Thousand Oaks, CA: Sage.

Crick, N. R., & Dodge, K. A. (1994). A review and reformulation of social information-processing mechanisms in children's social adjustment. *Psychological Bulletin, 115*, 74–101.

Dodge, K. A. (1986). A social information processing model of social competence in children. In M. Perlmutter (Ed.), *Minnesota Symposium on Child Psychology* (Vol. 18, pp. 77–125). Hillsdale, NJ: Lawrence Erlbaum Associates.

Dodge, K. A., Pettit, G. S., & Bates, J. E. (1994). Socialization mediators of the relationship between socioeconomic status and child conduct problems. *Child Development, 65*, 649–665.

Ellis, A. (2001). *New directions for rational emotive behavior therapy: Overcoming destructive beliefs, feelings, and behaviors.* Amherst, NY: Prometheus.

Glasser, W. (2001). *Counseling with choice therapy: The new reality therapy.* New York: HarperCollins.

Goleman, D. (1995a). *Emotional intelligence: Why it can matter more than IQ.* New York: Bantam.

Goleman, D. (1995b, September 27). Beyond IQ: Why some schools are adding "emotional intelligence" to their definition of what it means to be smart. *Education Week, 44*, p. 80.

Knoff, H. M. (1995). Facilitating school-based organizational change and strategic planning. In A. Thomas & J. Grimes (Eds.), *Best practices in school psychology* (pp. 239–252). Washington, DC: National Association of School Psychologists.

Meichenbaum, D. (1977). *Cognitive Behavior modification: An integrative approach.* New York: Plenum.

Parker, J. G., Rubin, K. H., Price, J. M., & De Rosier, M. E. (1995). Peer relationships, child development and adjustment: A developmental psychopathology perspective. In D. Cicchetti & D. J. Cohen (Eds.), *Developmental psychopathology: Vol. 2. Risk, disorder, and adaptation* (pp. 96–161). New York: Wiley.

Putallaz, M., & Gottman, J. (1982). Conceptualizing social competence in children. In P. Kardy & J. J. Steffen (Eds.), *Peer rejection in childhood* (pp. 189–216). Cambridge, England: Cambridge University Press.

10

Collaborating With Teachers on Social Emotional Learning

Karen Mildener
Cristi Riccio Keane
New York City Department of Education

It's mid-October, and an unfamiliar face shows up at my door to remind me about the first meeting of many that I'll be attending because she, a counselor, will be working with my class this year. It's been a busy first month of school, and quite frankly, I only vaguely remember getting the memo about this. All I can think about is "when"? When is there a free 40 minutes in an already over-packed schedule to have a counselor come in to teach my students about feelings? And meetings? What will I have to give up in order to attend them? How important is it really, that I add a social-emotional development component to my curriculum?

These are some of many barriers that school counselors must address in bringing social emotional learning (SEL) programs to the classrooms. SEL is based on the concepts and competencies of emotional intelligence (Boyatzis, Goleman, & Rhee, 2000; Mayer & Salovey, 1997) and is consistent with the personal-social development standards of school counselors (see Muller-Ackerman & Shelton, chap. 2, this volume). Teachers feel increased accountability and responsibility to prepare students for standardized testing, and their days are highly structured around these goals. Our challenge as counselors is to help teachers shift their thinking about SEL. Our view is that SEL should not be another subject that has to be taught. Teachers need to see this work not as an "add on" but as an "add in" to their day. It is essential that SEL counselors help teachers see the value of SEL to incorporate it into the classroom. We need to use our own social-emotional skills to support already overburdened teachers by understanding the pressure they experience to meet curriculum standards. In empathizing with teachers we can establish a working relationship that is critical in promoting an SEL program. By helping teachers develop SEL lessons that can be incorporated into their literacy and social studies classes and by coaching them in their classrooms, both SEL and academic goals can be met and some of the barriers to developing emotionally intelligent schools can be overcome.

There has been a good deal of media coverage of and widespread enthusiasm for the link between emotional intelligence and personal success in the last decade (Goleman, 1995). This has lead to an interest in emotional intelligence and social-emotional development in schools. Related social-emotional processes such as self-regulation, emotional competence, and social adjustment have been studied with regard to child development and education (see Salovey & Sluyter, 1997). The effectiveness of SEL programs in schools has also been examined (Topping, Holmes, & Bremmer, 2000; Zins, Travis, & Freppon, 1997).

As school counselors teaching SEL and consulting with teachers in several elementary schools, we have directly observed the role that social-emotional abilities play in the classroom. The SEL program that was implemented in these New York City public schools was part of Project EXSEL. It involved collaboration between the teachers and the counselors to create particular SEL lessons that were incorporated into the existing academic curriculum. The SEL counselor-consultant conducted weekly experientially based activities with the students in the participating classes. The social-emotional lessons that were taught (i.e., recognizing feelings, expressing self, managing intense emotions) were reinforced throughout the week by the classroom teachers' use of SEL material and activities in other subjects. Such a structure improves the learning about emotions by providing multiple exposures to the SEL material in varied contexts. It also allowed the students to practice the social-emotional skills that were the basis of the weekly lessons.

When teachers, counselors, and students work together through SEL programs, productive learning environments can be created not just for emotional learning but for academic achievement as well. The skills involved in emotional awareness, management, and expression enable teachers and students to solve conflicts as they arise and to work toward mutually beneficial goals. It has long been recognized that the classroom environment is a critical factor in student learning (Gredler, 2001). It is important that we define and support the importance of SEL in schools to enhance students' as well as teachers' emotional intelligence skills and social adjustment. To begin our work together, we first need to build a relationship with teachers based on mutual respect and trust.

TEACHER–COUNSELOR RELATIONSHIPS

The teacher–counselor relationship is a crucial component in SEL work in schools. The relationship itself serves as a model of effective collaboration for students. In working together, the counselor and teacher also demonstrate the very skills they are trying to teach. There are many opportunities to model a range of SEL skills, from empathy and perspective taking to social skills and conflict resolution. A strong teacher–counselor partnership allows students to know that the SEL work is important. The level of commitment on the part of the counselor and teacher dictates how extensive an SEL program will be and ultimately how successful it can become. "Having children see teachers and counselors collaborate and teach together helps build their level of commitment toward SEL work. My students know how important this work is to me, not just to someone coming in once a week," says Melissa, a teacher at the Manhattan New School.

Educators have recognized the benefit of encouraging collaborative work among students. However, we often observe teachers working in virtual isolation from the school community. SEL programs in schools are an opportunity to create such needed collaboration between educators. The teacher–counselor partnership needs to be grounded in a core belief that SEL is a critical element in any sound, cohesive instructional program that can enrich literacy instruction. With this shared belief the teacher and counselor can form an alliance and begin their journey into developing an SEL program designed particularly for their classes. Success at the classroom level can eventually build into a schoolwide program. The key ingredient at this stage of the process is for the counselor to develop in the teacher this core belief in the importance of SEL.

Working as a counselor in a classroom can be a challenging proposition. The collaborative relationship between the counselor and teacher is the foundation to making this a smooth transition. Teachers and counselors must have an understanding of each other's needs, goals, and roles in facilitating SEL lessons in the classroom. It's important that teachers don't feel that SEL work is being imposed on their classroom without their consent. It could also be detrimental to the relationship if teachers view the counselor as an authority who is in the classroom in an evaluative capacity. Teacher and counselor must form a partnership, working as a team toward clearly defined mutual goals, within specific roles that meet both of their needs. Open and regular communication and planning between teacher and counselor is important in developing and maintaining this partnership. Research in consultation, particularly when the consultant is in a teaching role, suggests that the classroom teacher's acceptance of the consultant is higher when the teacher's concerns about the consultation are accurately assessed and adequately addressed (Pedron & Evans, 1990). Each professional brings his or her own style and expertise that can be leveraged within the relationship. The teacher has a deeper understanding of the academic level of the students as well as a broad knowledge of books and other materials that can be used in developing a curriculum. The counselor has a deep understanding of social and emotional functioning in a broader context of human development. Together these resources contribute to designing a curriculum that infuses lessons using emotional intelligence competencies.

Counselors are often viewed as the social and emotional facilitators in the school. One of the three main focuses of counselors is on the personal-social development of the students (along with academic achievement and career development). Our work with individual students and small groups is heavily steeped in enhancing their SEL skills such as managing emotions, complex problem solving, decision making, and helping students understand themselves and others. Furthermore, many counselors organize schoolwide efforts such as peer meditation programs, antibullying initiatives, and so forth. Recently, there has been a trend in counseling toward having counselors conduct classroom guidance lessons, thereby providing psychoeducational counseling services to the broader population using the classroom as a forum. This is an ideal opportunity to implement an SEL program in your school. Teachers ultimately want their students to learn and master academics based on benchmarks appropriate to the grade they teach. They recognize that it is up to them to create a classroom that fosters learning. As educators, we know that students learn best when they are in an environment where they feel comfortable asking questions, sharing ideas with the teacher and classmates, and taking risks. They are better able to focus on learning when they are able to manage their emotions, express themselves in an effective way, and get along with others.

The teacher–counselor relationship is important in providing a consistent emotional learning environment for the students. The support of the counselor can positively affect the way the teacher works in various aspects of his or her pedagogy. The teacher's commitment and willingness to collaborate can also affect the counselor in the SEL teaching role, as illustrated by the following quote from a counselor in the project.

Personally I can feel the feel the difference when I am in a classroom where I am unsure about our relationship compared to a classroom where I feel a good/strong connection with the teacher. My comfort level in the classroom depends on this and certainly impacts how students perceive the lesson. A teacher that tells her students to listen to the SEL lesson being delivered by the counselor while she herself is disengaged sends a message that she either doesn't value this type of work or that she doesn't see it as being a part of the teachers role. Either way the students may not connect to this work as well. Given that my goal as a counselor is for students to learn these skills, I continue to go into classrooms and lead this work even when I feel that my relationship with the teacher is not as strong as I would like. However, I certainly notice that at times I have a lot of feelings about going into the classroom. Sometimes I find myself thinking "Why should I bother when the teacher doesn't work with me, I don't want to go, what's the point in doing a 45 minute lesson once per week if it won't be reinforced by the teacher throughout the week." At times I feel frustrated, anxious and discouraged. I need to tap into my own SEL skills to manage my emotions in order to stick to my goals. I tell myself that this is important work. Teachers could be having feelings such as being overwhelmed, having nothing to do with me. I just need to feel good about my part in this work.

It is important for the counselor to have well-developed social-emotional skills, not only for modeling and teaching but for adjusting to the many challenges of collaboration and SEL work in the classrooms.

SOCIAL EMOTIONAL LEARNING

As counselors working in the classroom, we plan out a sequence of lessons that teach SEL skills in a sequential, developmental way. Ideally, the teacher and counselor meet each week to review plans, select books, and discuss SEL competencies to be targeted. Roles are divided so that teacher and counselor each know their part in the lesson. Sometimes teachers address specific concerns they have about the behavior of a student(s) and ask that we create a lesson for it. As coaches, we try to guide the teacher in looking at the underlying SEL skill that needs to be addressed. By teaching and practicing a skill, it keeps the focus away from trying to "fix a problem" with a one-shot lesson and looks more at enhancing children's SEL skills so they can better handle situations as they arise. Lessons are created using emotional intelligence theory as our foundation. "We define emotional intelligence as the ability to perceive and express emotion, assimilate emotion and thought, understand and reason with emotion, and regulate emotion in the self and others" (Mayer & Salovey, 1997, p. 10). For example, students may need to enhance their ability to calm down when intense feelings arise. Using skills that have been targeted in previous lessons around awareness of feelings and their triggers, a new lesson can be created on regulating emotion. Students are asked to use their reflective ability to identify an emotion and to understand what caused, or triggered, this feeling. A book may be read in which the main character is having difficulty managing his or her emotions. The book can be read aloud and discussed from both an academic and social-emotional perspective. Students, counselors, and teachers brainstorm different calming techniques that the main character could have used by considering how they may have handled a similar situation. Through a series of role plays and activities, students are taught and are able to practice using various calming strategies. To encourage family involvement in the development and internalization of these skills, children are asked to practice these skills at home through homework assignments.

As our work together progresses teachers are encouraged to take a more active role in the weekly lessons. Initially, they are asked to read aloud the book chosen for the corresponding SEL skill-building lesson. Gradually, they take the initiative to take part in the discussion of the book's central theme and the SEL skill that we are attempting to highlight. Eventually, teachers become more active in the lesson, often participating in role plays or assisting students through more complex problem-solving activities.

When teachers participate in the lessons and model the SEL skills, students get the message that this work is important. According to Melissa, a NYC second-grade teacher, "The students really understood how important this work was when I rescheduled our Word Study in order to incorporate SEL into our day. They know how important our literacy program is, so by moving it they understood that social and emotional development work was equally if not more important." Melissa's personal commitment to doing SEL work set the tone for how involved and committed her students became. The teacher's influence not only reinforces the behaviors of the specific social skills but also facilitates the students' social-emotional development through her emotionally aware relationship with them. In turn, the students emulated her model and created a wonderful, warm, and caring classroom environment committed to SEL development.

Conversely, students can also get the message from the teacher that this work is not important. It is essential, therefore, that the counselor conduct the SEL work in conjunction with the teacher. When an outside person such as a counselor comes into a classroom once a week to do an SEL lesson, it can sometimes be seen as separate from their everyday learning and therefore not integrated into their daily lives. Furthermore, as a counselor working in a classroom, you are entering a teacher's domain. What happens or doesn't happen in a classroom, what succeeds or does not succeed in a classroom is truly up to the teacher. By working with a teacher in a joint effort to teach these skills, students are more likely to see its importance and relevance to their classroom environment and their lives.

A counselor may be the SEL "expert" of the school, but teachers are the "experts" of teaching their students. They have had time to assess where their students are socially and emotionally. They may have noticed that some students frequently call on the teacher to solve a problem for them, whereas others may be taking counterproductive, unsuccessful steps to work through issues. Students may lack the vocabulary or ability to let others know how they're feeling or may not be able to read accurately others' feelings. Spending so much time with her students, a teacher is able to see how well the class appears to be integrating lessons into practice. Mindy, a teacher at Manhattan New School, recalled the moment when she realized that her students were integrating the SEL skills we had taught and reinforced together throughout the year:

A group of kindergarten girls helped a new student, Lisette, to calm herself down when she arrived at their school feeling sad and alone and couldn't seem to stop crying. The girls began telling her about different techniques we had learned to calm ourselves down. One student suggested that Lisette try a technique called "Birthday Candles" in which the student holds up their open hand and imagines that each finger is a birthday candle. Through a series of deep breaths the child blows out the candles one at a time. Lisette tried the technique and not only felt calmer but made some new friends in the process. I was excited and proud when I realized that the girls had used many of the social and emotional skills we had been teaching together all year.

Amy, a first-grade teacher at the Elias Howe School, came to a realization that the probability of her students internalizing these skills relied on how far she herself was willing to take it. She stated, "There are times when I do need to stop what I had planned in order to deal with an issue or problem that comes up. However, if I've been teaching SEL skills consistently, and reinforcing them throughout the day, I can simply use this 'teachable moment' as an opportunity to practice these skills."

Abby, a kindergarten teacher at Elias Howe, realized that her students were really integrating the SEL skills after a troubling time in her classroom. "I was having a difficult day with my class," recalled Abby. "They weren't working to the best of their ability; they knew it, and I knew it. I told them, 'I'm really angry with you guys.' One student immediately responded, 'You're not really angry, you're frustrated.' It was certainly an experience that told me they were really getting this work. It made me want to continue."

OVERCOMING BARRIERS

So, what gets in the way of partnering counselors and teachers in doing SEL development work? Conversations with teachers led us to the realization that for some, time is just too great an obstacle. There are also teachers that don't feel comfortable with another person working in their room. Others expressed that they didn't feel that they had enough administrative support to focus on doing this work. Some teachers told us that they didn't feel that they had enough personal knowledge or training to do SEL work. Others felt that it was hard adding one more thing to their schedule, not being sure they'd see any real results. As SEL consultants working with teachers, we need to tap into our own emotional intelligence to understand teachers' feelings to overcome resistance to doing this work.

Amy, when asked what keeps her committed to this work responded, "There are times when I have a lot that I need to get done with my class, and having *anyone* come in can feel like an intrusion. Adding to my frustration is the fact that I don't often get to see the immediate results of this work. When I looked more closely, I began to see smaller instances of positive growth in my students. Ultimately I knew I wanted a classroom where kids care about and respect one another. I've come to realize that talking to them about it just isn't as effective as teaching them how to do it."

Social and emotional work is a natural component of classroom work. Whether it is acknowledged or not, each student comes to school with a full range of emotions to manage and an array of social situations to deal with. Ignoring this fact and not preparing students to deal with their emotions and social lives are equivalent to choosing not to teach math or literacy but expecting students to perform well on the SATs. Currently, our public education system focuses strongly on testing and standards. A single-minded focus on test preparation can lose sight of the goal to educate the whole child. To ignore the social and emotional life of children is a sad and dangerous mistake. Students who are unable or ill equipped to manage their emotions and solve the problems that life presents to them are not able to focus or concentrate on academics. They also grow up unable to deal with life.

School counselors have a great opportunity in schools by acting as SEL change agents and initiating teacher–counselor partnerships. In schools nationwide, teachers and counselors are partnering together to share the challenges and overcome the obstacles of doing this work. In this time of competing priorities, we seek opportunities for students to have exposure to SEL. Teachers, in creating a classroom climate that incorporates sound SEL approaches into instructional programs, can be powerful agents to reaching this goal. In doing SEL work, success is measured more qualitatively than quantitatively. Success would sound like students demonstrating self-reflection and identifying their emotions. It would look like students managing their emotions, practicing calming techniques, diffusing anger, demonstrating problem-solving skills, and working through interpersonal conflicts. It would feel like warm, caring, empathic schools.

REFERENCES

Boyatzis, R. E., Goleman, D., & Rhee, K. S. (2000). Clustering competencies in emotional intelligence: Insights from the Emotional Competence Inventory. In R. Bar-On & J. Parker (Eds.), *The handbook of emotional intelligence* (pp. 343–362). San Francisco: Jossey-Bass.

Goleman, D. (1995). *Emotional intelligence: Why it can matter more than IQ.* New York: Bantam.

Gredler, M. (2001). *Learning and instruction: Theory into practice* (4th ed.). Upper Saddle River, NJ: Merrill/Prentice Hall.

Mayer, J. D., & Salovey, P. (1997). What is emotional intelligence? In P. Salovey & D. Sluyter (Eds.), *Emotional development and emotional intelligence: Implications for educators* (pp. 3–31). New York: Basic Books.

Pedron, N. A., & Evans, S. B. (1990). Modifying classroom teacher's acceptance of the consulting teacher model. *Journal of Educational and Psychological Consultation, 1,* 189–200.

Salovey, P., & Sluyter, D. (Eds.). (1997). *Emotional development and emotional intelligence: Implications for educators.* New York: Basic Books.

Topping, K., Holmes, E. A., & Bremmer, W. (2000). The effectiveness of school-based programs for the promotion of social competence. In R. Bar-On & J. Parker (Eds.), *The handbook of emotional intelligence* (pp. 411–432). San Francisco: Jossey-Bass.

Zins, J., Travis, L., & Freppon, P. (1997). Linking research and educational programming to promote social and emotional learning. In P. Salovey & D. Sluyter (Eds.), *Emotional development and emotional intelligence: Implications for educators* (pp. 257–274). New York: Basic Books.

TABLE 10.1

Guides for Implementing a Social-Emotional Learning (SEL) Program

---

I. Guides for counselors in establishing SEL:
1. Make the work enjoyable for children and teachers.
2. Communicate regularly with teachers and administrators regarding the program.
3. Leverage teachers' strengths and interests.
4. Customize work to meet individual teacher's needs. Look at grade, age, population, and so forth.
5. Choose carefully which teachers you work with. (You'll feel better doing quality cooperative work with fewer teachers rather than working with a lot of teachers who aren't as invested in this work).

II. Guides for classroom teachers to reinforce SEL[a]
1. Use the morning meeting to do a daily emotional check-in with students.
2. Institute after lunch check-in to encourage students to problem solve conflicts that may have happened in the yard or lunchroom.
3. Use SEL language consistently and coordinate language and techniques used across grade levels so that teachers can continue to reinforce skills taught in previous grades.
4. Recruit other interested teachers.
5. Advertise your successes.
6. Share your ideas with others.
7. Leverage your school counselor as an SEL expert. They can be a tremendous resource if you ask for help.
8. Research existing SEL programs; don't try to reinvent the wheel.
9. Talk to your principal about how important this work is; with their buy-in you will have a lot more support for the work you are doing.

---

[a]The suggestions were developed by New York City school teachers participating in Project EXSEL, 2000–2003.

11

Emotionally Intelligent School Administrators: Developing a Positive School Climate

Kevin P. Brady

Queens College, CUNY

Great leaders move us. They ignite our passion and inspire the best in us. When we try to explain why they are so effective, we speak of strategy, vision, or powerful ideas. But the reality is much more primal: Great leadership works through the emotions.

—Goleman, Boyatzis, and McKee (2002, p.3)

Howard Gardner's (1983) theory of multiple intelligences has caused many educators to reevaluate their prior conceptions of student academic success and instructional best practices in the classroom. From the beginnings of Gardner's research, the field of emotional intelligence has developed substantially and has received increasing attention from a variety of professions, including business, organizational psychology, and education (Gardner, 1993; Goleman, 1995; Mayer & Salovey, 1993, 1997; Novick, Kress, & Elias, 2002; Salovey & Mayer, 1990). In 2002, Goleman, Boyatzis, and McKee published *Primal Leadership: Realizing the Power of Emotional Intelligence*. The major contribution of this book was that it detailed the significance of emotional intelligence in improving leadership competencies. Table 11.1 illustrates Goleman's emotional competence framework (Goleman et al., 2002).

TABLE 11.1
Emotional Competence Framework

Self/Personal Competences	Other/Social Competences
Self-awareness	Social awareness
Emotional self-awareness	Empathy
Accurate self-assessment	Service orientation
Self-confidence	Organizational awareness
Self-management	Relationship management
Self-control	Developing others
Trustworthiness	Influence
Conscientiousness	Communication
Adaptability	Conflict management
Achievement drive	Leadership
Initiative	Change catalyst
	Building bonds
	Teamwork and collaboration

Source: Adapted from Goleman et al. (2002).

Emotional intelligence refers to the ability to process emotional information as it relates to the perception, assimilation, expression, regulation, and management of emotions (Mayer & Cobb, 2000; Mayer, Salovey, & Caruso, 2000). Emotionally intelligent persons are commonly characterized as well adjusted, warm, genuine, persistent, and optimistic (Salovey & Mayer, 1990). Building on the cornerstone of research on emotional intelligence, there are numerous research findings that indicate that schools are significantly more successful in their overall goals and objectives when they integrate efforts to promote academic, social, and emotional learning (Zins, Weissberg, Wang, & Walberg, 2004).

School counselors play an indispensable role in improving the overall social and emotional health and well-being within schools. Some examples of how school counselors do this include the organization and development of parent education programs, the adoption of bullying prevention programs, the creation and management of service learning projects, and the facilitating of school environments for increased accessibility whereby students have a safe and proper venue for expressing personal concerns in a confidential forum. The primary purpose of this chapter is to highlight the pivotal role school counselors can play in informing educational leaders about positive school change through the enhancement of emotional intelligence competencies.

EMOTIONAL LEADERSHIP COMPETENCIES AND THE SCHOOL BUILDING LEADER

"As learners, principals have a bad reputation. Many in my own school community wondered whether, as a principal, I was educable. Parents, teachers, students, central office personnel, and even other principals sometimes had their doubts. Sometimes so did I" (Barth, 1990, p. 68).

As the time of the writing of this chapter, there exists a critical shortage of quality, experienced school leaders in America's elementary, middle, and secondary schools. For example, a significant percentage of the nation's approximately 93,000 principals are retiring, leaving their school leadership positions to novice educators with minimal or no school administrative experience (Fenwick & Pierce, 2002). Emotional intelligence can have a dramatic impact on school leaders and the individuals they lead. A central premise of emotionally intelligent leadership is that leaders are reflective practitioners concerning their own emotions and are continual, lifelong learners. By developing a more defined self-awareness and self-regulation of their emotions and what influences them, school leaders can place themselves in better positions to respond to significant changes in their schools and develop more trusting relationships with their school communities (Patti & Tobin, 2003).

In *Primal Leadership: Realizing the Power of Emotional Intelligence*, Goleman et al. (2002) argued that setting a "positive resonance" within our schools is critically important for school leaders. Often, leaders in any organization set the emotional tone and influence the emotional balance of everyone around them. Because the emotional health of an organization is often associated with the emotional well-being of its leadership, it is critical that persons in leadership positions have a realistic assessment of their own emotional status.

Recent innovations in brain research indicate why a leader's emotional moods and actions exert a significant impact on those whom they lead (Goleman et al., 2002). Additionally, this new brain research sheds light on the power of emotionally intelligent leadership within educational organizations and institutions. Emotional intelligence leadership characteristics, such as developing and maintaining high levels of motivation in others, has been shown to affect people's performance and potential (Goleman et al., 2002). Although initially applied to business leaders in corporate America, the benefits of emotionally intelligent leadership can be effectively applied to a variety of leadership organizational models, including school leadership.

Emotional intelligence can be defined as the intelligent use of one's own emotions. More specifically, it is the ability to be self-aware and manage one's self, to be socially aware and manage one's relationships (Goleman et al., 2002). Recent studies indicate that these abilities are driven by a neural circuitry that emanates in the limbic system (the mid-brain area in which emotional memory resides) and moves through to the prefrontal cortex to lead to action (Goleman et al., 2002). These major components of emotional intelligence—self-awareness, self-management, social awareness, and relationship management—enable us to establish the necessary relationships that bring out the best attributes in people (see Table 11.2).

Educators, especially school superintendents, principals, and assistant principals, should find it reassuring to know that as adults we can learn to change our leadership styles to be more effective. Indeed, the crux of leadership development is self-directed learning. As Boyatzis (2002) indicated, self-directed learning involves four "discoveries." These discoveries start with why we want to improve our emotional intelligence and are described in the following.

Motivation to Change

The motivation starts with the discovery of both the *ideal* and *real self*. The drive to change a person's ideal and real selves is called self-directed process learning. When you go through the process of uncovering an ideal vision of yourself, you feel motivated to develop these abilities. You see the person you want to be. This image is powerful. It fuels the drive you need, especially during the difficult and frustrating process of change. The motivation to change, or

TABLE 11.2
Emotional Intelligence Leadership Competencies

Personal Competence	Personal Attributes of Competencies
Self-awareness	Emotional self-emotional self-awareness, accurate self-assessment, and self-confidence
Self-management	Self-control, transparency, adaptability, achievement, initiative, and optimism
Social awareness	Empathy, organizational awareness, and service
Relationship management	Inspiration, influence, developing others, change catalyst, conflict management, and teamwork and collaboration

Source: Goleman, Boyatzis, and McKee (2002). Copyright © Harvard Business School Publishing. Reprinted with permission.

the discovery, is the process most overlooked in emotional intelligence leadership development efforts.

The motivation to change also comes from a sense of who you are, or the real self. The real self is similar to the analogy of looking in the mirror to determine who you actually are and realistically confronting that image for both its benefits and its flaws.

Readiness to Change

For change to be successful you need to develop an agenda for using your strengths and improving your abilities; this is called the *learning agenda*. A plan of action must be constructed, one that provides detailed guidance on what new activities and habits of mind to try. The plan should feel fundamentally satisfying, fitting your learning preferences as well as the realities of your life and work.

Metamorphosis

This process involves experimenting and practicing your new habits, thoughts, and feelings to the point of mastery. Experimenting with new behaviors and seizing opportunities to practice them eventually triggers in the brain the neural connections necessary for real change to occur.

Developing Supportive Relationships

This process can occur at any point in the self-directed learning process. Basically, this process acknowledges that although the journey toward acquiring emotional intelligence must be self-directed, a person cannot change alone. Individuals need others to help us identify our real self, discover our strengths and weaknesses, develop an agenda for the future, and experiment and practice.

PROMOTING SOCIAL
AND EMOTIONAL SCHOOL LEADERSHIP

The goal of SEL is to foster "knowledgeable, responsible, and caring students" (Elias et al., 1997). Research indicates that people can alter the feelings and moods of others around them. Successful school-based management programs are a recent example of what can happen when resource-starved classrooms are dramatically changed by dramatically altering the leadership style of a school toward a closer collaboration between school leaders and teachers, staff members, parents, and others. Positive resonance spreads by emotions, usually initiated by those in leadership positions, sent throughout the organization.

One major benefit of emotional intelligence is that positive emotional impacts can be applied to numerous leadership styles. There is no one "perfect" leadership style. Emotionally intelligent leadership depends not solely on the situation but on the emotional resonance of the individual leader. Not unlike other leaders, school leaders, either by habit or situation, adopt varying leadership styles. Recent research on emotional intelligence shows that leaders with the best results often do not practice only one leadership style (Goleman et al., 2002). Rather, similar to the analogy of a golf pro's golf club selection based on the demands of a particular shot, many leaders incorporate varied leadership styles depending on the situation. What is important is that the leaders use an individual leadership style demonstrating a positive resonance, or emotional tone. Table 11.3 depicts popular leader-

TABLE 11.3
Common Leadership Styles and Emotional Intelligence Capabilities

Leadership Style	Emotional Intelligence Capabilities
Visionary leader	Builds positive emotional resonance by moving people toward shared dreams and aspirations.
	To be used: When changes in an organization require a new vision, or when clear direction is required.
Coaching leader	Connects what a person wants with the organization's goals.
	To be used: Help an employee improve performance by building long-term capabilities.
Affiliative leader	Creates harmony by connecting people with one another.
	To be used: Heals rifts in a team, motivates during stressful times, or strengthens connections.
Democratic leader	Values people's inputs and gets communication through participation.
	To be used: Trying to build consensus or valuable input from employees.
Pacesetting leader	Used to meet challenging or exciting goals.
	To be used: Acquire high-quality results from motivated and competent employees.
Commanding leader	Soothes fear by providing clear direction in an emergency.
	To be used: In a crisis or with problem employees.

Source: Goleman, Boyatzis, and KcKee (2002). Copyright © Harvard Business School Publishing. Reprinted with permission.

ship styles along with a brief description of the underlying emotional intelligence capabilities required.

Common leadership styles can be readily applied to school leaders. More important, school leaders who adopt these leadership styles can incorporate effective emotional intelligence competencies to the myriad of decision-making scenarios they are confronted with on a daily basis. In the discussion that follows, six specific leadership styles—visionary, coaching, affiliative, democratic, pacesetting, and commanding—will be briefly outlined with an emphasis on the emotional intelligence capabilities each leadership approach brings and its potential impact upon the emotional climate of the organization.

The Emotionally Intelligent Visionary School Leader: The Transformative Leader

"Any leader would be wise to grab for the visionary 'golf club' more often than not. It may not guarantee a hole in one, but it certainly helps with the long drive" (Goleman, 1998, p. 59).

In a productive sense, visionary leaders assist their employees to see how their work fits into the big picture of the organization's goals and objectives. Of the six most common leadership styles discussed, research indicates that the leadership style approach is the most effective (Goleman, 1998). Inspirational leadership, transparency, and empathy (see Table 11.2) are the most significant competencies necessary for the successful visionary school leader using emotional intelligence.

School leaders react to a plethora of different interest groups, each advocating a different goal or mission. School leaders who attempt to pacify dissent by adopting a school vision that is disingenuous and antithetical to their vision are likely to be unsuccessful. Transparency, one of the emotional intelligence competencies, means the removal of barriers, or smokescreens, within a company (Goleman, 1998). In other words, employees often sense when leadership within an organization is dishonest or resistant to the sharing of information. Although some visionary leaders falsely believe that withholding information enhances leadership power and control, the dissemination of knowledge is often one of the major attributes of a leader's success within an organization.

Within schools, a visionary leadership style would be appropriate in many situations, especially involving a shared goal or objective. In one example, a school principal was transferred from a suburban, high-academic-performing school to an urban, low-academic-performing school. Once the principal arrived, she articulated a vision of increasing student test scores at the school to be the highest in the district. In a highly ambiguous imitative, this principal developed a 2-year plan to increase student math and reading scores 65%. Within weeks of her appointment as principal, she spoke at numerous school-sponsored conferences detailing her 2-year vision for increasing student test scores. The school also sent out a mailing to every parent or parental caregiver of a registered student in the school explaining her plan. Wanting to make sure that her message was out to everyone, she made personal house calls to people who were unable to attend the meetings or needed further clarification concerning the plan.

Fairly quickly, staff, parents, and the students themselves could see the passion and determination this principal had toward attaining her mission. The principal exemplified the emotional intelligence competencies of inspirational leadership, transparency, and empathy toward her staff, parents, and the students themselves. She not only told people her vision but she possessed the ability to sense how others felt and sincerely attempted to understand their perspectives. As Goleman (1998) indicated, a leader who misreads others cannot motivate and inspire others in an organization.

In the school leadership context, however, there are instances when the visionary leadership style is probably not either recommended or effective. One context when not to exercise visionary school leadership is when a school leader is working with a group on an issue with a team of experts more experienced and knowledgeable than the leader. By attempting to exercise the visionary leadership style in this situation, the school leader is often perceived as ill informed and out of touch by the expert members of the group. This perception of lack of experience and knowledge is a recipe for cynicism and potentially poor overall performance by the group.

For instance, developing sound technology plans for schools is a daunting task for school administrators who lack technological savvy. Nonetheless, a school leader lacking technology skills might want to incorporate a technology vision for her school based on what she has heard from other parties (colleagues, friends, etc.). A more realistic, emotionally intelligent option would be to develop a technology committee of school employees and perhaps students with a vested interest in technology and monitor, not micromanage, the committee.

The visionary, transformative school leadership model is a valuable one, especially if the leader has a definitive view of the big picture goals and objectives of the initiative. When a leader's big picture image is clouded, the emotionally intelligent school leader might want to refrain from using the visionary, transformative leadership model. Instead, the leader is encouraged to adopt a leadership style that is not only more collaborative but acknowledges reliance on experts whose role is to share their expertise to improve the overall organizational structure.

The Emotionally Intelligent Coaching School Leader: Leadership One on One

An emotionally intelligent "coach" helps employees identify their own unique strengths and weaknesses and connect them to their personal and career aspirations (Goleman, 1998). By creating a connection between an employee's daily work and long-term goals, leaders keep employees motivated. However, only by getting to know an employee on a more personal level can a leader become an emotionally intelligent coach.

As organizations, schools are extremely labor dependent. In other words, school employees are the primary agents of success, mediocrity, or failure in a school. Unlike other organizations, where some of the more important tasks are automated by computers, the teacher educates students, the school counselor counsels students, the school custodian maintains the school infrastructure, and so on. The school culture and environment are significantly influenced by their leadership. Good school leader coaches are adept at delegating responsibilities to their staff and providing employees with challenging assignments without making them feel undervalued. In assessing the emotionally intelligent coach, it is important to note that coaching only works well with employees who demonstrate initiative, do not lack motivation, or do not require inordinate personal direction.

Many leaders are either unfamiliar or not good at the coaching approach to emotionally intelligent leadership. Emotionally intelligent coaching is a learned behavior. Many leaders find it difficult when providing employee performance feedback to build motivation instead of either fear or apathy (Goleman, 1998). It is not surprising that the emotional intelligence competencies that work best in facilitating a one-on-one coaching leadership style are the emotional intelligent competencies that characterize the best counselors: emotional self-awareness and empathy toward others (Goleman, 1998). The competency of emotional self-awareness defines a leader that is authentic and provides advice to employees in their best interest. A successful coach is also empathetic to their employees and actively listens before reacting or providing feedback.

In the school context, an effective, emotionally intelligent leader coach can greatly improve only overall school morale to retain more of his or her staff with better levels of performance. In the current No Child Left Behind era of bottom-line results, the benefits of the coaching leadership style is important. For example, many current school leader positions are either maintained or lost based on student test results. An effective school leader coach can go a long way toward changing negative staff morale and perceptions. A school leader who actively empathizes with staff concerns and listens without automatically blaming others for poor student outcomes is in a much better situation to effect positive resonance and change. Similar to other employees, educators need to feel more valued not only by their peers but by those in leadership roles. An effective coach can identify problems in an organization with demeaning staff morale. When done effectively, good coaching by school leaders can positively boost staff self-confidence, allow employees to work more effectively, and increase staff performance levels. In return, employees have to be receptive to effective leader mentorship and alter their motivation and performance levels accordingly.

Of the most common emotionally intelligent leadership styles, the emotionally intelligent coaching school leader has the greatest potential to be significantly influenced by the school counseling profession. Many of the necessary skills required of a successful emotionally intelligent coach school leader are the same skills required of a successful school counselor. Some of these major skills include: empathy toward others, emotional self-awareness, adaptability, conflict management, and organizational awareness.

The Emotionally Intelligent Affiliative Leader

An effective affiliative leader values employees' emotional needs and concerns. The emotional intelligence competencies that are most imperative in the affiliative school leader are empathy toward school employees, students, and parents as well as skills in conflict management, especially when the school leader needs to bring together diverse employees into an effective and efficient cohesive unit. Unlike some of the other commonly accepted emotionally intelligent leadership styles, the affiliative leadership style is often ineffective if used solely as a leadership style. Instead, the affiliative leadership style is often used in conjunction with other leadership styles, most commonly the visionary leadership style. For example, a leadership style that focuses disproportionately on praise without constructive criticism often confuses employees as to what working attributes are positive compared to those that are negative. As depicted in Table 11.3, the affiliative leadership model is most appropriate in minimizing conflict or tensions within the workplace, motivating employees during stressful times, and strengthening positive working relationships among employees.

As Goleman (1998) indicated, many effective affiliative leaders use this leadership style in conjunction with other leadership styles. One successful combination that could be adopted in a school leadership scenario is the affirmative-visionary leader model. The visionary leader would state a mission, set standards, and actively inform employees whether they are positively satisfying the stated mission and standards. The visionary approach could be supplemented by the affiliative approach to assess whether positive personal relationships and amiable interactions are taking place within the organization.

The Emotionally Intelligent Democratic Leader: Listen to Employees and Neglect None

The democratic leadership style works best when a leader is uncertain about what direction to take in a particular situation and needs to require ideas from competent employees. For example, emotionally intelligent school leaders would seriously consider the democratic leader model if they were involved in a leadership decision involving assistance from experts. The democratic leadership builds on numerous emotional intelligence competencies. Some of these competencies include: teamwork and collaboration, conflict management, influence, empathy, and collaboration.

In *Primal Leadership: Realizing the Power of Emotional Intelligence*, Goleman et al. (2002) detailed a school leadership dilemma demonstrating the effective use of the democratic leadership model with positive emotionally intelligent resonance. In the example, a private, urban Catholic school, located in a poor neighborhood, had been losing money for some time, and the local archdiocese intended to close the school. The archdiocese told Sister Mary, the head school administrator of the local Catholic school system, to close the school immediately. Instead, Sister Mary called an emergency meeting of the school's teachers and staff, detailing the financial crisis at the school. At the meeting, Sister Mary asked school employees for any suggestions or comments they had for keeping the school open. After asking for suggestions and comments, Sister Mary listened to all of the offered suggestions and comments. Later, Sister Mary held a similar meeting for parents of students in the school as well as concerned members of the community. After the series of meetings and deliberations that lasted several months, a group consensus developed that the school should close. Collectively, it was decided by group consensus that parents who wanted students to attend another Catholic school several miles away would be transferred.

In another scenario, a priest who headed another Catholic school experiencing the same fiscal crisis as the school headed by Sister Mary was told to shut down the school immediately. The priest immediately shut down the school without holding any meetings or deliberations with parents. As a result, parents of the Catholic school filed lawsuits against the archdiocese, both teachers and parents picketed, and the local media, especially newspaper editorials, attacked the priest's decision to close the school. The disputes actually kept the school open 1 full year before it was allowed to close its doors.

Sister Mary's reaction to a very difficult situation reflected the emotionally intelligent democratic leadership style of gaining feedback from employees and constituents. Although the outcome was the same in both situations, the democratic leadership approach kept school morale high despite a negative situation and ultimate outcome.

The democratic leadership approach has its limitations. For example, if a school principal is over-reliant on employee feedback to the point of being incapacitated, the democratic leadership style should be avoided. Also, if a school leader actively does not make crucial decisions because the leader is attempting to force consensus among his or her employees, the democratic leadership approach should not be adopted. Instead, a major component of the democratic leadership style is inclusion. School leaders have many constituencies. Consequently, it is often nearly impossible for school leaders to have unanimous consensus, especially in controversial and polarizing decision-making areas. The leadership goal of the democratic leadership style is not to acquire uniformity in the decision-making process but to create an authentic organizational environment where staff, parents, students, and other interested parties truly believe their opinions matter and will be ultimately considered, if not adopted in decision-making outcomes.

The Emotionally Intelligent Pacesetter School Leader: Setting the Proper Pace for Organizational Success

The conventional wisdom regarding effective leadership management indicates that the pacesetting leadership is a proper venue for success. In the pacesetting leadership style, the leader personalizes high standards of employee performance. The leader also highlights poor employee performance and demands more. If the employee is unsuccessful at proper improvement, the leader intervenes and attempts corrective action.

Although the pacesetter leadership style sounds reasonable in the competitive and corporate context of business, emotional intelligence research indicates that the pacesetter leadership style must be used sparingly or it will lead to disappointing results (Goleman, 1998). If applied by leaders excessively, for example, employees can be left feeling pushed too hard and unclear concerning leader guidelines for employee success. The most common result is that employee morale plummets dramatically. Instead of creating positive emotional resonance, the pacesetting leadership style can create emotional dissonance. The major dilemma of an excessive pacesetting leadership style is that moderate pressure in an organization, which can create and even facilitate motivation, can also lead to constant high pressure among employees. Such an approach often results over time in a shift from a shared organizational vision to a "survival of the fittest" mentality by employees.

Effective pacesetting by leaders that fosters positive emotional resonance depends on the emotionally intelligent competencies of collaboration, effective communication, emotional self-management, and empathy. Too often, when pacesetting is applied exclusively or excessively, employees lack not only organizational vision but positive resonance.

Therefore, if a school leader is contemplating the adoption of a pacesetting school leader model, they need to be aware of the impact of this leadership model on employee morale. Tough love and zero tolerance models of school discipline adopted by school leaders are examples of a pacesetter school leadership model that are often extreme. In these examples, there is the potential to facilitate a school environment of emotional dissonance, where school employees and students feel that there exists too much pressure to achieve desirable school-level outcomes.

The Emotionally Intelligent Commanding School Leader: "Do So Because I Say So"

Of all the common leadership styles, the commanding leadership approach, or coercive style, is the least effective in most leadership situations. Unfortunately, however, it is a popular leadership style, heavily adopted by leaders across a variety of organizations and institutions, including schools. The continued legacy of command-and-control hierarchies that were the predominant management model of the 20th century are seen with alarming frequency as we enter the 21st century. Usually, a commanding leadership approach demands fairly immediate compliance to leader's requests with minimal attention to an explanation or reasoning behind the orders. Additionally, it is not uncommon under the commanding leadership approach for leaders to resort to threats if their orders are not properly followed by employees. Intense micromanagement is common with little, if any, delegation of authority. Performance feedback focuses disproportionately on what employees did wrong instead of what duties were performed well.

The emotionally intelligent leader can use the commanding leadership style, though under limited circumstances. The commanding leadership is effective when it is necessary to shock employees into new ways of thinking.

CONTRIBUTIONS FROM SCHOOL COUNSELORS

Emotionally intelligent school leaders create positive resonance through exemplifying the emotional intelligence domains of self-awareness, self-management, social awareness, and relationship management. However, many traditional school administrative courses on school management and administration practices do not include emotional intelligence in the literature on leadership practices. Instead, a predominant school leadership style covered is the command-and-control, commanding leadership style. Considerable empirical evidence has highlighted the shortcoming of this approach (Goleman, 1998).

The role of school counselors can be critical in creating the conditions for effective leadership in schools as counselors are increasingly taking leadership responsibilities (see Muller-Ackerman & Shelton, chap. 2, this volume). As the social-emotional experts in the school, school counselors need to educate not only students and teachers on the benefits of emotional intelligence but school administrators as well. Formally, through the promotion of SEL programs for students, school counselors have an opportunity to outline and describe the principles of emotional intelligence for school leaders. School counselors can draw on research that supports increased student learning and achievement through emotionally sensitive classroom environments as well as the benefits of SEL for the overall school ecology. Discussions of teacher leadership styles and their impact on students will draw a direct parallel to the effects of school building principal leadership styles on faculty. If the conditions are right, such discussions can be a springboard of productive discourse on the needs of the teachers and staff as to the best leadership approach to address these concerns.

Informally, the working relationships that school counselors have with various administrators in the school are another potential channel for influencing the conditions for emotionally intelligent schools. The emotional competencies of the school counselor are essential in developing a trusting and collaborative relationship that can positively affect the school administrator and his or her leadership styles. The school counselor needs to be able to assess which of the six most commonly used leadership styles the school administrator uses and how effectively they are matched to the situation being confronted. Next, the school counselor needs to determine at what stage of the four discoveries the school administrator is in (Boyatzis, 2002). In other words, what is the school administrator's degree of readiness and motivation to change and develop a more emotionally intelligent leadership perspective? The school counselor may need to create motivations for the school administrator to engage in self-examination or provide SEL information for the administrator to develop his or her own learning agenda. When windows of opportunity open, such as a critical decision point or a crisis, the school counselor can help facilitate the administrator's emotional learning and metamorphosis by examining the emotional factors that are at play. In this way, the counselor can be the supportive relationship for the school leader's emotional intelligence development and leadership style.

However one judges the performance or success of our schools, the research literature and common sense indicate that leadership is an indispensable ingredient in school reform process. The development and facilitation of a school climate that encourages emotionally competent school leadership can be enhanced significantly by school counselors. School administrators are the leaders of the school and therefore are a central part of the system that creates and maintains the school culture. School counselors are the social-emotional experts of the school and need to address administrators as critical in implementing systemic school-level change.

REFERENCES

Barth, R. S. (1990). *Improving skills from within: Teachers, parents and principals can make a difference.* San Francisco: Jossey-Bass.

Boyatzis R. E. (2002, April 24). Positive resonance: Educational leadership through emotional intelligence. *Education Week,* p. 52.

Elias, M. J., Zins, J. E., Weissberg, R. P., Frey, K. S., Greenberg, M. T., Haynes, N. M., et al. (1997). *Promoting social and emotional learning: Guidelines for educators.* Alexandria, VA: Association for Supervision and Curriculum Development.

Fenwick, L., & Pierce, M. C. (2002). *The principal shortage: Crisis or opportunity.* The National Association of Secondary School Principals. Retrieved September 13, 2004, from http://www.nassp.org

Gardner, H. (1993). *Multiple intelligences: The theory in practice.* New York: Basic Books.

Goleman, D. (1995). *Emotional intelligence.* New York: Bantam.

Goleman, D. (1998). *Working with emotional intelligence.* New York: Bantam.

Goleman, D., Boyatzis, R., &. McKee, A. (2002). *Primal leadership: Realizing the power of emotional intelligence.* Boston: Harvard Business School Press.

Mayer, J. D., & Cobb, C. D. (2000). Educational policy on emotional intelligence: Does it make sense? *Educational Psychology Review, 12,* 163–183.

Mayer, J. D., & Salovey, P. (1993). The intelligence of emotional intelligence. *Intelligence, 17,* 433–442.

Mayer, J. D., & Salovey, P. (1997). What is emotional intelligence? In P. Salovey & D. J. Sluyter (Eds.), *Emotional development and emotional intelligence: Educational implications* (pp. 3–31). New York: Basic.

Mayer, J. D., & Salovey, P., & Caruso, D. (2000). Models of emotional intelligence. In Robert J. Sternberg (Ed.), *The handbook of intelligence* (pp. 396–420). Cambridge, England: Cambridge University Press.

Novick, B., Kress, J. S., & Elias, M. J. (2002). *Building learning communities with character: How to integrate academic, social, and emotional learning.* Alexandria, VA: Association for Supervision and Curriculum Development.

Patti, J., & Tobin, J. (2003). *Smart school leaders: Leading with emotional intelligence.* Dubuque, IA: Kendall Hunt.

Salovey, P., & Mayer, J. D. (1990). Emotional Intelligence. *Imagination, Cognition, and Personality, 9,* 185–211.

Zins, J. E., Weissberg, R. P., Wang, M. C., & Walberg, H. (2004). *Building academic success on social and emotional learning: What does the research say?* New York: Teachers College Press.

12

Enhancing Emotional Intelligence in Parents: The Professional School Counselor's Role

Julaine Field
Jered Kolbert
Slippery Rock University

Parents are powerful, socializing agents in a child's life. Most children develop their values, beliefs, and emotional and behavioral skills from watching and emulating their parents or caregivers. Olds (1997) wrote, "Parents' behavior constitutes the most powerful and potentially alterable influence on the developing child" (p. 45). Included in this parental influence is the construct of emotional intelligence, or more specifically, how parents initiate and shape a child's emotional knowledge base (Mayer & Salovey, 1997). Zeidner, Roberts, and Matthews (2002) endorsed two main factors that influence a child's emotional intelligence: genetic endowment, or temperament, and parental socialization.

Additionally, parents facilitate their children's emotional intelligence through their teaching children about emotions through emotional dialogue and children's observation and modeling of their parents' emotional responses (Zeidner, Matthews, Roberts, & MacCann, 2003). Therefore, it seems likely that parents' emotional intelligence is most likely transferred to their children through daily interactions. Yet, systems theory (Nichols & Schwartz, 1995) suggests that parents' own capacity for emotional regulation and management is influenced by the temperaments, emerging personalities, and unique charac-teristics of their children (Zeidner et al., 2003). Therefore, "parents need to un-derstand how children think, interact, communicate, and change as much as clinicians do" (Donovan & McIntyre, 1990, p. 94) as this insight will be key in understanding the needs of individual children, the potential support needs of the parents, and how those mutual needs are addressed or neglected within the context of the family and community.

Deliberately promoting parent emotional intelligence enhances a child's most influential social climate, thereby creating a self-sustaining (Bond, 1998), positive influence on children's emotional growth and development. Goleman (1995) stated, "Family life is our first school for emotional learning" (p. 189). Parents foster emotional intelligence in their children through being aware of and sensitive to their children's emotions through acceptance and validation. This is not to suggest that children, who experience undesirable emotions, be immediately relieved of the emotions through their parents efforts. On the contrary, acknowledging the emotion with warm objectivity and using questions that include the child as an ac-tive problem solver assist with identifying the emotion's origin and specific strate-gies to cope with the emotion. The most influential strategy for developing adaptive emotional reasoning in children is for parents to model these steps in their own problem solving. Greene (2001) believed parents should deliberately teach children to recognize that problems are a normal part of living, stay calm in the face of frustration, identify the problem and various options for addressing the problem, and discover words that depict the individual's needs. Parents of adolescents can also assist with the discovery of faulty or irrational thinking, perspective taking, and interpreting others' motivations. This ongoing practice will most likely result in children's healthy, adaptive emotional habits.

How do parents or caregivers objectively monitor this emotional instruction if they are not consciously aware of these skills or reflective about their own emotional abilities? A parent's own emotional intelligence and knowledge of his or her child's development is crucial so that the parent is able to assess accu-rately degrees of emotion and respond with developmentally appropriate man-agement practices. Clearly, not all parents are equipped with the skills to address the emotional needs of their children. Childrearing strategies can range from generational practices to trial and error and be consistently applied with little critical reflection on the effectiveness of these strategies. Specifi-cally, the way parents respond to their children's emotions influences their children's emotional development.

Eisenburg et al. (1999) found that parents who respond to their children's emotions by being punitive, ambivalent, or dismissive are more likely to have children who express more negative emotions. Children of chronically depressed mothers are more likely to be depressed themselves as they age (Saarni, Mumme, & Campos, 1998), which is mostly likely due to the parent modeling a low degree of emotional regulation and being unable to facilitate emotional management within their children. Additionally, modern, fast-paced family life in the United States often translates into parents who are disconnected from their communities, resulting in mediocre or poor support systems when addressing parenting challenges.

SCHOOL COUNSELORS, PARENTS, AND EMOTIONAL INTELLIGENCE

Belenky, Bond, and Weinstock (1997) proposed that schools can serve as a "public homeplace" (p. 307) where community members are supported, nurtured, and challenged to be active participants in the full range of their children's developmental dynamics as well as in the school community by offering support to others. Because of their expertise in child development and a job description that typically includes serving as a liaison between parents and school, school counselors are in a unique position to enhance student's emotional intelligence through collaborative consultation, brief family counseling, and parental programming, which may include parent groups, workshops, or training.

Consistent with the primary prevention literature (i.e., Bond, 1998), early intervention with children and parents is often endorsed as the best way to influence positively children's subsequent life skills. Elementary school counselors are often involved with assisting families who face parenting challenges such as behavior modification, trauma or crisis, grief and loss, and divorce. Ritchie (1994) found that significantly more elementary school counselors conducted proactive parent training than did middle, junior high, or senior high school counselors.

Parents continue to influence significantly their children's accumulation of emotional skills throughout their school years. For example, Rice (1990) stated that strong parental bonds affect an adolescent's social competence with peers. Rice, Cunningham, and Young (1997) found a relationship between adolescents' attachment to their mothers and fathers and their ability to initiate, develop, and maintain friendships, ultimately influencing a teen's social and emotional adjustment. Finally, Pipher (1994) stated that adolescents need as much parenting time and intervention as do toddlers.

Therefore, school counselors in general must be equipped with the insight, skills, and energy to work with parents to influence student's home environment where children are gathering resources for coping with problems and developing emotional intelligence. Gazzard (2002) wrote, "Everyone can benefit from understanding emotions more fully and from having access to more constructive, creative, meaningful, and perhaps even productively useful ways to process emotion and its meaning" (p. 22).

Unfortunately, school counselors nationwide do not regularly enact parent interventions or work with the family system to help school-age children. In a study to assess the extent and nature of school counselor's parent interventions, Ritchie (1994) found that although 81.3% of school counselors believed that parent consultations were important, only 29.1% stated they met with the parents of the student they were counseling. One third of the school counselors reported that they did not have time to initiate parent consultation or parent training programs (Ritchie, 1994). Furthermore, when parents contact school counselors for assistance, it is often in search of tools to fix their child or alleviate immediate social, emotional, or behavioral symptoms.

The professional school counselor's challenge is both to recognize the far-reaching impact of parent interventions on students and to encourage parents to believe that they have a stake in and control over enhancing current family and social conditions. In response, parents will gain much needed support and insight into parenting responses that are more adaptive in bringing about the desired change in their child. Simultaneously, parents will be facilitating the development of adaptive emotional skills, which will positively influence students' social and academic success as well as the overall school environment.

The remaining sections of this chapter focus on strategies that shape and refine the school counselor's role as parent consultant, educator, and facilitator in emotional intelligence. However, our hope is to take an atypical approach to parent intervention that includes approaches and activities to enhance parents' emotional intelligence while inviting them to be involved in collaborative programming to benefit students, other parents, and the school community. Lewis (1996) claimed, "It is seldom that a school counselor can successfully intervene in the life of a student without considering the continuous influence of the family as the primary social system for the student" (p. 93).

CONSULTATION

The goal of school counselor–parent consultation is to address student needs through assisting parents with problem solving. Therefore, despite the indirect nature of this service, this triadic relationship ultimately benefits the student. Unfortunately, some school counselors shy away from consultation because they envision traditional consultation models that imply that the school counselor serves in the role of expert. School counselors, serving as the expert, may encounter anxiety over having to solve the problem and parental defensive-ness because of the implied power imbalance. Keys, Bemak, Carpenter, and King-Sears (1998) proposed a collaborate-dependent model of consultation that honors the parents and school counselor's knowledge and insight while addressing a problem collaboratively. "Together, the consultant and consultee establish mutual goals and objectives for the client and develop an interven-tion plan" (Erford, 2003, p. 176).

Before initiating consultation with a parent or guardian, it is essential to de-velop rapport and an atmosphere of open, caring dialogue. Nicoll (1992) re-ferred to "establishing the tone" or taking the time to get to know the parent and his or her concerns. Proper attending, nonverbal communication, eye con-tact, and active listening contribute to an amicable working collaboration without unnecessary defensiveness. Parenting can be complicated, stressful, and overwhelming. Adding to a parent's stress through patronizing, conde-scending, or blaming messages is counterproductive and will defeat efforts toward mutual problem solving.

After establishing rapport and gathering relevant information, the parent often begins to engage in problem talk or a detailed description of his or her child's current issues. Parents who are defensive or unaware of presenting prob-lems at school will often be presented with concerns about their child and asked to offer their insights or perspective. While establishing the nature of the problem, school counselors must be mindful of viewing this student's problem within a relational context, or understanding how the child is getting his or her relational needs met through his or her present behavior.

Emotions are intertwined with student academic and behavioral issues. Reframing a student's problem from a relational perspective, as well as brain-storming options to discuss how the student is feeling, offers a compassionate, alternative approach to punitive action. Frequently, behavior problems at school are unexpressed or misdirected emotions. For example, if an eighth grader is fearful of a teacher's critical response to his work, which may embar-rass him in front of his peers, the eighth grader may avoid turning in homework rather than discuss his anxiety over reaching his teacher's expectations. If the parent becomes angry at his or her child's lack of academic "productivity," this anger may further heighten a student's anxiety, potentially creating a circular reinforcement pattern for avoiding his homework.

When working with parents, school counselors must use cautious questions in a spirit of collaboration to create alternative means for understanding the student's presenting issue. Acknowledging this student's emotions while creat-ing a warm, inviting climate to talk about the purpose behind the behaviors may assist this student in examining any irrational beliefs about achievement

or adult expectations. In a family that traditionally uses authoritative, neglect-
ful, or indifferent means to address issues, this approach will be a welcome opportunity to facilitate new coping strategies for unresolved problems.

The following scenario demonstrates an approach to collaborative-depend-
ent consultation in which awareness of emotion is key to effective problem
solving. The counselor–parent dialogue demonstrates a warm, genuine approach to greeting a parent and initiating dialogue, which examines a student's
presenting issue within a relational context. Furthermore, questions to address
awareness and exploration of a student's feelings are used to create this
alternative framework for viewing the problem.

Mr. Jones is an elementary school counselor at Sunshine Elementary School.
He has initiated a parent meeting with Ms. Williams, mother of LeShauna, a
6-year-old first grader who is frequently absent from school. LeShauna is the
youngest of three children.

Mr. Jones: Hello Ms. Williams, it is nice to see you today.

Ms. Williams: Hello, how are you?

Mr. Jones: I am fine and so glad that you were able to come in and talk
                with me today.

Ms. Williams: LeShauna liked having me drive her to school. She seems
                excited that I am here today.

Mr. Jones: (smiles) I spoke with LeShauna's teacher and Mrs. Abbott
                reports that LeShauna is doing well in school. She is partic-
                ularly talented in her art and reading classes!

Ms. Williams: Yes. Her last report card was good; however, I know she has
                missed a lot of days in the past two months and I am afraid
                she is getting behind.

Mr. Jones: That is one of the issues that I would like to talk with you
                about today. I am wondering if there is anything the school
                can do to assist LeShauna with school attendance.

Ms. Williams: I don't think so. She has been sick a lot lately. She will wake
                up and tell me that she doesn't feel good—her stomach
                hurts, her head hurts. I don't want to send her to school
                when she is not feeling well because she may get the other
                children sick.

Mr. Jones: So she wakes up, tells you she is sick, and then you keep her
                home from school?

Ms. Williams: Yeah. Sometimes she starts to feel better about mid morn-
                ing and I would like to send her to school, but she has
                missed the bus and I don't always have the car.

Mr. Jones:	So sometimes she recovers quickly and seems ready to go to school.
Ms. Williams:	Right. I wonder if she is really sick all the time, but I hate the thought of her going to school and not feeling well. She can be hard to deal with when she doesn't feel well.
Mr. Jones:	I see. You are thinking that perhaps she is not physically sick and is trying to avoid school.
Ms. Williams:	Maybe. She loves school, but lately she isn't as excited about it.
Mr. Jones:	Okay, I think we may be on to something. LeShauna might actually feel a little sick in the morning because she is worried. Can you think of any school circumstances that might cause her to feel anxious about going to school?
Ms. Williams:	I am not sure. I know she recently told her grandmother that her teacher doesn't like her because she gives her "red marks." The teacher uses a red pen to correct student's answers on homework and quizzes. I told LeShauna to try hard in school and do what the teacher tells her to.
Mr. Jones:	So LeShauna is concerned when Mrs. Abbott corrects her papers. I am wondering what LeShauna feels like when she believes her teacher doesn't like her.
Ms. Williams:	LeShauna has to get used to getting feedback from her teacher. She has to try harder and understand that correcting papers is the teacher's job.
Mr. Jones:	I hear you and that is something that you and I understand as adults. I am wondering what a six-year-old might feel like if she believes her teacher doesn't like her.
Ms Williams:	Well, she could get mad or sad I guess. But that is not the point here.
Mr. Jones:	Okay, so LeShauna may be frustrated when she believes her teacher doesn't like her. I am wondering if she may also not know how to talk about those feelings so instead she experiences them as stomachaches or headaches. (pause) Do you think that is possible?
Ms. Williams:	Yes, it is possible. Come to think of it, LeShauna says she has a stomachache and wants to lie down when she and her friends argue over toys.

The previous dialogue represents how to initiate consultation from a relational perspective while guiding the parent to consider the role of emotions in her child's behaviors. This parent has good intentions; however, she may not recognize the value of addressing her daughter's emotions rather than solely focusing on the behavior or reported "illnesses." By helping LeShauna identify her emotions and link them to the real problem, LeShauna's mother will help her child learn to manage her emotions, which will most likely lead to new behaviors. Furthermore, LeShauna may gain the support she needs to put teacher feedback into proper perspective. Finally, although this example involves a young child, it is appropriate for school counselors to collaboratively "uncover" strategies for emotional processing with adolescents. Often, parents of young adults are searching for different approaches to deal with the emotional intensity created between themselves and their teens. Attending to a teen's emotions through attending, active listening and warm, open-ended questions often works wonders when working through various problems. Perhaps time invested in this type of approach can be subtracted from the hours of arguing, cajoling, and silence that result when parents engage in typical power struggles without addressing the emotions of their teens.

Consultation is an invaluable tool to creating alternative perspectives for viewing problems experienced by children and teens. Furthermore, if a school counselor invests an appropriate amount of energy in making the parent believe that he or she is welcome and that his or her opinion is valuable while brainstorming solutions, the school counselor will have the opportunity to model and discuss strategies for facilitating emotional intelligence in children and adolescents.

BRIEF FAMILY COUNSELING

Bowen's family systems theory provides a useful framework for conceptualizing school counselors' intervention and prevention efforts in helping parents promote their children's emotional intelligence. According to Bowen family systems theory, the family represents an emotional unit in which the thinking, feelings, and behaviors of members have a reciprocal influence on each other. Emotions are not viewed as residing solely within the individual but rather are more the product of the transactions that transpire between people (Kerr & Bowen, 1988).

Bowen (Kerr & Bowen, 1988) believed that higher levels of emotional maturity can only be achieved when parents foster an environment in which children's feelings and thoughts are less dictated by the expectations of parents and the community and more guided by the child's emerging unique value and goals. In other words, the ultimate aim of parental endeavors is to facilitate their children's development so that they become fully functioning individuals who are responsive to but not dictated by the emotions of others.

Through open dialogue with the counselor, parents can become aware of and learn to reduce their tendency to escalate the family's emotional intensity by failing to contain their own emotional intensity, allowing it to spill over onto the children. Bowen (Kerr & Bowen, 1988) believed, similarly to Freud, that individuals in the family with more power have a tendency either consciously or unconsciously to displace their anxiety onto less powerful family members, which is particularly the case for less mature parents. Subsequently, children, who are typically the most vulnerable members, are more likely to absorb the anxiety within the emotional system. For example, if two parents are going through divorce without appropriate adult support or being mindful of what emotions they display in front of their children, they are transferring their hurt, frustration, anger, and so forth onto their children. Because of their emotional and financial dependency, children and adolescents are sensitive to the prevailing emotional issues of their parents, meaning that when the emotional transfer occurs, they are left to work through emotions that are not necessarily their own or that they do not fully understand. This supports many school counselors' observations regarding how children's maturity is often highly correlated to family's level of functioning.

The emotional process is often most readily apparent in families in which there is marital tension. Bowen's (Kerr & Bowen, 1988) research regarding emotional process within families revealed that tension within the marital dyad often resulted in the inclusion of a child, which stabilizes the tension, but often at the cost of the child's development. The over-involvement with the child enables parents to remove their focus from their partner, whom they blame for their emotional distress, but results in the impairment of the child as the parent's anxiety is displaced onto the child. In essence, the parent unconsciously needs the child to have difficulties to justify the parent's intense focus. The child becomes overly sensitive to the parents, becoming reactive to their emotional intensity. In turn, parents become overly reactive to their child's emotions, getting pulled in. Normal developmental challenges for the child, such as conflicts with peers and siblings, and academic struggles, cause considerably anxiety for the parent, as the parent makes overly negative interpretations of the issue, assuming something is wrong with the child. The child, in turn, becomes reactive to and concerned about the parent's anxiety, thus diluting energy to resolve the initial concern of the child. The long-term result of such a pattern is that the child becomes relationship oriented in being worried or angry with his or her parents' emotional intensity and being less able to use his or her intellectual system in resolving problems.

The first step in reducing emotional fusion is for a family member with more mature intellectual capabilities, meaning either parents or fully physically and intellectually mature children, to learn use their intellectual abilities, primarily the capacity for reflective self-awareness, to gain insight into the emotional process of the family system. School counselors can encourage parents to step outside and observe their interactions with their child, enhancing their awareness of particular patterns and the family's emotional process. Parents may be reluctant at first to consider how they are being affected, so initially it is helpful to paraphrase their concerns about their child and validate them as being concerned parents. Once you sense that you have joined the parent in that he or she believes that you understand his or her concerns, you may initiate the step of helping them to explore how they are affected by the emotions of their child. For example, the following statements seek to normalize the issue for the parents but also help them consider the reciprocal nature of emotions: "Parents often tell me about how difficult it is to have a child entering adolescence. I am wondering how it has been for you and how you deal with this transition in your family." If the parents seem receptive to discussing how they have been impacted by changes or emotions in their child, the counselor may engage in process oriented questions that broaden the parents' perspective of the issue. Parents are asked to consider in minute detail their cognitive, emotional, and behavioral response to the behavior in question, and their child's subsequent reaction. The counselor continues this form of dialogue as parents gradually develop an understanding of the interactional nature of family functioning. Examples of process-oriented questions include the following: "What do you notice about your thoughts and feelings when you think about your son's issue, and then how do you respond to him?" "When your anxiety increases, how does it impact your daughter?" The emotional process can also be demonstrated through a graphic display. The school counselor may draw two overlapping circles, shading the part that overlaps, explaining how it represents the emotional fusion that often occurs in families.

Once parents develop greater emotional awareness of the family's emotional systems, the school counselor can assist the parents with exploring how to reduce their own emotional intensity. In focusing on managing their own emotional intensity, parents reduce the overall level of tension within the family, which is likely to reduce their child's emotional intensity. Furthermore, parents' focus on their own emotional intensity both provides their child with a model of emotional management and demonstrates appropriate emotional boundaries, exhibiting to their child the importance of assuming responsibility for one's emotional reactions. Bowen asserted that maturity, or what he referred to as differentiation, is the capacity to be in contact with another without either absorbing or displacing anxiety (Kerr & Bowen, 1988).

Although Bowen would most likely argue that parents are most helpful to their children by focusing on their emotional management, parents may also use a more direct and didactic approach to promoting emotional intelligence. Parental modeling of emotional management is enhanced when parents verbalize their cognitive process, meaning that parents can be encouraged to share their own emotions and the thoughts related to those feelings. However, as with all parenting techniques for teaching emotional intelligence, it is essential that parents educate their children about emotions when the level of family tension is low to moderate. Research reveals that high levels of emotional tension interferes with cognitive functioning. Given that children are in such a vulnerable position in regard to their parents, they are prone to regard emotional sharing as an indication that they should assume responsibility for the family's mood. School counselors can explore with parents situations when they would most likely want to engage in emotional processing and signs that their child is available for such dialogue. For example, the school counselor may ask parents, "When is your child more likely to hear you?" Also, parents must be selective in deciding what issues they share with their child to demonstrate their emotional process. Parents are urged not to share issues about a spouse or partner that may lead the child to infer that the parent is seeking an alliance against the other parent.

WORKING WITH GROUPS OF PARENTS

An effective and efficient mean for collaborating with several parents is through parent training. For example, presentations at PTO meetings and parent workshops that address proactive problem solving and its relationships to student social and academic success are opportunities to engage parents in a discussion about fostering emotional intelligence. Furthermore, parent newsletters are a cost-effective way to facilitate school–parent dialogue and cohesion on behalf of the student body.

Emotional intelligence programming may be limited in effectiveness when parents are not included in the development and implementation of such programs. It is important for school counselors to identify approaches to parent development that honor and acknowledge parents' expertise on child development and how they seek to facilitate social and emotional skills that are needed for future success. Kolb and Hanley-Maxwell (2003) emphasized the unique perspective that may be offered by parents when they are asked to participate in program development. Furthermore, parent input can contribute to parent ownership of such programming.

Parent training groups provide an opportunity to engage parents in more didactic instruction regarding children's emotional development. Ivey and Ivey (2003) provided a developmental framework that may be taught to parents to assist them in understanding how the age and developmental level of their child is likely to influence how their child experiences emotions. Between the ages of 2 and 7, most children are in Piaget's preoperational stage of development. Cognitive limitations of this stage include difficulty in distinguishing between one's point of view and that of others and confusion about cause and effect. Preoperational children tend to experience and describe their feelings in terms of behavioral actions and physiological sensations. Parents can promote their preoperational child's emotional intelligence by helping their child connect their physiological sensations to emotions. For example, parents may ask children to put words to what is going on in their body, asking them if they feel tightness or butterflies in their stomach, or whether their head is getting hot. Or, parents can ask children to "tell me where you feel the hurt." Next, parents seek to provide children with the emotional vocabulary to give the experience an emotional label. Parents may say, "A lot of times when you have a knot in your stomach it means that you are feeling scared or worried. Are you feeling scared or worried?" Parents may also model this process by disclosing their own unique physiological sensations that serve as clues to what they are feeling. Parents can first teach the four basic feelings—mad, sad, glad, and scared—and over the years introduce more differentiated feelings, such as annoyed, hurt, and lonely. Preoperational children's limitations in understanding cause and effect often mean that they will have difficulty understanding the potential contributions to their feelings, in other words, why they might be feeling a certain way, and parents can explore with their children the preceding events that may be causing their feelings. Preoperational children generally lack cognitive coping mechanisms for reducing their emotional intensity, and thus parents can explore behavioral mechanisms for reducing emotional intensity, which may include going for walks, drawing, listening to music, playing a video game, punching a safe object such as "bop bag," and so forth.

Cognitive limitations of the concrete operational stage, which characterizes most children between the ages of 7 and 11, include difficulty in identifying patterns and understanding abstract concepts. Concrete operational children's emotional processing is usually limited to describing feelings in terms of linear, sequential events and how they responded behaviorally, explaining how they "walked off," or "lost their cool," or "yelled and kicked." They are also likely to refer to emotions in the past tense, given that their emotions are tied to specific behavioral actions. As with preoperational children, parents can assist concrete operational children with identifying what emotional labels might best fit their behavioral actions. Also, once children have emotional words for their experience, parents can explore how their emotions influenced their behaviors, as concrete operational children are better able to engage in cause-and-effect thinking.

During the later stages of the concrete operational stage, parents can help children identify patterns regarding their emotions by asking questions such as: "Do you often have this feeling in this type of situation?" "What usually happens next?" At this stage, emotional coping mechanisms will also largely include behavioral strategies. However, concrete operational children may not be able to generate positive coping statements independently but may be provided specific statements for particular situations. It is helpful for parents to model their own internal dialogue for managing emotional intensity.

Upon entry into adolescence, most students develop the capacity for formal operational thinking, which is defined as the ability to think logically about abstract concepts. Formal operational children are more readily able to reflect on their thinking and feelings in a variety of ways that one can perceive or feel in a situation. In the preoperational and concrete operational stage, parents must be fairly structured in guiding children's awareness of their emotions through the use of close-ended questions. However, in the formal operations stage, the role of the parent, in terms of promoting emotional intelligence, is to ask more open-ended questions. Also, it is crucial for parents to respect adolescents' developing desire for autonomy. The following question and statement respect adolescents' increasing desire for independence and cognitive abilities: "Would you like to tell me what is going on for you?" and "I get the sense that you might be having some big feelings and I would be interested in hearing them when you are ready." Adolescents have the cognitive capacity for a much greater array of potential coping mechanisms. Helpful questions parents can ask to prompt the consideration of various possibilities or multiple perspectives include: "What is your thinking about how to handle this situation?" "What are you thinking about doing?" "How have you seen others deal with situations like this?" "How have you handled past situations like this?"

SUMMARY

The role of parents and the family environment in facilitating children's emotional development is significant. The emotional intelligence of parents has a direct impact on emotional learning in their children. Although school counselors rarely engage in providing ongoing family therapy, they can enhance parents' emotional functioning through several channels. As consultants, school counselors can help parents find alternative perspectives to their children's issues and use emotional intelligence in problem solving. Through brief family counseling, school counselors can educate family members on the emotional processes within the family system and assist with parents' ability to develop emotional management skills. Presentations and parent training groups provide instruction about emotional intelligence and children's social-emotional development to larger groups of parents. Each of these methods can enhance the emotional awareness of parents and lead to positive impacts on the emotional development of children.

REFERENCES

Belenky, M. F., Bond, L. A., & Weinstock, J. S. (1997). *The tradition that has no name: Nurturing the development of people, families, and communities.* New York: Basic Books.
Bond, L. (1998). Investing in parents' development as an investment in primary Prevention. *Journal of Mental Health, 7,* 493–503.
Donovan, D. M., & McIntyre, D. (1990). *Healing the hurt child: A developmental contextual approach.* New York: Norton.
Eisenburg, N., Fabes, R. A., Murphy, B. C., Shepard, S., Guthrie, I. K., Mazsk, P., et al. (1999). Prediction of elementary school children's socially Appropriate and problem behavior from anger reactions at age 4–6 years. *Journal of Applied Developmental Psychology, 20,* 119–142.
Erford, B. (2003). *Transforming the school counseling profession.* Upper Saddle River, NJ: Merrill Prentice Hall.
Gazzard, A. (2002). Emotional intelligence, the witness, and education. *ENCOUNTER: Education for Meaning and Social Justice, 15*(4), 20–29.
Goleman, D. (1995). *Emotional intelligence: Why it can matter more than IQ.* New York: Bantam.
Greene, R. W. (2001). *The explosive child: A new approach for understanding and parenting easily frustrated, chronically inflexible children* (2nd ed.). New York: HarperCollins.
Ivey, A. E., & Ivey, M. B. (2003). *Intentional interviewing and counseling: Facilitating client development in a multicultural society.* Pacific Grove, CA: Thomson/Wadsworth.
Kerr, M., & Bowen, M. (1988). *Family evaluation.* New York: Norton.
Keys, S. G., Bemak, F., Carpenter, S. L., & King-Sears, M. F. (1998). Collaborative consultants: A new role for counselors serving at-risk youth. *Journal of Counseling and Development, 76,* 123–133.
Kolb, S. M., & Hanley-Maxwell, C. (2003). Critical social skills for adolescents with high incidence disabilities: Parental perspectives. *Exceptional Children, 69,* 163–179.
Lewis, W. (1996). A proposal for initiating family counseling interventions by school counselors. *School Counselor, 44,* 93–99.
Mayer, J. D., & Salovey, P. (1997). What is emotional intelligence? In P. Salovey & D. J. Sluyter (Eds.). *Emotional development and emotional intelligence: Educational implications* (pp. 3–31). New York: Basic Books.
Nichols, M. P., & Schwartz, R. C. (1995). *Family therapy: Concepts and methods.* Needham Heights, MA: Allyn & Bacon.
Nicoll, W. G. (1992). A family counseling and consultation model for school counselors. *School Counselor, 39,* 351–362
Olds, D. (1997). The prenatal/early infancy project: Fifteen years later. In G. W. Albee & T. P. Guliotta (Eds.), *Primary prevention works* (pp. 44–45). Thousand Oaks, CA: Sage.
Pipher, M. (1994). *Reviving Ophelia: Saving the selves of adolescent girls.* New York: Ballantine.
Rice, K. G. (1990). Attachment in adolescence: A narrative and meta-analytic review. *Journal of Youth and Adolescence, 19,* 511–538.

Rice, K. G., Cunningham, T. J., & Young, M. B. (1997). Attachment to parents, social competence, and emotional well being: A comparison of Black and White late adolescents. *Journal of Counseling Psychology, 44*, 89–101.

Ritchie, M. H. (1994). Parent education and consultation activities of school counselors. *School Counselor, 41*, 165–170.

Saarni, C., Mumme, D. L., & Campos, J. J. (1998). Emotional development: Action, communication, and understanding. In W. Damon (Ed.), *Handbook of child psychology: Vol 3* (pp. 237–309). New York: Wiley.

Zeidner, M., Matthews, G., Roberts, R. D., & MacCann, C. (2003). Development of emotional intelligence: Towards a multi-level investment model. *Human Development, 46*, 69–96.

Zeidner, M., Roberts, R. D., & Matthews, G. (2002). Can emotional intelligence be schooled? A critical review. *Educational Psychologist, 37*, 215–231.

V

APPLICATIONS
WITH SPECIAL MODALITIES

Counselors live and work in a rich world of new technologies, therapies, and other creative modalities that can be used to enrich their work. In creating emotional learning opportunities, certain students may respond to various experiential activities in play therapy, art therapy, music and movement therapy, the martial arts, or lessons presented on a computer. This section provides a snapshot of two of these emerging modalities. In chapter 13, music therapy is presented as a means of enhancing counseling and as a way of infusing emotional learning experiences into other subjects (i.e., music education). In chapter 14, computers and other technologies are described within the context of the SDM/PS program as a means of engaging students. We believe that these chapters represent only the beginning of the many creative ways counselors can work toward developing emotionally intelligent schools.

13

The Use of Music to Facilitate Emotional Learning

John Pellitteri
Queens College, CUNY

Music is an inherently human activity that was part of primitive societies and has evolved along with the human species. All cultures throughout human history have created music, and music in turn has served as an expression as well as an embodiment of culture. Radocy and Boyle (1988) noted the various functions of music across diverse societies as emotional expression, aesthetic enjoyment, communication, entertainment, ceremonial purposes, and religious rituals as well as more contemporary use in commercial, industrial, and therapeutic settings. Music no doubt plays a powerful role in the world of children, particularly adolescents, as evidenced by the music media industry and the influence of music pop stars. Certain styles of music, in fact, tend to be identified with the teenage culture. Music itself has naturally reinforcing qualities and can be a transformative force. It can sooth and calm as well as move and energize. Given its significance, there is an enormous, though often untapped, potential for music to be incorporated into various educational processes. There is a natural connection between music and emotions, which makes it a well-suited modality for psychoeducational programs that focus on SEL. School counselors, who are typically trained in verbal approaches, can benefit from the use of music in their clinical work. In addition, music education programs can be used as a channel for supporting emotional intelligence in diverse areas of the school environment.

This chapter first presents a brief description of music and its relation to emotional processes. The next section describes music therapy, which is a clinical specialty related to counseling, and highlights some music therapy techniques that may be applicable in school-based SEL programs. The last two sections focus on the two major avenues where school counselors can incorporate the potential of music to facilitate emotional learning: One is in direct work through individual and group counseling, and the other is as a consultant to music educators and other aesthetic education initiatives.

THE INTIMATE CONNECTION OF MUSIC AND EMOTION

Music has always been a part of the natural world in forms such as bird songs, mating calls, and even the sounds of inanimate forces of rain and wind. Theories on the origin of music and on its neuropsychological development consider how early humans imitated these sound patterns in their environment (Joseph, 1990; Mache, 1992; Radocy & Boyle, 1988). Such imitation may have served the adaptive function of understanding one's surroundings and developing a relationship with nature. Other theories of music have noted the structural similarities between music and language and considered how music developed out of emotional speech and the melodic intonations of spoken sound (Radocy & Boyle, 1988). It is evident that changes in the musical qualities of speech (i.e., pitch, tone, and intensity) convey emotions to listeners.

It is interesting to note that emotions, like the natural sounds of early human environments, can be considered as signals that convey information about one's surroundings. Schwarz (2002) considered emotions as intrapersonal indicators of the environment, with positive and negative moods reflecting benign and problematic situations, respectively. When one feels uncomfortable in a situation, it is likely that the internal affective state was influenced in part by stimuli in the immediate environment. A sudden loud sound, for example, creates a startled feeling in a person and directs attention to the source of the sound to determine whether there is an immediate threat. Thus, sound (the very substance of music) is intricately linked with affective responses.

In any interpersonal encounter, emotions are a means of communication. The affective state of a speaker influences the nonverbal tone quality (i.e., musical quality) of the speaker's voice, which in turn creates a feeling state in the listener. The listener then evaluates the message of the speaker based in part on the emotional characteristics of the communication. A person's attitude toward someone else depends on this nonverbal level of interpersonal exchange.

"The affect-as-information hypothesis assumes that actual liking [another person] depends not so much on cognitive beliefs about a person, as on direct, affective experience with the person" (Gohm & Clore, 2002, p. 90). Similar to the environmental view of sound, emotions are the "music" of the interpersonal environment. The emotional expression of a teacher's communication style, for example, significantly influences the emotional tone of the classroom atmosphere, such as when a positive mood conveys the message that the environment is safe. Effective counselors in a clinical situation attend to the nonverbal cues such as vocal tone as much as to the verbal content of what a client says to attain a deeper understanding of the person.

The perception of emotional communication in vocal expression can be explained through acoustic properties such as pitch, timing, rhythm, and intensity (Pittman & Scherer, 1993). These acoustic properties are the same dimensions used to analyze music and are referred to as speech prosody, or the "musical aspects of speech ... used to convey a speaker's emotions" (Thompson, Schellenberg, & Husain, 2004, p. 48). Hodges (1980) described the physiological responses to music and reviewed research supporting the influence of music on heart rate, pulse rate, blood pressure, respiration, galvanic skin responses, muscular responses, and brain waves. Although results have been inconsistent, there is general support that music described as simulative tends to increase arousal (of heart rate, respiration, galvanic skin response, etc.) whereas music described as sedative decreases activity of these physiological indicators. The connection between music and physiological states is important in explaining how music creates emotion. The James–Lange theory of emotion posits that emotions arise from an interpretation of bodily states (Cacioppo, Klein, Berntson, & Hatfield, 1993). Thus if someone's heart rate or breathing increases, he or she may experience this undifferentiated physical arousal as excitement, fear, or joy depending on the cognitive interpretation of the situation. The etiology of certain anxiety disorders, such as panic attacks, for example, is based on the cognitive interpretation that follows an initial state of physical arousal. In this way, music can alter one's emotional state by directly influencing the person's physiological arousal. This is a basic principle in the rationale for music as a form of therapy, which is described in the next section.

The link between music and emotions is also supported by the literature on neuropsychology that examines how music and the recognition of emotional vocal tone are processed predominantly in the right hemisphere of the brain (Joseph, 1990; Lezak, 1983). Damage to particular brain regions can result in the loss of these related functions. Likewise, the musical functions in the brain have been known to compensate for the loss of other functions. Stroke patients who have lost the capacity to speak words because of left hemisphere damage retain the capacity to sing the lyrics to songs.

The association between music and emotion has been described from evolutionary, linguistic, interpersonal, and neuropsychological perspectives. The importance of this connection serves not only as a rationale for supporting music as a medium in emotional learning programs but also as a basis for psychoeducational and clinical interventions. The next section focuses on a clinical specialty based on the emotional and motivational aspects of music.

THE FIELD OF MUSIC THERAPY

"Music therapy is a systematic process of intervention wherein the therapist helps the client to achieve health, using musical experiences and the relationships that develop through them as dynamic forces of change" (Bruscia, 1989, p. 47). The musical experiences referred to in this definition are broad but usually involve the client in creating music with instruments, voice, or both, although some approaches to music therapy are based on listening to recorded music, performing composed music, or being systematically exposed to sound. The relationships that develop within music therapy include the client–therapist relationship, the client–client (in group therapy) relationship, and the client's relationship to the music or musical instruments.

Music therapy has been used in a wide range of settings, including medical, rehabilitation, hospice, educational, recreational, psychotherapeutic, pastoral, and healing/wellness programs. As a therapeutic approach, it draws on the same psychotherapy theories as the counseling profession. Music therapy has been practiced within various frameworks such as psychoanalytic, humanistic, behavioral, gestalt, and transpersonal psychologies (Wigram, Pedersen, & Bonde, 2002). It has been used with all age groups from infants to the elderly, and with individuals presenting any range of disorder or conditions such as: psychiatric, neurological, medical, special educational, developmental delays, or bereavement.

The profession of music therapy, which formally began in 1950, has long struggled to clarify its identity. Music therapy is not a recreational activity, it is not music education, and it is not entertainment. Wigram et al. (2002) distinguished music therapy from music education based on several parameters. One difference is the goals of the activity. In music therapy, the change is focused on clinical, nonmusical functions (such as improved impulse control, increased verbalization, increased social interactions, sense of self-esteem); in music education, the change is pedagogical (increasing knowledge about music, technical skill on an instrument, preparing for a performance). Another difference is the place of music within the activity. In music therapy, "music is a means ... [whereas in music education], music is the purpose" (Wigram et al., 2002, p. 35). There is also a difference in the level of disorder of the participants, with therapy clients exhibiting a greater degree of psychological, social, or physical problems than music students. The use of music therapy with the special education population, however, tends to fall between these two ends of the continuum, as such students have psychosocial or physical needs, or both, along with their academic needs.

A major clinical technique is musical improvisation (Bruscia, 1987), where a client creates spontaneous music as a means of self-expression and interpersonal communication with the therapist or other clients. The music that a client creates does not have to adhere to any specified format or be "accurate" according to prescribed notes. There is no right or wrong way to improvise. Improvisation is free and arises from the inner emotional states of the client in the exact moment of musical creation. In terms of traditional verbal therapy techniques, musical improvisation is akin to free association in psychoanalysis, although the music therapist's use of a client's improvised material need not be analytic.

A music therapy group that uses improvisation in a free, unstructured form or within a semistructured musical format allows communication on a nonverbal level. This nonverbal communication is much the same as the emotional dimensions of vocal expression described earlier. Clients can express emotions through music in a way that is not limited to the written or spoken words. This is especially powerful for children with speech impairment, developmental delays, or autism whose language limitation may have created tremendous frustration or disengagement from others. As the acoustic qualities of music parallel the structure of emotion (i.e., loud music can express a more intense affect), the improvised music of the client is a means of externalizing inner affective tensions in a meaningful form that establishes a relationship with listeners and others who are making music.

The potential for socialization experiences is limitless, as various combinations of instrumental orchestration and accompaniment can be devised. Each client's musical part is a contribution to the whole group "song" or musical creation. It is extremely important that there is a nonjudgmental attitude toward all types of music making, as the created music of the client is a reflection of the self. When the music of each person is accepted without criticism or comparison to a standard, the individual develops a greater sense of acceptance from the therapist and the group.

Music therapists are trained professionals (usually at the master degree level), are proficient in several musical instruments, and use specific clinical techniques. School counselors therefore cannot actually practice music therapy unless they have had the specified training. It is important, however, to understand basic aspects of this clinical specialty, as techniques and approaches can be adapted for use in a related manner. With regard to emotional learning and the development of emotional intelligence, music therapy methods can provide a unique modality for reaching these psychoeducational goals. Bruscia (1989) distinguished different levels of therapeutic practice where at the highest levels music takes a singular or a central role (primary and intensive levels, respectively) compared with a less central role of enhancing other treatment modalities (augmentative level) or a nonclinical role (auxiliary level). The next section considers how a school counselor can work at the augmentative level by using music therapy methods as a springboard for emotional activation and expression, thus enhancing the counselor's clinical work. The last section describes how the counselor can consult with music educators and other teachers in applying music therapy methods at the auxiliary level to develop emotional intelligence.

MUSIC AND EMOTIONAL LEARNING IN THE SCHOOL COUNSELING PROCESS

The relationship between music and emotion has been described and basic aspects of music therapy methods have been presented. There are several means by which the use of music can enhance the clinical work of the school counselor in general and facilitate emotional learning in particular. These methods include (a) music as an emotional stimulus, (b) music as aesthetic experience, (c) music for relaxation and imagery, (d) music making as self-expression, and (e) music as a group experience. This chapter introduces the use of music in school counseling. Some of these techniques might require additional training or level of skill to be implemented effectively.

Music as an Emotional Stimulus

Considering the powerful potential for music to arouse and alter affective states, a basic application of music in emotional learning programs is to use it as a stimulus for emotional experience. A counselor conducting psychoeducational groups or classroom presentations that focus on emotional learning can have the students listen to recorded music and discuss the emotional qualities of the music. The discussions can involve identifying the student's emotional reactions, examining how they can identify these reactions within themselves, and exploring the meanings of such emotions. Music is not just a springboard for discussion about emotions but an actual experience with an emotional stimulus that can be responded to in the moment. The counselor can choose different musical pieces and musical styles to represent varied emotional qualities. Music without words is preferable so the students can react only to the acoustic qualities of the music and not to the cognitive associations of the words, although a discussion of the poetic meaning and message of lyrics can prove useful for rich discussions.

Activities that use music in this way can benefit the development of the emotional intelligence abilities outlined by Mayer and Salovey (1997). One of their four subcomponents of the emotional perception branch of their emotional intelligence model is the "ability to identify emotion in other people, designs, artwork, etc., through language sound, appearance, and behavior" (p. 11). A subtest of the MEIS (Mayer, Caruso, & Salovey, 1999) uses musical passages to measure an individual's perception of emotion. The *music as stimulus* activities work directly on perceptual abilities through a recognition of emotions in the music and a recognition of affective reactions in the self. The discussions that develop from this can lead to learning about other emotional intelligence components such as emotional knowledge.

Music as Aesthetic Experience

The aesthetic engagement with a work of art is similar to identifying emotional reactions to music as described in the previous section; however, it involves a broader range of processes. Aesthetics is "concerned about perception, sensation, imagination, and how they relate to knowing, understanding, and feeling about the world" (Greene, 2001, p. 5). Through aesthetic engagement with various works of arts (visual arts, music, dance, theater) students can explore their inner world, make cohesive connections within and between works of art, and develop new vistas about themselves and their world. Aesthetic experience includes emotional reactions; thus, it can be a source of emotional learning. However, it also includes the student's awareness of his or her thoughts, sensations, and imagination in reaction to the music or other artwork. In this way, activities focused on *aesthetic experience* have broader potential beyond the emotional intelligence components of emotional identification and emotional knowledge. Students can begin to make connections between their personal reactions and other aspects of life, the artists intentions, and others participants in the group or community. To the extent that aesthetic experience is the creation of meaning in one's self and one's life, it can be used to understand the place of emotions in this deeper life meaning.

Noting how the cognitive and imaginative reactions can be activated along with the emotional reactions can be used to illustrate what Mayer and Salovey

(1997) referred to as emotional facilitation of thinking. The development of multiple perspectives, of new connections, and of the synthesis of the meaning of an art work is related to the flexibility often described as emotionally intelligent. The tolerance and nonjudgmental acceptance of various aesthetic reactions to art works contribute to pluralistic, multicultural perspectives.

Music for Relaxation and Imagery

Another method for incorporating music into emotional learning is using music as a means of relaxation. Hodges (1980), as noted previously, described how soft and slow music can reduce heart rate and respiration, which corresponds to the physiological state of relaxation. Counselors may use a variety of relaxation techniques for anxious students to assist them in developing emotional regulation. Such techniques can include deep-breathing exercises, progressive muscle-tension-release activities, and imagery. Music can be used to enhance any of these techniques. For example, when a student in a counseling session is working on slowing down his or her breathing, listening to gentle music can assist in the effort. Music itself can be used as a primary means to create a relaxing atmosphere in the counselor's office. The emotional learning aspect of relaxation is for the student to become more aware of his or her physical cues and of the relation of those cues to emotional arousal, and to learn how to modulate emotional states. A particular song can become a conditioned stimulus if it is used systematically to induce relaxed states and then be used by the student in anxious situations (i.e., before an exam) to reduce tension.

A related use of music used by trained music therapists is guided imagery and music (GIM). This technique, developed by Bonny (1978; Bonny & Savary, 1983), is used to create altered states of consciousness for self-exploration and analysis. The method begins with progressive relaxation techniques and then introduces specified classical music scores. With the close observation and guidance of a facilitator, the client creates imagery while listening to the music. The images that emerge from the experience can serve as metaphorical themes to understand the client's issues or as symbols of unconscious dynamics. The client in a GIM session has the potential to enter a very deep altered state of consciousness (similar to being in a dream state or in hypnosis), which is why this method should only be used by highly trained therapists. GIM therefore is not appropriate for use in school settings but is applicable in psychotherapeutic settings for older teenagers and adults. It is essential for clients to have satisfactory ego strength because they enter a regressed state (i.e., altered state of consciousness). GIM is an intensive psychotherapy rather than a counseling method.

There are, however, adaptations to GIM that can be used by counselors in small-group settings. The counselor can use a short piece of relaxing music and have the students listen to it with the instructions to focus on any imagery or associations they choose. Without the progressive relaxation in the beginning of the session, with shorter pieces of music, and without the particular sequence of classical music selections developed by GIM researchers, the students are unlikely to enter a deep altered state of consciousness. Instead, they may have a relaxing experience that can focus their thoughts and bring an emotional centeredness. This approach can be used by skilled school counselors to help students who are anxious or stressed. The imagery that emerges from the session can still be useful in understanding the student as each image is a unique creation of that individual. It is important that the counselor have some additional training in general guided imagery techniques if this method is to be used systematically with students.

Music Making as Self-Expression

Creating music is a natural human activity. Infants naturally vocalize and sing even before the development of formal language (thus paralleling human evolution where it was believed that primitive humans made music before developing organized languages). Young children are usually motivated to tap sticks or other objects in a percussive manner and are drawn to experimenting with the sounds of various musical instruments. Self-expression is a naturally rewarding aspect of creating music.

Depending on his or her level of music skill, the school counselor can use music making in clinical sessions in various ways. Just as music therapists improvise music along with their clients and create a musical connection with them, so too can the school counselor use music making to establish a deeper rapport with a student. There is a bond that develops when two people share a piano in the same musical piece or when there are two instruments playing a duet. Even if the counselor has minimal skills in music, there can be a musical connection simply by keeping a beat with a drum or tambourine. The steady beat of the counselor can be a stable and grounding support for the music that the student is making (whether the student is playing a composed piece of music or improvising spontaneous music). When both student and counselor have limited skills, playing simple percussion instruments together can be a tension-releasing experience or a means of enhancing the therapeutic relationship. Simple percussion instruments such as drums, maracas, and tambourines require little skill to produce sounds. Counselors and students can play instruments along with recorded music (from a CD or radio), which may be less threatening for students who are resistant to playing or do not believe that they have musical talent (remember that clinical uses of music have nothing to do with talent).

More important than musical skill is the attitude that musical expressions are accepted and not judged. This involves a high degree of emotional flexibility on the part of the counselor and complete freedom from the mindset of good verses bad music. The counselor needs to convey the belief that music is music and to look at music making only as a means of personal expression and communication, not as a performance. At times students may benefit from playing music for the counselor. If the counselor's role is to be therapeutic when listening to a student make music, the counselor must listen in a nonjudgmental manner (i.e., no critique about skills, never describe the music as good because this can imply the possibility of being bad). When the student is creating music, the counselor listens to the essence of the person—his or her way of being in the musical moment—as much as listens to the actual song.

The activity of making music can be used as a means of emotional expression that has the therapeutic value of releasing inner tensions. It can also be a means of emotional learning when the counselor discusses the students' reactions during and after the music. Pellitteri, Stern, and Nakhutina (1999) used music with a fourth-grade special education class as part of an emotional literacy program. One activity involved a student making music to a particular emotion. The other students had to determine what was the target emotion. This activity developed several emotional intelligence abilities. The student making the music had to decide how to represent a certain feeling through sound and in doing so had to examine the qualities and dynamics of that feeling. The other students developed emotional perception by listening to the quality of the music and the emotions suggested or experienced by the sounds. This activity also allowed one child to be the center of focus and the other students to invest attention into understanding that child.

An interesting opportunity of emotional learning occurred when one boy played loud and intense music with a drum. The other students consistently interpreted the music as expressing anger. When asked which emotion the boy was trying to express, he said "sadness." "Feedback from the other children as well as the teacher brought attention to the discrepancy between his verbalized emotion and his [musical] expression of it" (Pellitteri et al., 1999, p. 28). Part of this boy's social-emotional difficulties may have stemmed from poor emotional knowledge (he had confused or unclear concepts about emotions), poor emotional expression (he could not coordinate a response that accurately expressed what he was feeling), or deficits in emotional processing (he had both anger and sadness but the former impaired the expression of the latter). The music activity along with the group feedback of the students was the channel for this type of learning to take place.

Music as a Group Experience

Making music as a group can be therapeutic when it strengthens bonds among the participants. Each sound is an expression of the individual, yet all of the sounds contribute to the one group song. Rather than verbal means of expression where one person speaks at a time to be heard, group music allows everyone to express themselves simultaneously. Just as improvised music making between a client and counselor creates a unique connection, so too are the multiple duos, trios, and quartets within a group setting a unique creation of those participants. If you change one person, you change the group creation.

In a group setting, the music therapist or counselor can use the structure of the song to create learning opportunities. Group music can be improvised (everyone playing spontaneously) or can re-create a familiar song where everyone knows the different sections of the musical piece. At mentioned previously, the counselor may have the group play along with a CD or radio, as the music itself structures the experience (the way a music therapist would structure a song if he or she were leading). One activity (the group–soloist structure) involves playing as a group but then allowing each participant to play a solo at prescribed moments in the song. This allows the benefits of playing together but also the opportunities for individual self-expression in front of peers. If a student is resistant to playing a solo, the counselor can explore the feelings related to that. Students will seek the opportunity for attention, as the other members must listen to what they "say" with the musical solo.

A uniquely therapeutic opportunity exists when using the group–soloist structure. For the soloist to be heard, the other students must be able to not play or to moderate their playing so that it is notably softer than the soloist. This involves a particular degree of self-control. In the special music therapy/emotional literacy groups described earlier (Pellitteri et al., 1999), emotional regulation (i.e., impulse control) was a major issue in the group music making. The students with affect regulation deficits would get very excited when making music, and this interfered with their abilities to stop during the soloists' turn (or even when the counselor would end the song). The turn-taking structure of the activity (play together, stop during soloist; play together, stop for another soloist, etc.) allowed the students to practice impulse control. The emotional arousal during the music making provided a particularly potent opportunity for learning emotional regulation. To be able to exert control when emotions are intense (i.e. highly aroused in the music) involves a greater de-

gree of ability than if the student were not aroused. The music provides therapeutic agents to motivate emotional regulation in that it is naturally rewarding
to make music, the student desires to be part of the group song, and there is reinforcement for being a soloist. Turn taking during a music-making activity is
potentially more powerful than during a purely verbal activity for these students because the learning is experiential in an emotionally active state. Real
emotional learning must obviously involve emotional experiences. The music
is what activates emotions in the student and the emotionally oriented
counselor is able to capitalize on these windows of opportunity.

THE SCHOOL COUNSELOR AS AN EMOTIONAL
LEARNING CONSULTANT WITH MUSIC EDUCATORS

The previous section illustrated how music can augment the clinical and educational work of the school counselor. Another approach to using music for
emotional learning purposes comes through the counselor's role as a consultant. If emotional intelligence is to be developed in students, there should be
a schoolwide commitment or at least a critical mass of educators in the school
interested in emotional learning. Such a commitment is necessary to develop
a sensitive school ecology that supports emotional learning. The emotional
intelligence abilities that students might develop in counseling sessions or
psychoeducational class presentation need to be reinforced and supported in
a variety of experiences throughout the school. Several educators from different disciplines may want to incorporate emotional learning or to support the
efforts of counselors in developing emotionally intelligent schools. Given
that this chapter is focused on music, I emphasize how emotionally intelligent
counselors can consult with music educators, although the ideas presented
may be adaptable to visual arts, drama, dance, or academic disciplines. The
infusion of emotional learning in any discipline is a creative process that
emerges out of the collaboration between the educator and the emotional intelligence counseling consultant. The major ingredients for success are the
willingness of the educators and the emotional awareness and knowledge of
the emotionally intelligent counselor.

Many of the methods described in the previous section can be adapted, perhaps more practically, to a music education class setting. Music educators
would readily understand the music–emotion connection and be able to incorporate instinctively an emotional orientation in their work. The role of the
consulting counselor would be to provide the emotional intelligence terminology and componential model. For example, if the goal of the emotional learning
is the perception of emotions, a *music-as-stimulus* activity can be used. The

music teacher may already have lesson plans that involve eliciting emotional reactions to music. The counselor can provide an emotional intelligence framework for understanding the acoustic qualities of the musical stimuli that evoked such emotional responses. Recognition of emotions in music was used as a subtest of the original MEIS. The lessons of the music teacher can be broadened to include emotion identification in tone of voice (speech prosody) and facial expression, thus increasing a student's emotional perception.

The type of music class and the teaching style of the teacher is important in determining how emotional intelligence can be applied. If the class is a type of music appreciation where there are many opportunities to listen, then music-as-stimulus activities may be appropriate. For a band class that focuses on playing instruments, improvisations and music-making activities may be better suited. In special education settings or inclusion classrooms, music can be an important aspect of the adjustment process for the special needs student. Pellitteri (2000) outlined the application of music therapy with various special education clinical services (i.e., speech and physical therapies) and suggested that music be included in IEP planning.

The counselor's role as an emotional intelligence consultant is primarily to motivate the teachers to adopt an emotional learning dimension to their work and to provide the emotional intelligence terminology and concepts that will frame the learning. Consultants may have to explain to music educators the specific links between music and emotional intelligence in particular and, more important, may have to justify to administrators why music should be part of an emotional intelligence curriculum. Current research in the field has increasingly provided empirical support for such justifications. Thompson et al. (2004), for example, established an association between music training in adults and children and an increased capacity in the accurate identification of emotions. This association is believed to be based on the improvement of speech prosody as a result of music lessons. Thompson et al. (2004) also referred to research that supports links between music training and several academic domains such as general intelligence, symbolic reasoning, reading, mathematical abilities, verbal recall, and spatial abilities.

CONCLUSION

When a counselor works to develop an emotionally intelligent school he or she must focus not only on direct counseling and psychoeducational approaches but also on incorporating emotional learning throughout the school ecology. Music education programs can be a unique and effective channel for supporting emotional learning. The close association of music and emotion allows for the activation of emotional states, which can form the basis of ex-periential learning. Music therapy provides clinical approaches such as im-provisation, relaxation and imagery techniques, and group processes that can be adapted for use as emotional learning tools. Counselors can incorporate music into their own clinical work or collaborate with music educators to in-volve emotional intelligence in their existing curricula. Essential aspects of using music in emotional intelligence programs are the willingness, flexibility, and creativity of the educators along with the counselor's knowledge base of emotional intelligence.

REFERENCES

Bonny, H. (1978). *Facilitating guided imagery and music sessions*. Baltimore: Institute for Con-sciousness and Music.
Bonny, H., & Savary, L. (1983). *Music and your mind: Listening with a new consciousness*. Port Townsend, Washington: Institute for Consciousness and Music.
Bruscia, K. (1987). *Improvisational models of music therapy*. Springfield, IL: Thomas.
Bruscia, K. (1989). *Defining music therapy*. Spring Lake, PA: Spring House Books.
Cacioppo, J., Klein, D., Berntson, G., & Hatfield, E. (1993). The psychophysiology of emo-tion. In M. Lewis & J. M. Haviland (Eds.), *Handbook of emotions* (pp. 119–142). New York: Guilford.
Gohm, C. L., & Clore, G. L. (2002). Affect as information: An individual-difference ap-proach. In L. F. Barrett & P. Salovey (Eds.), *The wisdom in feeling: Psychological process in emotional intelligence* (pp. 89–113). New York: Guilford.
Greene, M. (2001). *Variations on a blue guitar: The Lincoln Center Institute lectures on aesthetic education*. New York: Teachers College Press.
Hodges, D. (1980). Neurophysiology and musical behavior. In D. A. Hodges (Ed.), *Hand-book of music psychology* (pp. 195–224). Dubuque, IA: National Association for Music Therapy.
Joseph, R. (1990). *Neuropsychology, neuropsychiatry, and behavioral neurology*. New York: Plenum.
Lezak, M. D. (1983). *Neurological assessment*. New York: Oxford University Press.
Mache, F. B. (1992). *Music, myth, and nature*. Chur, Switzerland: Harwood.
Mayer, J., Caruso, D., & Salovey, P. (1999). Emotional intelligence meets traditional stan-dards for an intelligence. *Intelligence, 27*, 267–298.
Mayer, J., & Salovey, P. (1997). What is emotional intelligence? In P. Salovey & D. J. Sluyter (Eds.), *Emotional development and emotional intelligence* (pp. 3–31). New York: HarperCollins.
Pellitteri, J. S. (2000). Music therapy in the special education setting. *Journal of Educational and Psychological Consultation, 11*, 379–391.
Pellitteri, J. S., Stern, R., & Nakhutina, L. (1999). Music: The sounds of emotional intelli-gence. *Voices from the Middle, 7*, 25–29.
Pittam, J., & Scherer, K. R. (1993). Vocal expressions and communication of emotion. In M. Lewis & J. M. Haviland (Eds.), *Handbook of emotions* (pp. 185–197). New York: Guilford.

Radocy, R., & Boyle, J. D. (1988). *Psychological foundations of musical behavior* (2nd ed.). Springfield, IL: Thomas.

Schwarz, N. (2002). Situated cognition and the wisdom in feelings. In L. F. Barrett & P. Salovey (Eds.), *The wisdom in feeling: Psychological process in emotional intelligence* (pp. 144–166). New York: Guilford.

Thompson, W. F., Schellenberg, E. G., & Husain, G. (2004). Decoding speech parody: Do music lessons help? *Emotion, 4,* 46–64.

Wigram, T., Pedersen, I. N., & Bonde, L. O. (2002). *A comprehensive guide to music therapy: Theory, clinical practice, research and training.* London: Kingsley.

14

Integrating SEL and Technology Within the Curriculum

Maurice J. Elias
Brian S. Friedlander
Steven E. Tobias

Although many may see the use of computers and technology in the development of SEL as an oxymoron, there is much to be said for its integration into the school curriculum and the work of the school counselor. To some people, it strikes them as odd that one would want to use computers to help in social-emotional development. However, computer technology provides students with a wonderful way to practice important social-emotional skills. There is something alluring and engaging about the computer, as it is a tool with which many students enjoy working. For children with special learning needs, the computer offers them the capacity to relate their personal experiences using something other than just words. From work done in the field of multiple intelligences (Gardner, 1983), the computer provides many students with alternative ways of expressing their experiences that would not be possible with just pencil and paper. This chapter explores the role of computers and technology and how counselors can integrate them into the curriculum to help students develop a core set of skills related to emotional intelligence.

Before discussing the role of computers and digital technologies in SEL it is important to identify the core set of skills that constitute emotional intelligence. Although many theorists have postulated hundreds of skills that would fall into the domain of SEL, from our perspective (Elias, Tobias, & Friedlander, 1999), the skill set for emotional intelligence could be summarized into these five areas:

1. Be aware of one own feelings and those of others.
2. Show empathy and understand others' point of view.
3. Regulate and cope positively with emotional and behavioral impulses.
4. Be positive goal and plan oriented.
5. Use positive social skills in handling relationships.

It is in this framework that this chapter explores digital technologies and their assistive role with SEL. When one looks in a typical classroom today it is rare to see the teacher standing in the front of the room teaching to the whole class. Rather, it is more typical to see children working in small groups or working independently on assigned tasks. Over the past 20 years there has been a transformation in the classroom—one in which the teacher's role has changed from disseminator of information to facilitator of learning. This change has had a large impact on the style of instruction now taking place. Children are spending more time working on projects and thematic units across the curriculum, usually taking into account multiple disciplines. Working in cooperative groups has meant that teachers now have to spend time understanding the dynamics that the varied personalities bring to learning. It is within this group context that many children are learning not only about the content but, more important, also about key social-emotional skills that will prove to be critical skills for life long after their formal education has been completed. With this in mind, we next explore how digital technologies can be used in SEL. Many of the examples included in this chapter come out of the work we have been doing in SEL with children, particularly under the rubric of the SDM/PS program.

TOOLS TO AID IN RECOGNITION
AND EXPRESSION OF FEELINGS

Learning about one feelings and those of others is sometimes a difficult process for children and, for that matter, for some adults. From our perspective, understanding one's feelings is key to decision making, and in particular, to the social decision-making process. It is important to understand that our feelings give us information about what is happening inside of and around us. Not using this valuable information can be critical in more ways than one. For this reason it is important to sensitize children to the range of feeling states and the richness of the words we use to describe feelings.

Using off-the-shelf software applications, it is now possible to have children use painting programs to help express their feelings. Key to developing social-emotional skills is the ability to become aware of one own feelings. To help students develop their feelings vocabulary, we often have a discussion of the various range of feeling states people can have. We know it is through these feelings that a child perceives his or her world. If children have a limited feelings vocabulary, such as mad, glad, and sad, their world is colored by it. Likewise, when you are mad you do one thing, but if you are bored you do another. Using the computer we can have children draw different facial expressions and discuss the key facial characteristics that define the feeling. In a group context it is wonderful to see the excitement that is generated when the children print out their pictures and share them with others. The children really enjoy this activity and benefit from the discussion of how facial expressions reflect feelings. Although this is a simple application, the students are highly engaged and focused on the activity. Software programs such as ClarisWorks, Appleworks, Microsoft Paint, and Kid Pix can be used when doing this activity.

Using a digital camera adds another dimension. In this activity, the leader of the group asks the children to display various feeling states, which are captured with the digital camera. The leader, for example, asks the child to show a happy face, which is recorded by the digital camera. The pictures are then downloaded to the computer and added to a multimedia software package such as HyperStudio, Media Blender, mPower, or PowerPoint for viewing. Creating a digital feelings vocabulary scrapbook is really exciting and just one activity that students enjoy. The students enjoy seeing themselves on the computer monitor. If you are looking to expand this activity, it is easy to create a written language activity. One suggestion is to have the students write a story about a time when they felt like the picture portrayed on the computer monitor. The students enjoy talking about their different feeling states, which helps them cue into facial features and develop their feelings vocabulary. In the counseling process these digital applications can enhance discussions and provide a springboard for emotional learning.

One of the skills introduced early on in our social skills program is BEST (Elias et al., 1999). You may be aware that we use many prompts and cues when teaching social-emotional skills. We have found that when prompts and cues are used consistently over time, students remember and use the skills outside of the context where they were learned. BEST is our mini-assertiveness training program and each letter describes a specific behavior. We found that students often did not have the communication and social-emotional skills to express themselves appropriately when they were under stress. Using BEST, students learn a set of skills, which allows them to assert themselves through confident communication. In fact, confident communication can be summarized as being one's BEST. Each letter in the acronym stands for an observable behavior.

B   Body posture (Stand up straight; be confident in yourself but not arrogant.)

E   Eye contact (Look at the person appropriately; cultures differ on this dimension.)

S   Speech (Use appropriate language; say what you really feel but don't be insulting, no put downs.)

T   Tone of voice (Use a calm voice, no whispering or shouting.)

BEST is a way of communicating, that when mastered, enables someone to be sure of himself or herself and increases the chance of being understood and respected by others.

When working with students in a social skills groups it is a good idea to model two other styles of interacting that are not as effective as BEST, which we have labeled Shrinker and Blaster. Shrinker is mild and meek and uses a whispering voice, which can hardly be heard. Shrinker exhibits poor body language and cannot communicate his ideas in a confident manner. Blaster, on the other hand, is loud and in your face and does not display appropriate body language, speech, or tone of voice. Both of these styles of communicating are contrasted with BEST. When students have the opportunity to role play they are sensitized to the behavioral components that make up confident communication.

For elementary-age students who are just learning the BEST approach, it is helpful to have activities that reinforce the steps needed to exhibit this communication strategy. In this enjoyable activity, students work in small groups to create a book that depicts the behaviors that make up the BEST strategy. The students use the digital camera to capture others communicating and in so doing create a literal snapshot of posture, overall body language, and eye contact of two students engaged in conversation. This activity enhances awareness of others' nonverbal aspects of communication. After the students capture a number of pictures they then have to decide as a group which will be used as part of the book. The book lists all of the BEST behaviors. Students can also draw pictures and color the pages as well as use digital photographs. It is exciting to see the students using their BEST skills as they learn the key steps in confident communication.

For middle school and high school students who need to learn these skills, the approach is somewhat different. One may want to think about setting up a digital video club to create a digital video that can be used to teach younger children the skills. With today's computer technology and digital video cameras coming down in price, it is possible to set up a reasonably priced editing workstation that would allow students to edit digital video in real time. Using the popular iMac and iMovie software, students can quickly create instructional videos with the power to edit. The creation of the video is exciting for students and allows them to practice a core set of skills essential for SEL. Group collaboration in working on these projects is good preparation for teamwork and problem solving in years to come. When employers are asked what types of skills they are looking for in their employees, they often are quick to reply that they are seeking, individuals who can solve problems and work well in groups. Activities such as these allow students the opportunity to practice their organizational skills, goal setting, collaboration, and negotiation. When one considers what is involved in creating a short instructional video, the real value in this activity becomes apparent. There are few more motivating and stimulating activities educators can use to hook students who are hard to reach. Using digital technologies, we can open the door to such students and give them opportunities that are meaningful and challenging, and give them a reason to use appropriate social-emotional skills. Once you have hooked students in the process of creating their own project, you are much more able to help them understand the social-emotional skills that they need to help create the digital video.

BUILDING STUDENTS' SDM/PS SKILLS

One of the most essential life skills that students need to develop is the ability to engage in social problem solving. Working in groups and collaborating on group-based project provide an excellent vehicle for testing and developing the social skills of students in the group. The Personal Problem Solving Guide (1993–2001) is a software application that was developed to help students work thorough problem situations in a format ideal for the counseling context. The program acts as coach or therapist on the disk and guides the student to look at the problematic situation in a different light. The program was designed so that students can look at their problem from a new perspective and brainstorm novel ways to handle the situation if it comes up again in the future. The Personal Problem Solving Guide brings ideas, events, feelings, and ideas into new relationships. The computer format helps connect thinking with behavior; this releases students—and those who work with them—from emotional logjams that jumble feelings, stifle thinking, and disrupt positive goal-directed behaviors.

Over two decades of research and practice have led our team members (Elias et al., 1999) to develop an acronym that clearly delineates the steps needed to do effective problem solving. It is this problem-solving process that is at the core of the Personal Problem Solving Guide (1993–2001). We call our social problem-solving acronym FIG TESPN (pronounced Fig TES-pin). When we introduce FIG TESPN to students, we explain it as sort of a Jiminy Cricket, or a coach who stays on the sideline but helps you out if you need it. Although a coach may give you some advice or direction, we tell students, you are the one on the playing field and ultimately you have to make the decisions for yourself. FIG TESPN is our way of speaking about the steps people can take to go from ideas to responsible, thoughtful actions.

Each letter in the FIG TESPN acronym stands for a discrete step in the social decision-making process and gives the students a framework for thinking clearly about the decisions they are making. We caution children that the FIG TESPN process is dynamic: at times, they may enter the process in the middle, work backward from the end to the beginning, or take it sequentially, step by step. The computer program takes students through the steps in a natural, interactive process that engages the students in the flow of problem solving inductively. Here are the steps for social problem solving using the FIG TESPN model:

1. Feelings cue me to thoughtful action.
2. I have a problem.
3. Goal gives me a guide.
4. Think of things I can do.
5. Envision outcomes.
6. Select my best solution.
7. Plan the procedure, anticipate pitfalls, practice, and pursue it.
8. Notice what happened, and now what?

The Personal Problem Solving Guide (1993–2001) can be used in detention, discipline situations, counseling sessions, and dispute and conflict resolution. It can be used any time there is a problem that students need to think through and work out. The Personal Problem Solving Guide can be used to teach prevention skills to high-risk youth, either as an adjunct to an existing prevention program or by itself. The Personal Problem Solving Guide is designed for middle school and high school students. It can be used in both regular and special education and is effective with individuals and in group settings.

Two versions of the Personal Problem Solving Guide are included with the application. The first is entered by clicking the keyword *problem* and is used when children have a problem, issue, or decision that they are thinking about.

The second is entered by clicking the keyword *trouble* and is used when children have gotten into detention or other discipline-related or academic difficulty and need to think through what happened and how they can resolve it or avoid the same trouble in the future. Both versions yield an action plan that students can use to implement their ideas.

The Personal Problem Solving Guide is unique way to have students both apply and learn how to become better problem solvers. The program guides users through the FIG TESPN process and helps them look at the problem from a new perspective (see Fig. 14.1). Once the student has gone through the entire program, the Personal Problem Solving Guide prints out an action plan, which can be followed up by the counselor or by whomever is working with the students. The second program, which is still under development, takes a different approach, still using the computer, to teaching social problem-solving skills. Using a multimedia authoring tool, iBuild (2000), the second author has created an interactive software application designed to focus on a wide variety of skills that are generally part of the social problem-solving curriculum. When they start the program, students can jump to any section of the program by clicking on the topic. The program keeps track of where the student has left off and marks the page that the student has previewed as part of the lesson. The Interactive Course in Social Problem Solving (1999–2001) uses digitized speech, sound effects, and QuickTime video to enhance the presentation of skills. Some of the screens were designed in a game-like format to engage students in an educational and fun experience. Throughout the course students are asked to interact with the program by typing in information, clicking on buttons, and moving objects on the screen.

```
┌─────────────────────────────┬─────────────────────────────┐
│      NEXT STEP              │     FEELINGS I HAD          │
│                            │                             │
│  Describe how you FELT just │  ◆ I felt bored.           │
│  BEFORE the trouble started.│                             │
│  Use a new sentence for     │                             │
│  each feeling, like "I was  │                             │
│  really mad at Jan." Use as │                             │
│  many different feeling     │                             │
│  words as you want to.      │                             │
│                            │                             │
│  Press ↵ after each         │                             │
│  sentence.                  │                             │
│                            │                             │
│  Press PgDn to PROCEED      │                             │
└─────────────────────────────┴─────────────────────────────┘
```

FIG. 14.1.   Screen shot from the Personal Problem Solving Guide (1993–2001).

The Interactive Course in Social Problem Solving was designed to be used as an adjunct for students who are learning new skills as part of their participation in social problem-solving groups (see Fig. 14.2). Many of the skills that would be introduced as part of the social problem-solving curriculum have been included in this application module. There are numerous opportunities for the students to practice the readiness skills that are generally part of any social problem-solving curriculum. The students are taught to recognize bodily signals and sensations that let them know when they are feeling stress and are taught a simple relaxation technique to help them deal with stress when it occurs. The computer guides the student through the list of steps that are part of a mini-relaxation training called keep calm. Once the students have mastered the relaxation steps, they can apply these skills by measuring their pulse rate before and after a physical activity using the relaxation technique. Student can type in their pulse rates and the computer will graph the difference before and after they use keep calm.

At a later stage in the program, the students are introduced to FIG TESPN. FIG as we affectionately call him (or her) can be thought of as a coach who assist you when you have problems. The program reviews the steps with the student using a text-to-speech algorithm so it sounds as if FIG TESPN is having a dialogue with the student. There are also some skill builders noted so that additional activities can be built around this centralizing theme.

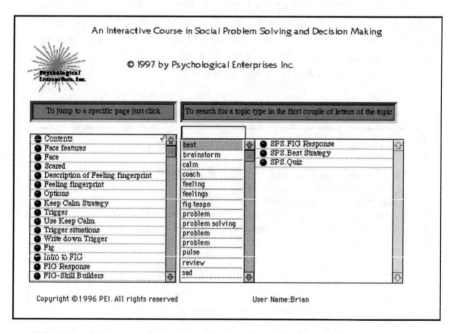

FIG. 14.2.   Main menu: Interactive Course in Social Problem Solving.

Although we have just scratched the surface of what the programs offer, students will find the programs a fun way to learn or to practice their skills as part of a social problem-solving curriculum. Both programs discussed offer different approaches to reinforce and teach students critical skills to become better problems solvers and decision makers. With the advent of faster computers, we are confident there will be many more software applications designed to address social problem solving and decision making.

One particular commercial software package, Hollywood High (1996–2001), is terrific for teaching a variety of social-emotional concepts. Hollywood High is a multimedia application that allows students to direct and create their own, play on the computer screen. The students have the opportunity to change the backgrounds for the sets and then add characters on stage to bring their story to life. Once the backgrounds and the characters have been added, the student can write the scripts and give each character the appropriate action before running their movie. The program is unique in that it runs on both the Macintosh and Windows platforms and it allows the students to change the facial features of the characters on the stage.

What is exciting about this program that it has many flexible applications for individual, dyad, small-group, and whole-class usage. It is a format for setting up a variety of common social scenarios, which the students then have to complete. Imagine that you are teaching a lesson on peer pressure and want to simulate the interaction on the computer for students to resolve. Hollywood High uses the computer to provide a simulation of the complexity and nuance of live action, but with an element of fun. The counselor, alone or with a teacher in a classroom context, can set up a scenario on the computer whereby several characters on the screen are pressuring a student to do something the student is not comfortable doing. The counselor can then assign students to groups and have them discuss what is happening and how the problem could be resolved. Using Hollywood High, the students could write or rewrite the scripts using the social problem skills they have been taught. When the groups of students have finished creating their productions, they could all have an opportunity to share them with their classmates and show how they resolved the conflict. This application provides a wonderful way for students to reflect on social interactions and practice their skills in an environment where there are no real-life consequences for their actions and reactions.

USING PORTFOLIOS TO PROMOTE
GOAL SETTING AND PLANNING

Goal setting and a positive orientation to planning is an important social-emotional skill, sometimes difficult to convey to students. Many students are unaware of how critical this skill, goal setting and planning, is to a full, rewarding, and successful life. In fact, many students have a hard time shaping and then articulating short- and long-term goals. School counselors and others in the mental health professions know that children without goals may be headed down an uncertain and possibly dangerous path. Goals give us our bearing and point us in a purposeful direction. Computer technology affords students a way to track their goals and keep a record of how they are doing—in fact, tracking in this way allows short-term goal planning to inspire and translate into long-term planning.

One activity that has received a lot of interest in educational circles is the use of portfolios. Portfolios are wonderful vehicles to show off students' work and give them goals to pursue. Two different types of portfolios have been identified in the literature that are relevant to use by counselors. They have been conceptualized as best work portfolios and growth portfolios. The best work portfolio is used to highlight and show evidence of the best work of the learner. The best work portfolio allows students to select the items, which may be called artifacts, they want in their portfolio and allows them to explain why they have selected the item. Students who use best work portfolios often feel a great sense of pride and accomplishment in their work. Best work portfolios are an excellent vehicle to exhibit a student achievement or can be used for postsecondary admissions or for employment (Rolheiser, Bower, & Stevahn, 2000). On the other hand, growth portfolios can be used to demonstrate a student's progress or development over time. Growth portfolios allow the student and teacher to view the progress of the student in many different areas (e.g., content areas, thinking skills, self-knowledge). The artifacts represented in the portfolio can be selected based on the core curriculum standards and be tied to existing educational goals and objectives. Growth portfolios are a wonderful vehicle for students to mark their achievement and to learn how effort and goal setting are directly connected to this achievement. When students are placing an artifact into their growth portfolio they need to be self-reflective and identify their rationale for selecting the item. Many educators often use growth portfolios to evaluate: knowledge, skills and attitudes, teamwork, and career decision making (Rolheiser et al., 2000). The process of creating portfolios is a wonderful educational activity. In creating individual portfolios, students focus on what they are doing in the classroom and identify goals to work toward.

Two of the our favorite programs for creating portfolios with a variety of digital media are PowerPoint and Hyperstudio. Both software applications are wonderful tools for creating stand-alone digital portfolios that include sound, graphics, scanned material, animation, and text (see Fig. 14.3). Although the students may need more time to complete a digital portfolio than

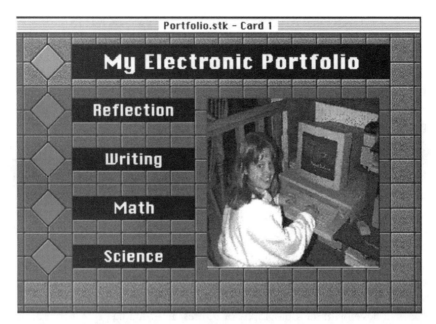

FIG. 14.3.   Digital portfolio in Hyperstudio.

a traditional paper-and-pencil version, the investment is well worth it. As is true of any portfolio, students will spend time planning and reflecting as to what is going to be included and why. Although the teacher will give overall criteria for what is to be included in the portfolio, it is really up to the students to decide what artifacts should be included. It is in the process of self-evaluation and reflection that students begin to view themselves as learners with individual goals and standards. Creating a digital portfolio allows students quick access to their material and allows them to review and reassess the direction for their learning. In this time more than ever, students need to learn how to set goals and reflect on how they are doing on the way to achieving these goals. This digital application allows for that process. As students collect artifacts for their digital portfolio it is now possible to include written reports that are scanned, digitized speech, students artwork, test scores, and digital photos. This gives the students a great deal of leeway and allows them to craft a product that reflects their style and thinking. If you have access to a computer and to any of the new multimedia applications, try developing a digital portfolio with your students and see how it helps them set goals and see the larger picture. The concept can also be used in setting goals and making plans in the counseling arena as well.

CARING AND SUPPORTIVE CLASSROOMS

The role of the classroom environment in promoting learning—both academic and social-emotional—is well known to both teachers and counselors. Practitioners often find themselves listening to students talk about the teachers they like and dislike. Many students say that when they come across a teacher they perceive as unfair, uncaring, and not willing to listen, they frequently write off the course and decide not to do the work. Even with extensive cajoling and pointing out that it is the student, not the teacher, who is ultimately being harmed, many of these students will not engage in the course and will ultimately fail. Is it no wonder that when teachers are responsive to the needs of their students and go out of their way to learn more about their interests, desires, and aspirations, students are more willing to engage in their work and behave in an appropriate manner? After all, students want their teachers to show them that they take an interest in them that goes above and beyond whether they perform well in the subject area.

One exciting project that can be done at the beginning of the year is for students to develop an autobiography or interest multimedia project that allows them to craft a digital story about themselves. This is a wonderful way for teachers to learn about their students at the beginning of new school year. Having opportunities to create a presentation about oneself opens doors not only for building a stronger relationship with the teacher but for developing and identifying interests that other students may share. The most essential tool needed is access to PowerPoint or Hyperstudio. Both of these generally available programs allow students to express their ideas and interest using multimedia technology. The projects could be structured so that students need to incorporate something about their interests, hobbies, clubs, and sports groups. Each student could then put together their presentation, which when completed could be viewed by their classmates and by the teacher. We (Elias, Friedlander, & Tobias, 2001) have outlined and provided step-by-step directions on how to help students create autobiographies.

CONCLUSIONS

The role of the counselor continues to be essential to the functioning of schools. As technology changes, counselors find themselves possessing new tools to aid in their work. However, as technology changes, the learner also changes. More and more students will be less receptive to traditional, one-to-one talking approaches to helping and to building students' social-emotional competencies. Throughout this chapter, we explore ways that technology can be introduced into the curriculum to support the work being done in SEL. These explorations are based on our direct practice in school and counseling contexts for more than a decade each. The activities we have presented allow the students, both in the counseling office and in the classroom, to apply and practice newly learned skills that may be introduced as part of their more formal SPM/DS program or introduced for the first time in the activities themselves. As counselors bring technology into their efforts to support and enhance students' academic and SEL, they will be rewarded with greater student engagement, learning, and generalization.

REFERENCES

Elias, M. J., Friedlander, B. S., & Tobias, S. E. (2001). *Engaging the resistant child through computers: A manual to facilitate social and emotional learning.* Port Chester, NY: National Professional Resources.

Elias, M. J., Tobias, S. E., & Friedlander, B. S. (1999). *Emotionally intelligent parenting: How to raise a self-disciplined, responsible, and socially skilled child.* New York: Harmony.

Gardner, H. (1983). *Frames of mind: The theory of multiple intelligences.* New York: Basic Books.

Hollywood High [computer software]. (1996–2001). New York: Scholastic.

iBuild [computer software]. (2000). Amsterdam, Netherlands: Acrux Software.

The Interactive Course in Social Problem Solving [computer software]. (1999–2001). Port Murray, NJ: BHC.

Personal Problem Solving Guide [computer software]. (1993–2001). Morristown, NJ: Psychological Enterprises.

Rolheiser, C., Bower, B., & Stevahn, L. (2000). *The portfolio organizer: Succeeding with portfolios in the your classroom.* Alexandria, VA: Association for Supervision and Curriculum Development.

VI

SUCCESS STORIES

As school counselors traditionally include perspectives that range from local to global, the final section of this book focuses on success stories that capture SEL implementation in one school campus, within a district, and at a state level. In chapter 15, we highlight Bartle School, a 3rd through 6th grade building set in suburban New Jersey that has adopted the SDM/PS program throughout its building to increase social-emotional competence. Chapter 16 describes the grant-funded Project EXSEL in District 2 in the New York City Public School System and shares the successes and challenges of a districtwide commitment to infuse SEL into its elementary school literacy programs. The last chapter, 17, presents a state model in Illinois for ensuring that all of the students have social-emotional competencies integrated into its kindergarten through 12th grade schools. These stories are presented to inspire the reader to replicate the models showcased. It is our hope that in reading this book, you will want to begin the process of applying emotional intelligence and SEL at various levels of the education system.

15

Social and Emotional Learning Through Comprehensive School Counseling: A Case Study

Linda Bruene Butler
The University of Medicine and Dentistry of New Jersey
University Behavioral HealthCare

Victoria A. Poedubicky
Highland Park Public Schools

Joseph Sperlazza
Fairleigh Dickenson University

Character cannot be developed in ease and quiet. Only through the experience of trial and suffering can the soul be strengthened, vision cleared, ambition inspired and success achieved.

—Helen Keller

"I'm stupid! Everybody knows it! Kids make fun of me!" Keisha, Grade 4, classified with a specific learning disability

"A kid in the cafeteria started poking me and I got so angry I pushed him. Then I ran out and cried in the hall. That happens to me a lot.... I can't control my temper." Andrew, Grade 4, classified as emotionally disturbed

"I don't know why I get in trouble all the time. Other people do the same thing I do and they never get caught."

—Carlos, Grade 6, recently diagnosed with ADHD

These students (who were introduced in chap. 9) are describing but a few of the many emotionally laden social situations that special needs students encounter, sometimes on a daily basis. In counseling students with a wide variety of classifications and needs, the most common denominator is their difficulty in navigating and managing social and emotional situations. SEL goals are often at the heart of effective intervention plans for the vast majority of classified students.

In the following pages we examine how in one school, Bartle School in New Jersey, counseling students such as Carlos, Andrew, and Keisha is embedded within a comprehensive, research-based SEL program. A research-based program serves as an organizing framework and provides a consistency of language and instructional methods that can enhance learning for special education students. We describe how all students receive multiyear exposure to systematic skill-building methods and extensive and varied practice of social-emotional skills through a programmatic approach. In this context, classified students have a greater probability of internalizing and generalizing the abilities they need to manage difficult emotions and social situations.

SOCIAL EMOTIONAL LEARNING (SEL)

SEL is an approach to character education that is often considered the missing link (Elias, 1997; Elias, Lantieri, Patti, Walberg, & Zins, 1999) that students need to perform to their highest academic potential (Welsh, Parke, Widaman, & O'Neil, 2001).

The concept of SEL refers to "a process that strengthens a person's ability to understand, manage and express the social and emotional aspects of life" (Elias & Norris, 2003, p. 3). SEL has emerged as an outgrowth of work in emotional intelligence, defined as "the ability to monitor one's own and others' feelings and emotions, to discriminate among them and to use this information to guide one's thinking and actions" (Salovey & Mayer, 1990, p. 189). These abilities or skills are distinct from nonability aspects of one's personality or temperament (Mayer, Salovey, & Caruso, 2000). School-based efforts to promote emotional intelligence are referred to as social and emotional learning to emphasize that these are abilities and, that as abilities, they can be learned and developed through education and training.

During the past decade there has been a dramatic increase in our knowledge regarding effective strategies for promoting social and emotional abilities through systematic, consistent, and developmental programming in schools (CASEL, 2003; U.S. Department of Education, 2001). Under the federal No Child Left Behind Act of 2002, schools are required to implement programs that are grounded in scientifically based research and proven to be effective. Increasingly, the need for program-level efforts to promote SEL as an integral part of education for all students has been recognized. (Elias et al., 1997; CASEL, 2003).

COMPREHENSIVE SCHOOL COUNSELING

School counselors are ideally positioned to play a central role in coordinating SEL programming for the general population while fortifying and tailoring these efforts to meet special needs. This emphasis on program—as opposed to relatively random, individual counselor efforts—is consistent with the National Model for School Counseling Programs of the ASCA (2003). The National Model emphasizes system change and provides a framework for designing, coordinating, implementing, managing, and evaluating programs to support measurable student success. This updated National Model shifts the role of the school counselor from seeing only students in crisis, test coordination, and other random duties to being program centered, focused on assisting every student, and demonstrating program-generated student outcomes within the academic, career, and personal-social domains. In short, the model positions school counselors to play a clear, significant, program-based role in helping students learn, learn how to earn, and learn how to live.

This trend toward unification and coordination is also consistent with inclusion efforts that unite general education and special education staff to provide coordinated services for special education students within general education settings. These trends have all helped to set the stage for developing schoolwide SEL programs.

RESEARCH-BASED SEL
FRAMEWORK FOR PROGRAMMING

Our case example, Bartle School in New Jersey, is used to illustrate how school staff can use a research-based model for SEL as an organizing framework to link the school's guidance program coherently to a school's other offerings. The model used in this study is SDM/PS, which is an empirically based and research-validated program (Bruene Butler, Hampson, Elias,

Clabby, & Schuyler, 1997; CASEL, 2003; Elias, 2004; Elias, Gara, Schuyler, Branden-Muller, & Sayette, 1991; Elias, Gara, Ubriaco, Rothbaum, & Clabby, 1986). This model provides a curriculum-based approach to systematically build students' social-emotional skills and teach children to be aware of emotions in themselves and others, to manage these emotions, and to use emotions to fuel problem-solving action. The targeted skills and systematic skill-building methods used by this model provide the foundation and shared language that underlies individual and group counseling sessions, specialized groups such as the school's Anger Management group, as well as the counselor's delivery of social skills development lessons in classrooms. Shared skill-building methods strengthen collaborations between the school counselor and teachers, fortify school and classroom discipline policies, and assist teachers' delivery of curriculum content that can infuse the application of social decision-making skills that relate to academic content. School staff work together to teach SDM/PS skills and help students apply those skills in the real world. For example, in a third-grade classroom, the counselor uses a giant fictitious report card and first models how to identify problem areas and then has all of the students identify a personal problem and develop a plan to improve their work in that subject. The model establishes and supports the knowledge, skills, attitudes, and beliefs that individuals need to regulate emotions, think clearly, and negotiate with others in an emotionally intelligent and socially competent way across situations and over time (Bruene Butler et al., 1997; Elias & Tobias, 1996). The goal is to provide all students with concrete skills to help them think rationally in stressful situations.

The SDM/PS model targets a repertoire of skills that helps students be more self-aware and socially aware and prepares them to be good decision makers. A self-control unit, for example, focuses on skills for regulating emotions in self and in others and helps students learn to recognize physical cues and situations that put them at risk of fight-or-flight reactivity that can result in negative consequences and poor decisions. Students learn specific strategies, such as a Keep Calm strategy, to maintain emotional control. The strategy includes self-talk and breath control that helps calms the autonomic nervous system while dealing with emotionally charged situations. Another strategy, BEST, helps students learn to self-monitor their body language, eye contact, speech or use of words, and tone of voice, communication variables that affect the feelings and reactions of others (see chaps. 9 and 14, this volume, for a more detailed description).

Because emotional reactivity is natural, the objective in teaching these strategies is to help students become aware of their own emotions and to recognize feelings as cues to use skills such as Keep Calm and BEST. Students learn to self-monitor, self-regulate emotional reactivity, and communicate effectively. Skill-building lessons establish a shared language, prompts and cues that can be used by staff and students to call forth the skills when needed. Skill prompts are also shared with others such as parents, paraprofessionals, sports coaches, and bus drivers to promote the transfer and generalization of skills to real-life situations.

Another central component of the SDM/PS model teaches students an eight-step FIG TESPN problem-solving framework (see also Poedubicky, Bruene Butler, & Sperlazza, chap. 9, this volume; Elias, Friedlander, & Tobias, chap. 14, this volume).

The most important component of the SDM/PS model is providing students with multiple, varied, and structured opportunities to practice the cognitive and behavioral skills learned within the academic content areas and transfer them to real-life problems and decisions.

THE IMPORTANCE OF "OVERLEARNING" FOR STUDENTS WITH SPECIAL NEEDS

Gresham (2000) found that efforts to teach students with special needs social skills are often not effective because the training occurs in restricted settings without adequately programming for transfer, generalization, and maintenance of skills.

If there is any aspect of SEL that is not understood by the general public, it is what it takes to build a skill to a level that it is accessible under stress. Such learning goes beyond the mere acquisition of knowledge. The learning curve for skill development is more gradual and develops over time through many cycles of practice coupled with performance feedback. The only way individuals can integrate a skill into their personal repertoire is through an ongoing series of practice and feedback trials (Gagne, 1965).

A skill is only accessible under stress if it is overlearned (Elias & Bruene Butler, 1999). Overlearning refers to a point in skill mastery when the skill becomes almost automatic. Can you think of a skill you have internalized to the point that it has become almost automatic? Perhaps you can parallel park and talk at the same time. Could you do that at your initial stages of skill acquisition? Skills such as dribbling a basketball, knitting, playing the piano, teaching, or counseling can only become internalized and automatic after much time and practice. Thus, the goal of having social and emotional skills readily accessible to—and independently used by—students with special needs in stressful contexts can only be achieved if these students are taught the skills and provided with sufficient practice and feedback.

COMPREHENSIVE AND INTEGRATED
SEL PROGRAMMING

A fully operational SEL process encompasses three major areas:

1. *Prevention,* which includes schoolwide comprehensive SEL programming for *all* students;
2. *Intervention,* which focuses on individual and small-group opportunities,
   provided by school counselors and other qualified staff, that helps students use skills to address real-life problems that have resulted in a referral for support services; and
3. *Comprehensive School Counseling,* which brings the school counselor into
   partnership with other school professionals in activities using a common
   language, skills, and frameworks in the classroom and beyond for helping
   individual students with special needs.

A comprehensive program supports student academic, personal-social, and
career development. Within such a context, classified students and all students
referred for counseling are familiar with the SEL language and skills that are
taught in their classrooms. These can then be used and supported by the counselor who applies them in an individualized way that reflects each student's
unique strengths and deficits. Under this model, counseling becomes a matter
of accessing and using what students have learned, practiced, and applied in
their classrooms in a more individualized context. For a more detailed description of how SDM/PS skills can be fortified and infused within individual counseling sessions to help students apply the skills to specific identified problems,
see Poedubicky et al. (chap. 9, this volume).

PROGRAMMING FOR SEL AT THE BUILDING LEVEL

Bartle School has been developing its SEL program since 1989. In 2002, the
school was designated as a demonstration site for SEL by the New Jersey
Center for Character Education at the Center for Applied Psychology,
Rutgers University.

All staff members at Bartle School are expected to teach and apply SEL-es-
tablished skills, prompts, and thinking frameworks as they work with students
within the full range of school contexts. First, we articulate the range of SEL
program components, followed by some illustrations of how the school counselor works in combination with other areas of programmatic effort to support
continuity and consistency of skill building for students with special needs.

The current Bartle School plan includes the following features (illustrated in the Appendix).

Basic Skills Instruction in Health Class

A scope and sequence of skills across grade levels are taught within the health curriculum. Students then use the skills to address health content areas such as coping with peer pressure to use drugs, alcohol, and tobacco; making food choices; and practicing safety.

Skill Practice Infused in Academics

All other subject-area and grade-level teachers have been trained to review and reinforce skills, and to infuse the practice of skills into various curriculum content areas and linked with core curriculum standards.

Skill Practice Infused Within Behavior Management Systems and Prereferral Interventions

Classroom and school rules incorporate SDM/PS skills to provide clear behavioral expectations that are stated positively. For example, Respect Speaker Power (take turns talking), Keep Calm, Be our BEST, Work to Solve Problems, and so forth. Discipline becomes a matter of identifying and achieving appropriate decision-making and problem-solving goals. In many classrooms, a problem-solving corner is used to provide a place for children to think about their behavior and ways to improve it. The problem-solving corner serves as a prereferral intervention that provides students with an opportunity to make plans for improvement. Students who are unable to resolve problems can be referred to the Social Problem Solving Lab.

Social Decision Making Lab

The Social Decision Making Lab is a place where students experiencing behavioral or interpersonal difficulties can be supported in applying skills learned in the social decision-making curriculum to develop a plan for solving their real-life problems.

Students can be referred to the lab by staff and parents, or students can ask to use the lab if they are having trouble solving a problem or making a decision.

Students are supported in the Social Decision Making Lab by school staff or trained undergraduate or graduate psychology student interns from Rutgers

University. Issues are generally approached through one of two tracks: (a) "I got in trouble today because ..." (the most common teacher referral), or (b) "A problem I am trying to solve is ..." (the most common student self-referral). Students use a wide variety of methods to work out plans for self-improvement or to solve a problem (e.g., drawing, worksheets, role plays, peer coaching). A computer-based personal problem-solving guide (Friedlander, 1993) is often used to help prompt students to think through a problem and develop a plan.

Peer Mediation

Students can also work with peer mediators to help them resolve conflicts. The peer mediators are nominated by teachers, peers, or themselves, and are trained and supervised by teachers and the school counselor. The mediation process students use has been articulated to include SDM/PS skills and language. This helps students realize that the same skills they use to solve their own problems can also be used to solve a conflict by having both parties engage in problem solving together.

The Keep Calm Force

Students are also trained to provide support for use of SDM/PS skills in the playground and other less structured school settings. The Keep Calm Force is a trained group of students who are supervised by school staff to help other students remember to keep calm and focus on problem solving when problems or conflicts arise. Members of the force wear identifying shirts or other gear, provide encouragement and coaching to other students when needed, and seek adult help when necessary.

Professional Development

Training for staff, including physical education teachers, music teachers, art teachers, the school nurse, the school librarian, and cafeteria and playground aides is provided. The district has invested in training teachers and the school counselor to become certified trainers of SDM/PS to allow for ongoing training of teachers new to the district. In addition to formal training sessions, newly trained teachers are paired with a master teacher mentor. Opportunities to observe each other and colead lessons, and time to process what the new teacher is learning are scheduled as a part of the training process.

Certified trainers also intermittently conduct booster sessions for the full staff, and opportunities for teachers or staff to share new and innovative application lessons are scheduled regularly at staff meetings.

Parent Awareness, Involvement, and Training

Parents are encouraged to participate in developing their children's SDM/PS skills. Workshops are held in the evening, right after child drop-off time, and right before child pickup time after school. This may be a particular concern for parents of students with special needs or students whose behavior is problematic. Parents can become involved their child's learning of the specific SDM/PS skills, just as they can become involved in their child's learning of math or language arts skills. Use of the model creates opportunities to bring parents into an SDM/PS partnership through newsletter articles, letters from teachers, student assignments, and e-mails from staff working with students in counseling groups or the Social Problem Solving Lab. Both in workshops and in informal communications staff demonstrate and help parents practice specific activities that help their children apply the skills they are learning at school in home and community situations.

Comprehensive School Counseling

The school counselor works with parents, individual students, and groups of 5 to 10 students by targeting specialized needs, such as coping with a divorce, anger management, and others.

Shelton and Stern (2004) published a chapter describing a visit to Bartle School in their book *Understanding Emotions in the Classroom* for those interested in a detailed description of what they observed while sitting in on many examples of SEL activities.

The following case studies illustrate how multiple SEL program components and coordinated efforts of school staff work together with counseling activities to enhance student's skill development and ability to generalize these skills to real-life problems.

THE IMPORTANCE OF INTEGRATED PROGRAMMING FOR STUDENTS WITH SPECIAL NEEDS

Case Study 1

The following is based on the personal reflections of Victoria Poedubicky, school counselor. The importance of consistency in what we are teaching the children was never made more salient to me then when I happened to observe Carlos, a student that was referred to me at the beginning of the year for a high frequency of getting into fights on the playground. Through

SEL, Carlos learned and was helped to practice Keep Calm in classroom situations but was having a hard time remembering to apply this skill in less structured situations, such as the cafeteria and playground. Through a combination of problem-solving sessions that occurred during time spent in the problem-solving corner in his classroom, several sessions in the Social Problem Solving Lab, and individual sessions with me, Carlos had developed a strategy to help him remember to use Keep Calm. He realized that he often put his hands in his pocket when he started to feel angry. Because of this he constructed a "Keep Calm card" and kept it in his pocket as a physical cue to remind him to use keep calm. This strategy was working and the number of fights was steadily decreasing.

One day I stopped at the door of Carlos' classroom when I saw him sitting with his teacher in the problem-solving corner. He had just served lunch detention for getting into a fight. Carlos explained that a boy in the cafeteria was making him angry and he did put his hands in his pocket and remembered to use Keep Calm. He got confused, however, because a visitor to the school had taught a different self-calming strategy during a presentation on resisting peer pressure to do drugs. When it came time to use Keep Calm he wondered if he should count to three or five and should he change what he said to himself? He said that he became confused and frustrated so he "just pushed him."

I will never forget that story. Especially for students with special needs I think we need to keep our strategies and language consistent. I realized that in this case confusion created by disjointed programming contributed to the feelings behind that push.

Case Study 2

The SDM/PS approach is helpful when working with students, like Andrew, who have been classified as emotionally disturbed. Translating the eight problem-solving steps of FIG TESPN into open-ended questions yields helpful, full-bodied responses from students rather than a barren yes or no. This productive approach is called facilitative questioning in the SDM curriculum, and it provides students such as Andrew with the help they need to implement many of the SDM/PS strategies. Let's take a look at what this might look like.

In a third counseling session with Andrew, he was asked to apply SDM/PS strategies to hypothetical situations, with some based on situations in which he had actually found himself. One of the actual situations involved Andrew becoming emotionally unstable because he had forgotten an assignment at home. Helping him put the problem into words is essential. The following dialogue shows how we used the eight-step FIG TESPN decision-making approach to deal with the situation.

Counselor: Hi Andrew, let's try to put your problem into words and talk about how it make you *feel* when you think about the problem.

Andrew: Okay, I think the problem is that the work is hard for me plus the fact that now I don't have this English assignment and it's due in 1 hour! I left it home and I won't be able to get it here. I feel sad, frustrated, and angry because I know I'm going to get in trouble again from my teacher. What am I going to do?

Counselor: Okay, let's try to Keep Calm and think about controlling what's going on in your head.

Andrew: The most pressing problem is that I don't have my English assignment here in school and it's due in less than 1 hour!

Counselor: Very good. Now letting your *Goal* guide you, what do you want to have happen?

Andrew: I want to turn it in or at least not get in so much trouble.

Counselor: Good, so think and name at least three *Solutions* to reach your goal.

Andrew: I could call my mom to bring it to me. I could just go home when I get that funny feeling in my stomach and say I'm not feeling well. I could try to do it here … now! Maybe I could just tell her the truth and say that I left it home. Maybe I could even bring it back after school today!

Counselor: WOW, that's five! Great, now let's *Envision Consequences* for each solution.

Andrew: Well, my mom is sick and won't be able to bring it to me. The nurse will NEVER let me go home! She will see right through me and know I'm not sick! I could do it now … here but I will NEVER get it done in time and I don't have all of the materials. Plus it will be a lot of work that I already have done. I could just tell her the truth and take the lowered grade. And if I bring it in after school maybe she won't count it down too badly.

Counselor: Okay, so which one will you *select?*

Andrew: I think I'm going to tell her the truth and bring it after school.

Counselor: Great! Let's figure out how we can make this happen. What are *you* going to *do?*

Andrew: Well, when I get to class and she collects them, I'll go up to her and just say I don't have it but I'll bring it after school and leave it in the main office for her.

Counselor: Now what we did was use *FIG TESPN* to help solve this problem. This is what you need to call up in your head once you are calm. I'm going to give you some additional *Hassle Logs* that have the steps of FIG TESPN on it to help guide you towards making good decisions.

Counselor: Next time we meet we're going to take a look at how you handle those situations when someone makes a comment about
your family or what you're thinking when someone is staring
at you. Between now and then, let's see how many times you
can appropriately remind yourself to use Keep Calm.

DISCUSSION

Weissberg and Elias (1993) pointed out that ongoing and long-term SEL
programs yield stronger, enduring results and a greater likelihood of generalization. Planning for school-level implementation of a program that involves all staff provides opportunities to "wrap" students in an SEL
supportive culture and shared language; foster the affective, cognitive, and
behavioral development of the whole child; infuse targeted knowledge,
skills, and attitudes in a variety of settings and academic content area; and
facilitate the use of skills in less structured settings. It must be borne in
mind, however, that schools are complex organizations and that the SEL
program implementation planning process must reflect this complexity.
Guidelines and recommendations for those interested in bringing a program into their school can be found in *Safe and Sound: An Educational
Leader's Guide to Evidenced-Based Social and Emotional Learning Programs*
(CASEL, 2003) and *Promoting Social and Emotional Learning: Guidelines for
Educators* (Elias et al., 1997). There are also resources available to provide
recommendations for institutionalizing and sustaining SEL programming
once it is in place (i.e., Bruene Butler, Kress, & Norris, 2003).

Bartle School suggests but does not constrain the universe of possibilities
that are available to school counselors as they help create the supports necessary for students to overlearn skills they need for academic, personal, and career success. In the busy lives of counselors we are forced to make hard choices
about how to use our precious time and energy. We hope that the Bartle School
example helps spur your thinking toward developing comprehensive SEL programming in a way that is most likely to yield significant results for students
with special needs and all students, our schools, and our profession.

REFERENCES

American School Counselor Association. (2003). *National Model for School Counseling Programs.* Alexandria, VA: Author
Bruene Butler, L., Hampson, J., Elias, M. J., Clabby, J. F., & Schuyler, T. (1997). The Improving Social Awareness-Social Problem Solving Project. In G. A. Albee & T. Gullotta
(Eds.), *Primary prevention works: Issues in children's and families Lives* (Vol. 6, pp.
239–267). Thousand Oaks, CA: Sage.

Bruene Butler, L., Kress, J. S., & Norris, J. A. (2003). Institutionalizing programming for social emotional learning: Lessons and illustrations from the field. In. M. J. Elias, H. Arnold, & C. S. Hussey (Eds.), *E.Q. & I. Q. Best Leadership Practices for Caring and Successful Schools* (pp. 199–212). Thousand Oaks, CA: Corwin.

Collaborative for Academic, Social, and Emotional Learning. (2003). *Safe and sound: An educational leaders guide to evidence-based social and emotional learning (SEL) programs.* Chicago: Author.

Elias, M. J. (1997, December 3). The missing piece. *Education Week,* pp. 36–38.

Elias, M. J. (2004). Strategies to infuse social and emotional learning into academics. In J. E. Zins, R. P. Weissberg, M. C. Wang, & H. J. Walberg (Eds), *Building academic success on social and emotional learning* (pp. 113–134). New York: Teachers College Press.

Elias, M., & Bruene Butler, L. (1999). Social decision-making and problem solving: essential skills for interpersonal and academic success. In J. Cohen (Ed.), *Educating minds and hearts: Social emotional learning and the passage into adolescence* (pp. 74–94). New York: Teachers College Press.

Elias, M. J., Gara, M. A., Schuyler, T. F., Branden-Muller, L. R., & Sayette, M. A. (1991). The promotion of social competence: A longitudinal study of a preventive school-based program. *American Journal of Orthopsychiatry, 6,* 409–417.

Elias, M. J., Gara, M., Ubriaco, M., Rothbaum, P., & Clabby, J. (1986). The impact of a preventive social problem solving intervention on children's coping with middle-school stressors. *American Journal of Community Psychology, 14,* 259–275.

Elias, M. J., Lantieri, L., Patti, J., Walberg, H. J., & Zins, J. E. (1999, May 19). Looking past Columbine: Violence is preventable. *Education Week,* pp. 45–49.

Elias, M. J., & Norris, J. (2001–2002). Social and emotional learning: A crosswalk to standards and assessments. *New Jersey Journal of Supervision and Curriculum Development: Focus on Education, 45,* 1–11.

Elias, M. J., & Tobias, S. E. (1996). *Social problem solving: Interventions in the schools* (pp. 1–10). New York: Guilford.

Elias, M. J., Zins, J. E., Weissberg, R. P., Frey, K. S., Greenberg, M. T., Haynes, N. M., et al. (1997). *Promoting social and emotional learning: Guidelines for educators* (pp. 1–10). Alexandria, VA: Association for Supervision and Curriculum Development.

Friedlander, B. (1993). Incorporating computer technologies into social decision making: Applications to problem behavior. In M. J. Elias (Ed.), *Social decision making and life skills development* (pp. 315–318). Gaithersburg, MD: Aspen Press.

Gagne, R. M. (1965). *The conditions of learning.* New York: Holt, Rinehart & Winston.

Gresham, F. M. (2000). Social Skills. In G. G. Bear, K. M. Minke, & A. Thomas (Eds.), *Children's needs II: Development, problems and alternatives* (pp. 39–50). Bethesda, MD: National Association of School Psychologists.

Mayer, J. D., Salovey, P., & Caruso, D. (2000). Models of emotional intelligence. In R. Stenberg (Ed.), *Handbook of intelligence* (pp. 000–000). Cambridge, England: Cambridge University Press.

Salovey, P., & Mayer, J. D. (1990). Emotional intelligence. *Imagination, Cognitions and Personality, 9,* 185–211.

Shelton, C. M., & Stern, R. (2004). *Understanding emotions in the classroom: Differentiating teaching strategies for optimal learning.* Port Chester, NY: Dude Publishing.

Weissberg, R. P., & Elias, M. J. (1993). Enhancing young people's social competence and health behavior: An important challenge for educators, scientists, policymakers, and funders. *Applied & Preventive Psychology, 2,* 179–190.

Welsh, M., Parke, R. D., Widaman, K., & O'Neil, R. (2001). Linkages between children's social and academic competence: A longitudinal analysis. *Journal of School Psychology, 39,* 463–481.

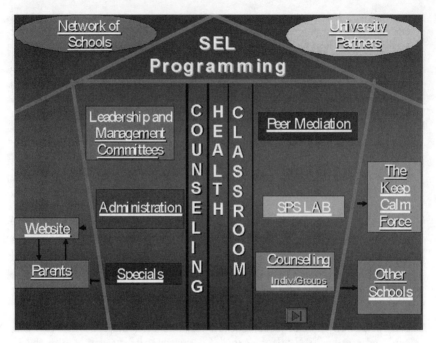

FIG. 15.1.   Comprehensive programming for social and emotional learning.

16

Emotionally Smart School Counselors: A School District's Initiative to Create Emotionally Intelligent Schools

Sheila Brown
New York City Department of Education

James Tobin
Independent Consultant

Robin Stern
Teachers College of Columbia University

I feel that it is my calling to share what I have learned about social emotional learning with the students and the teachers I work with. I envision that someday students will stand up for each other using their own strategies rather than depending on the adults around them.

—Valerie Radetsky, District 2 school counselor

Beginning in 2000, New York City Community School District 2 implemented an SEL program that was one of the first in the nation to systematically use counselors as agents of change. The initiative, called Project EXSEL, was viewed as a pilot project. It also came to serve as an example of how a commitment to emotional literacy can enable one school district to cope with a horrible disaster such as the events of September 11, 2001.

Before this initiative, District 2 established a national reputation for its standards-based educational system, one whose mission was to provide an accountable, world-class education for every student. Although the district made great strides in achieving its mission, changes in the larger society affected students' social and emotional needs and began to undermine the district's ability to create caring learning communities. Although schools cannot possibly remedy all the social and economic problems that construct barriers to learning, it was the district's belief that these factors could be lessened, to a large extent, by implementing a comprehensive approach to promoting SEL while also promoting academic learning. A comprehensive approach to SEL has been shown to be effective (Greenberg et al., 2003; Johnson & Johnson, 2003), and District 2 hoped this approach would increase the collaboration among counselors and teachers, which may be essential for promoting social and emotional competence throughout the school community (Marlow, Bloss, & Gloss, 2000). The district viewed counselors as uniquely qualified to be catalysts for change because of their training and schoolwide role. According to Massachusetts School Superintendent Sheldon Berman, a recognized leader in championing socioemotional education, counselors can be "instrumental in moving the district forward in social-emotional learning" (Mid-Atlantic Regional Educational Laboratory, 2003, p. 12).

In this chapter we first describe the design and implementation of this project, highlighting the major challenges encountered along the way. These challenges not only included the typical systemic forces encountered in any change initiative but also the powerful and persistent impact of September 11, which placed a unique burden on the emotional resources of the district. Next, we present the outcomes of the project and some recommendations for school districts based on lessons learned. Finally, we summarize the chapter and voice our hope for the continued development of this work.

THE DESIGN PROCESS

Based on a preliminary needs assessment, it was clear that SEL needed to be integrated into the curriculum in such a way that it fostered collaboration and valued diversity. Based on this perspective, the design team created a set of project goals:

- To develop the capacity of District 2 elementary schools to infuse a standards-based approach to SEL into literacy and social studies instruction in kindergarten through fifth grade. The National Standards for School

Counseling Programs developed by the ASCA (1997) was used as a framework.

- To enhance the skills of District 2 guidance counselors to enable them to design, implement, and assess a developmental, proactive, and preventative approach to school counseling. Counselors would act as leaders and mentors of this approach with school staff and parents.
- To expand the repertoire of District 2 parents with regard to SEL competencies so these competencies can be reinforced in students' homes.
- To capture the learning of this project and assist other interested educational communities in replicating its most effective practices in their own schools and districts.

In the design process, which was funded by a grant from U.S. Department of Education, a number of important factors were considered. The first factor was the tremendous diversity of the school population. Although diversity is one of the greatest strengths of the school district, it poses great challenges in addressing the myriad ethnic, socioeconomic, linguistic, and cultural backgrounds of the students. Project EXSEL, therefore, collaborated with several community-based organizations that provided key insights throughout the design and implementation phases of the project. A second factor was the awareness that it was crucial to begin the process of developing social and emotional literacy as early as possible; therefore, Project EXSEL targeted kindergarten through fifth grade. A final factor was the need to ensure that the project was replicable, so the designers targeted six elementary schools that reflected the enormous diversity of the district and could serve as demonstration sites. Once piloted and refined, this design and resulting strategies could be shared throughout the district, the United States, and in other countries.

The initial design included:

- training of counselors;
- follow-up coaching of counselors;
- developing curriculum with teachers, counselors, and curriculum consultants;
- creating manuals detailing lesson plans developed by teachers around SEL competencies;
- parent workshops for SEL skill building;
- ongoing communication with parents;
- technology training to increase teacher ability to incorporate the use of technology into classroom activities; and

- statistical measurement to track gains of students' SEL skills and competencies.

IMPLEMENTATION AND CHALLENGES

The EXSEL team began by putting several interrelated steps into action. We recruited four schools whose student populations, taken together, represented the diverse ethnic and socioeconomic makeup of the district. Two EXSEL project counselors were hired to support the principal, counselor, and six volunteer teachers in each school. Forging relationships with these educators, the project counselors' goal was to model the effective teaching of guidance-based lessons and facilitate collaboration among the counselors and teachers in the design and teaching of standards-based lessons that integrated literacy, social studies, and SEL. To assist in this process, an EXSEL curriculum developer met with each school team on a regular basis. The teams began by selecting children's books that were rich in emotional literacy and piloting lessons that they derived from these books.

As EXSEL was being implanted in the four schools, however, it was also nurtured in the larger school community. For example, monthly workshops and presentations were conducted for all district counselors to increase their ability to provide culturally competent and developmentally appropriate counseling to students and their families. At the same time, SEL parent workshops were created and led by various EXSEL team members so parents could reinforce students' SEL within the context of the home and family. These workshops were adapted to each school community's unique needs and culture (e.g., Chinese and Spanish interpreters were often used to ensure that all parents in attendance could participate).

As in any change process, obstacles emerged that the EXSEL team had seen reported in the literature. In a survey of 500 teachers and counselors (Marlow et al., 2000), for example, investigators found that respondents reported that the major obstacles to collaborative SEL teaching were: (a) inadequate time for implementation, (b) higher priority placed by schools on other curriculum areas, (c) a lack of useful instructional materials and adequate funding, (d) teachers' existing workloads, and (e) low parental expectations. Although the design of this project was intended to eliminate or lessen these obstacles, the Project EXSEL team still found it faced similar obstacles.

For example, an assessment of the 1st-year implementation found that a missing element in the teacher–counselor collaboration was the teachers' lack of a deep understanding of SEL. Without that mastery, most teachers were unable to be true partners to counselors in teaching SEL and in developing lessons for the curriculum manual. The draft of the curriculum manual revealed that the lessons contained few SEL skill-building activities and that the concepts presented were sometimes incorrect.

A second major problem was the resistance of most of the school counselors to teaching SEL lessons in the classroom. In interviews with the project counselors, three of the school counselors reported that they found that the usual demands of their position seemed to conflict with the new demands on their time of Project EXSEL. Role conflict has been found to be a prevalent factor in the practice of school counselors (Coll & Freeman, 1997). As a result, only one of the counselors was avidly teaching lessons and, notably, she had a principal who relieved her of some of her other duties. Based on these interviews and other assessments, it was clear that Project EXSEL needed to provide more professional development for teachers, revise the curriculum, and engage the principals in problem solving around expectations on the counselor.

As Year 2 began, however, an unanticipated event occurred that both challenged Project EXSEL and underscored its importance. On September 11, the overwhelming tragedy of the attacks on the World Trade Center shook, to their foundations, the school communities of District 2—especially those schools that were near the World Trade Center. After the disaster, some schools had to be abandoned. Others had to find space for children who had been displaced. Even the district schools not physically affected found themselves dealing with the human response to emotional trauma. Uncertainty, fear, anger, sadness, grief, and hope were suddenly part of the hidden curriculum.

In response, the Project EXSEL team, with a new director in place, put action plans on hold while they worked with teachers, counselors, parents, and others to help school communities deal effectively with the emotions of each passing day. Since children's books have been often been used by counselors to open up communication about fears (Nicholson & Pearson, 2003), Project EXSEL was often called on to help adults learn how to talk with children. As a result, it seemed as if the school communities involved came to deepen their commitment to ensuring that emotional literacy became more of a priority in the classrooms.

As the urgent needs subsided after several months, Project EXSEL focused on how it could meet the SEL needs of its teachers as well as the larger community. To meet the needs of the teachers, a series of in-school workshops was created and a consultant was hired to revise the manuals so they would be more effective and user friendly in the teaching of SEL skills and concepts. In addition, a video of best SEL practices was produced and a Project EXSEL Web site was developed that could both support project schools and meet the SEL needs of a much larger community (see www.projectexsel.net).

The EXSEL Web site made available the following valuable SEL resources:

1. a description of the project and its development;
2. current information about SEL concepts, practices, and resources;
3. a video clip showing a model Project EXSEL classroom lesson;
4. interactive creative games and role-play scenarios for children that can enhance their SEL skills; and
5. a parent component in English, Spanish, and Chinese, with interactive exercises for parents designed to offer helpful hints on a variety of parenting topics and SEL skill development.

OUTCOMES OF THE PROJECT AND LESSONS LEARNED

Overall, it was found that the implementation of Project EXSEL was very successful. Data collected by Metis Associates using focus groups, individual interviews, observations, and program documentation revealed that a large majority of the staff members found the project beneficial to themselves, their schools, students, and families. Staff members reported that, through participation in the program, students were able to increase their SEL skills, becoming more aware of their social and emotional states and more able to employ SEL techniques for self-regulation and positive behavioral change. Counselors were able to improve their counseling skills as well as their general SEL knowledge. Administrators reported that they felt Project EXSEL contributed to an improved social climate in their schools.

The district's schools and the larger public are increasingly using the products developed by Project EXSEL. The EXSEL Web site provides a wealth of information in English, Chinese, and Spanish. The revised manuals are much more teacher friendly and will be disseminated in kits complete with children's literature used in the lessons. Experienced counselors are already developing their own imaginative ways to piggyback on the Project EXSEL program to create emotionally intelligent schools.

The implementation of the program, however, has not always progressed smoothly, and there are lessons to be learned from this pilot. A key lesson is that project goals and policies need to be flexible enough to respond to unanticipated events. A second lesson learned, after encountering resistance during early implementation, was that active involvement by school leaders, especially principals, was an essential element in the beginning of this project. In addition, SEL training needs to be provided to school leaders, specifically in emotionally intelligent leadership development (Patti & Tobin, 2003). Another important step related to involving principals is to find ways to relieve counselors of the many administrative tasks they are often given that are unrelated to their core mission. Freed from unnecessary tasks, school counselors are then able to focus on the promotion of SEL. Finally, we discovered that classroom teachers often need a great deal of training and follow-up coaching to both understand and teach SEL concepts and skills. As part of this teacher learning, teachers also need both the physical and emotional space that allows them to communicate frequently and openly with guidance counselors and fellow teachers, enabling them to feel comfortable with their own emotions and those of their students.

SUMMARY

This chapter describes a pilot program that was designed by one school district to enable counselors and their school communities to create emotionally intelligent schools. Focusing on the school counselor as the agent of change in the school, Project EXSEL developed a comprehensive plan to integrate academic learning and SEL, employing a series of strategies that ranged from curriculum and professional development to the use of video and the Internet. In addition to the usual obstacles to change, educators also had to deal with the traumatic effects of the attack on September 11 of the World Trade Center that once stood at the southern end of the district. Testing the emotional resilience of the people in the district, the disaster confirmed the importance of emotional literacy in education.

At the center of that education, acting as a fulcrum to tip the scales toward this work, is the school counselor. The counselor often has the skills, the wider perspective, and the calling to serve as a catalyst. In reviewing the process and outcomes of this project, however, it is clear that the counselor needs the support of the district, the school principal, and other key members of the school community to succeed in that role. It is hoped that this chapter will help in this mission.

REFERENCES

Coll, K. M., & Freeman, B. (1997). Role conflict among elementary school counselors: A national comparison with middle and secondary school counselors, *Elementary School Guidance & Counseling, 31*, 251–261.

Greenberg, M. T., Wiessberg, R. P., O'Brien, M. U., Zins, J. E., Fredericks, L., Resnik, H., et al. (2003). Enhancing school-based prevention and youth development through coordinated social emotional and academic learning. *American Psychologist, 58*, 466–474.

Johnson, S., & Johnson, C. D. (2003). Results-based guidance: A systems approach to student support programs. *Professional School Counseling, 6,* 180–184.

Marlow, L., Bloss, K., & Gloss, D. (2000). Promoting social and emotional competence through teacher/counselor collaboration. *Education, 4,* 668–674.

Mid-Atlantic Regional Educational Laboratory. (2003). Creating safe, supportive, high-achieving schools: Superintendents talk about programs for better student outcomes. *Laboratory for Student Success Field Notes, 1–12.* Retrieved June 12, 2004, from htttp://www.temple.edu/lss/pdf/fieldnotes/spring2003.pdf

Nicholson, J. I., & Pearson, Q. M. (2003). Helping children cope with fears: Using children's literature in classroom guidance. *Professional School Counseling, 7,* 15–19.

Patti, J., & Tobin, J. (2003). *SMART school leaders: Leading with emotional intelligence.* Dubuque, IA: Kendall-Hunt.

17

A State Mandate for Social-Emotional Literacy: Implications for School Counselors

Maria McCabe
Illinois Children's Mental Health Partnership

Toni Tollerud
Northern Illinois University

Jennifer Axelrod
Collaborative for Academic and Social Emotional Learning

HISTORICAL PERSPECTIVES OF SCHOOL COUNSELING IN ILLINOIS

School counselors in Illinois have long struggled to define their roles as mental health professionals working in the schools. This phenomenon is nothing new, as noted in earlier chapters. Historically, there was little written in Illinois School Code that directly defined the role of the school counselor and the duties essential to being effective professionals. As a result, administrators were often unaware of the transformation of the school counseling profession to a more developmental and comprehensive program, the activities school counselors are asked to do often do not reflect how school counselors are trained, especially in addressing social-emotional issues. Rather, these duties often parallel teachers' duties. Duties such as mental health prevention programming, crisis intervention, and individual counseling or small-group work are not emphasized.

School counselor training programs may contribute to some of this struggle. In Illinois all certified school counselors were required to have a bachelor's degree, be eligible for a state school teaching certificate, and complete a master's degree in school counseling. Therefore, nearly all students in training programs were already school teachers or they were in the process of completing a teaching area of specialization. A major change in the state certification rules occurred in May 2004. These rules allow non-teacher-certified people to become school counselors by completing a master's in school counseling or its equivalent and covering knowledge and skill indicators representing four additional areas of educational training. Because new professionals will be graduating with school counseling certificates who are not school teachers, it is possible that these school counselors will be less prone to continue to act as teachers or to get overly involved in doing noncounseling activities.

In Chicago, every school has a school counselor position. In Chicago high schools, school counselors have traditionally been used primarily for scheduling, testing, paperwork, career counseling, and college counseling. Elementary school counselors have digressed even further from the role of counseling and have focused on case management issues for their students. The elementary school counselor has accomplished minimal success at addressing academic, personal-social, or career development goals to prepare students to enter high school with knowledge and practice regarding these important skills. More emphasis is given to intervention than to prevention. Additionally, an accountability system is not in place. Crisis issues are rampant and get the bulk of the attention. The important issue of teaching students SEL skills is spotty and inconsistent.

In the suburbs and rural areas, most schools, except high schools, employ school social workers instead of school counselors. Federal reimbursements for school psychologists and school social workers encourage school districts to hire them to do the work of the school counselor when budgets are tight. Less emphasis is given to prevention and SEL programming because of a lack of time and expertise. More of an emphasis is given to crisis intervention and remedial treatment.

Even in Chicago, where positions are available, qualified personnel are not. Many positions remain vacant. Fewer teachers have chosen to enter school counseling for a number of valid reasons. Chicago has been creative in addressing this problem by creating positions for school counselor candidates to fill, with pay, while they are completing their programs and internships.

Finally, an additional issue occurs in rural and suburban areas when school counselors are hired for elementary or middle school positions but they serve more than one school. Partial positions make program development and consistency difficult. These factors have contributed to an identified personnel shortage in school counseling by the Illinois State Board of Education.

In 1992 the Illinois Counseling Association along with the Illinois School Counselor's Association and the Illinois Counselor Educators and Supervisors organized a joint task force to work on a developmental school counseling program for Illinois. In 1996 the *Developmental Counseling Model for Illinois Schools: Guidelines for Program Development* was published. This document served as a model for well-defined programs that would integrate school counselors into the fiber of the school and allow them to collaborate directly with the educational system and with the broader community. The availability of this model provided an opportunity for school counselors to work in a way that was developmental, preventive, collaborative, goal oriented, and measurable. The model provided a framework for role definition and accountability. Most important, it provided a vehicle for the design and implementation of a curriculum including SEL.

Instead of looking at the responsibilities of the school counselor as services, the model proposed a philosophical change and began to look at those responsibilities as components. This change made the counseling service no longer ancillary but instead an integral part of the educational system. School counselors were defined as prevention specialists who would give intentional attention to the social-emotional development of children. Counselors and administrators were encouraged to look at the opportunities for prevention and collaboration that would result from the adoption of a developmental counseling approach. The model encouraged collaboration and discouraged fragmentation of services to children.

As counselors headed into their schools with the developmental model under their arms, they continued to face the barriers mentioned earlier. As a result, the Illinois School Counselor Association asked for an amendment to Illinois School Code, which defined the role of the Illinois school counselor. This definition in the Illinois School Code gave specificity to counseling programs and articulated the broad, comprehensive role of the counselor. In some school districts the model and the new definition were embraced. In other districts the definition was misunderstood and caused some to lose their jobs. The struggle continued. The Illinois School Counseling Association took big steps to create partnerships with agencies outside of the schools and to engage in conversations with other professional organizations in an attempt to be understood in a way that would allow them to provide the prevention services they knew would make a difference for all children.

In 1992 the governor of Illinois signed a bill that provided licensure for counselors on two levels: licensed professional counselors and licensed clinical professional counselors. School counselors who met the education requirements were eligible to sit for the National Counselor Exam and thereby acquire the first license, the licensed professional counselor. Though this did not bestow the rights of the licensed clinical professional counselor to conduct an independent private practice, many school counselors jumped at the chance to gain professional recognition as mental health counselors working in the schools.

Additionally in Illinois, professional development opportunities for school counselors in schools were limited. As a result, the Illinois School Counselor's Academy was formed in 1999. This program's mission focused on the development of leadership for school counselors by advocating, supporting, and promoting the role of the professional school counselor so as to positively affect students' academic, career, and social-emotional development. The academy, working through Regional Offices of Education, began providing opportunities for professional development.

Progressive school counselors in Illinois also knew that they needed to look outside of the school system for opportunities to collaborate on behalf of children's mental health if they were to be successful at providing the services needed. They became involved with a statewide violence prevention program called Safe to Learn. This organization received money that provided grants to schools to address student needs and offer services. School counselors became involved with this initiative and were asked to give input by serving on its advisory board. School counselors also participated with other statewide organizations to create a group called Partners for Peace, which designed conferences to provide information for communities, including students and parents, about school violence prevention programs. As a result of their involvement in Partners for Peace, school counselors, counselor educators, the Illinois School Counselor's Academy, and the Attorney General's office formed a pilot study to determine the value of providing small focus groups in schools called Listen to Youth. The results of that program were overwhelmingly positive. Later, school counselors collaborated with the Illinois Mental Health Association of Illinois to address the issues of eating disorders and provided training for school counselors through the Illinois School Counselors Academy and the Illinois School Counselors Association.

In 2000, the professional standards for school counselor education programs were examined and changed to reflect a comprehensive, developmental school counseling program. State standards were aligned with national standards. The current role of the school counselor emphasized working directly with students using a counseling curriculum, individual and group counseling, prevention work, and planning meetings to address the developmental needs of *all* students in the school. Within the new state document there was also a recommendation to change the endorsement area from "guidance" to "counseling." This recommendation emphasized a more integrated role for the school counselor in the educational system.

At the same time the new standards were being developed, the committee also recommended changes in the criteria for certification as a school counselor. In 2004 these changes were adopted by the state school board and written into rules. These new rules designate the process necessary for professionals who do not have teaching certificates but who want to become certified school counselors in Illinois.

In summary, much has happened over the past 4 to 6 years that has had a positive impact on school counseling in Illinois. It is safe to say that school counseling has moved forward in defining itself more clearly, establishing state standards and certification requirements that support the transformation of the profession, working collaboratively with other state entities that promote prevention and wellness for children, and developing advocacy. Although there is much to do, this is a commendable start. School counselors, across all the grades, stand ready to design and implement models that will intentionally and concisely address the mental health needs of children and adolescents. They are in a key position to identify students (and their families) for early intervention testing and services, provide curriculum that teaches knowledge and skills to students developmentally, make meaningful interventions and referrals, and ensure student mental and emotional safety and wellness.

THE RISE OF SEL PROGRAMS

At the same time counselors were struggling to define their role in schools, a movement was beginning that recognized that health and well-being of students were affected by SEL skills. In 1995, *New York Times* science writer Goleman wrote *Emotional Intelligence: Why It Can Matter More Than IQ.* The book synthesized the advances that had been in made educational theory and practice, human development, neurology, cognitive psychology, and other applied behavioral and psychological science as researchers began to address the development of children's emotional awareness, their social problem-solving skills, and their avoidance of risky health behaviors, and to apply the findings in school classrooms. The need for this work was supported by the recognition that the sheer numbers of mental health issues presented by school-age youth overwhelmed any ability to respond effectively to them all and that there was a pressing need to develop interventions in classrooms to prevent many behavioral and adjustment problems before they developed. At the same time, re-searchers recognized the need to enhance the social and emotional functioning of all children through promoting assets and protective factors.

The interest and enthusiasm that under girded Goleman's desire to write *Emotional Intelligence* (1995) also led to his cocreation of an organization de-voted to promoting social and emotional learning in all schools, from preschool through high school. In 1994, the Collaborative to Advance Social and Emo-tional Learning (CASEL) was established and was initially housed at Yale Uni-versity's Child Study Center. In 1996, CASEL's Leadership Team (composed of scientists, educators, and philanthropists and practitioners to provide direc-tion to CASEL) asked Roger Weissberg to be CASEL's executive director. When Weissberg agreed to the Leadership Team's request, CASEL moved to the University of Illinois at Chicago. Financial support for the transition was provided by the University of Illinois at Chicago, the Surdna Foundation, and the Fetzer Institute. At that time, CASEL began to work with local schools in the Chicago area to address issues of implementation and integration of inter-vention services for at-risk youth with classroom-based social competence pro-motion. In 2001, CASEL changed its name to reflect an increasing recognition of the importance of the relationship between social and emotional learning and academics. Currently, the acronym of CASEL stands for the Collaborative for Academic, Social and Emotional Learning. Concurrently, the provost of the University of Illinois provided seed funding to allow CASEL to have a more fo-cused and strategic plan to support SEL in state. To that end, CASEL has cre-ated an advisory board of state leaders to provide guidance to the initiatives, cohosted a number of statewide conferences on Working Together for Student Success and has been actively involved in a number of collations and state planning efforts to support children's wellness and development (e.g., Children's Mental Health Task Force).

The movement toward the integration of SEL into the educational practices of schools has expanded in Illinois in recent years. As educational leaders have become more aware of the principles of SEL and the impact that SEL program-ming can have on students' academic success and well-being, interest has grown in the strategies for enhancing programming efforts. SEL is defined as the "process of developing the ability to recognize and manage emotions, de-velop caring and concern for others, make responsible decisions, establish posi-tive relationships, and handling challenging situations effectively" (CASEL, 2003). Embedded within this definition is a framework for preventing problems and promoting success for students through the integration of SEL into a schoolwide effort. In the past, there have been a number of state initiatives that have been implemented with short-term gains for students. However, these initiatives frequently were fragmented and had little success in creating sustainable programs to improve the health and well-being of students. Illinois is now embarking on a new vision for SEL in schools. This vision supports the best practices guidelines of comprehensive, coordinated, and sustainable programming for children and youth.

To support these efforts, CASEL, through a grant from the governor's office, is working with schools to develop model sites of programming. These sites selected from around the state highlight the complexities of implementing SEL programming and the remarkable impact that the programming may have on students, staff, and families. In the schools that are doing the work well, evidence has been gathered that proves that SEL programming enhances children's skills and creates an environment of caring, nurturing connectedness.

ILLINOIS CHILDREN'S MENTAL HEALTH ACT 2003

In the spring of 2001 a group of interested individuals spent a day in the Chicago public schools. They left disturbed by the number of students depressed and traumatized by the violence in their homes and communities. These students needed someone with whom to talk about their concerns and anxieties. As a result, the Illinois Violence Prevention Authority convened a workgroup to explore the status of children's mental health in Illinois and they produced a white paper (Mental Health for Children Working Group, 2001)—an important first step in identifying the key issues facing children and youth in Illinois. Based on that document and information contained in The Social-Emotional Health Committee of the Birth to Five Project, a state project supported by the Robert Wood Johnson Foundation, a joint resolution was passed to convene and administer a multidisciplinary Illinois School/Community Mental Health Task Force to study further the status of children's mental health. The Illinois Violence Prevention Authority, under the leadership of Barbara Shaw, convened the Children's Mental Health Task Force in 2002. More than 100 groups and individuals participated in the work. School counselors were summoned to the table! Recognized at last!

Members of the Children's Mental Health Task Force represented key agencies (e.g., mental health, child welfare, public health, education, juvenile justice), professional organizations, and interested individuals. Some of those groups involved on the executive committee of the task force included the following: Chicago public schools, Office of the Attorney General, Mental Health Association in Illinois, Ounce of Prevention Fund, Community Behavioral Health Care Association of Illinois, Illinois Violence Prevention Authority, Illinois Department of Children and Family Services, Illinois Department of Human Services, Illinois School Counselor's Association, and Voices for Illinois Children, to name only a few.

The group started by identifying individuals who had demonstrated an understanding of children's mental health systems and who had been involved in creating meaningful change. They also identified other groups, legislators, and individuals who not only represented significant roles in children's mental health but who were consumers and workers in the current children's mental health system. These individuals were invited to join the Children's Mental Health Task Force and to help in drafting recommendations for developing and advancing a comprehensive and coordinated children's mental health system.

The task force was divided into three committees—Early Childhood, School Age, and Policies and Resources—charged with forming recommendations that would be included in a report to Illinois policymakers. The task force's executive committee was composed of the cochairs of the three committees and key state agency representatives. Together, these committees provided valuable information regarding existing state systems and services. State agencies were integral partners in the effort. For instance, Carolyn Cochran Kopel, Associate Secretary, Illinois Department of Human Services, conducted a survey of state agencies that provided the task force with critical information regarding existing state systems and services.

Recommendations were deliberated and consensus was reached. The Children's Mental Health Task Force Report was published in April 2003 and presented to Illinois Governor Rod Blagojevich and the General Assembly, with wide dissemination to key stakeholders throughout the state. It states:

> Research clearly demonstrates that children's healthy social and emotional development is an essential underpinning to school readiness, academic success, and overall well-being. Prevention and early intervention efforts heave been shown to improve school readiness, health status and academic achievement, and to reduce the need for more costly mental health treatment, grade retention, special education services and welfare dependency. Unfortunately, a significant number of Illinois children experience serious mental health problems and many of them do not receive the service they need. (Illinois Children's Mental Health Task Force, 2003)

The report's key findings and key principles, together with input from the committees, helped guide the development of the recommendations included in the final report. Among the five pages of recommendations put forth by the task force, a core set of priority recommendations was identified. The following priority recommendations were identified in the report "as critical to achieving immediate successes, generating additional funding sources, and advancing a comprehensive system of children's mental health." (Illinois Children's Mental Health Task Force, 2003):

    I.   Make Children's Mental Health a priority in Illinois.

   II.   Maximize current investments and invest sufficient public and private resources over time.

  III.   Build a qualified and adequately trained workforce with a sufficient number of professionals to serve children and their families.

  IV.   Develop a comprehensive, multicultural, and multifaceted public awareness campaign to reduce the stigma of mental illness; educate families, the general public and other key audiences about the benefits of children's social and emotional development; and inform parents, providers and others about how to access services.

   V.   Create a quality-driven children's mental health system with shared accountability among key state agencies and programs that conducts ongoing needs assessments, uses outcome indicators and benchmarks to measure progress, and implements quality data tracking and reporting systems.

  VI.   Establish a Children's Mental Health Research and Resource Center(s) to collect and facilitate research on best practices and model programs, share information with Illinois policymakers, practitioners and the general public, develop training and educational materials, provide technical assistance, and other key activities.

 VII.   Provide funding for culturally competent and clinically relevant research, including longitudinal studies that: address evidence-based practices in children's mental health prevention, early intervention, and treatment; are translated into practice standards and policy implications for key groups; and are used to improve programs and services.

The task force agreed that if children's mental health was to become a priority in Illinois, policymakers would need to be educated about the issues facing children and youth and the solutions identified in the task force report. Furthermore, legislation was needed to codify some of the priority recommendations so that the task force effort would have a life beyond the report.

The state of Illinois acknowledged that its children's mental health system was fragmented, underresourced, and underfunded by passing the Children's Mental Health Act of 2003. The results of that legislation created the Illinois Children's Mental Health Partnership, on which school counselors are represented. The partnership is responsible for developing a children's mental health plan for Illinois that provides direction for building an effective children's mental health system that addresses the prevention, early intervention, and treatment needs of children 0 to 18 years old. In addition, the law mandates that the Illinois State Board of Education incorporate social-emotional development standards into the Illinois Learning Standards. As of August 2004, all schools in Illinois are responsible for developing policies to address the role of social-emotional development in their district education programs. The law allows Office of Mental Health funds to be used for children 0 to 18 years old and

improves methods of capturing Medicaid funds that could be used to support
children's mental health. Senate Bill 1951 passed both houses with no
opposition in August 2003.

On March 4, 2004, Illinois Governor Blagojevich appointed 25 members to
the Children's Mental Health Partnership and appointed Shaw as the chairper-
son. Representatives from key state agencies are also members of the partnership. Four committees were formed: Early Childhood, School Age, School
Policies and Standards, and Public Awareness. School counselors, school social
workers, psychologists, and school administrators are represented on the executive committee of the partnership.

The partnership met and reviewed the work of the task force and the final
report, with a charge of building on the recommendations of the report to develop an action plan and strategies for the systems change. Applications for
subcommittee work were published. The partnership was overwhelmed with
the interest shown by the number of people interested in working to develop
the children's mental health plan. Committee members were selected and the
work of the committees was under way.

Much of the work of the partnership up until this point had been conducted
with a relatively small budget from the Illinois Violence Prevention Authority
and the Irving B. Harris Foundation, and support from Blue Cross Blue Shield.
Once the partnership was initiated, a more aggressive fundraising plan and
budget were identified to support the work of the partnership. Initial funds
were identified and secured for some of the following areas: stipends for parents
working on the committees, staffing, consultation, development and implementation of the public awareness campaign, development and implementation of the evaluation plan, and pilot projects. Once the partnership's plan is
submitted to the governor, the partnership will embark on raising funds for top
priorities identified in the plan.

In a short time changes were being made. SEL was finally recognized as integral to the mission of schools and a critical component of student academic
readiness and school success. Schools would be mandated to take concrete
steps to address their students' social and emotional development.

The elements of the Children's Mental Health Act that relate directly to
SEL are:

- Section 15(a) incorporating SEL into the state learning standards:
  The Illinois State Board of Education shall develop and implement a
  plan to incorporate social and emotional development standards as
  part of the Illinois Learning Standards for the purpose of enhancing
  and measuring children's school readiness and ability to achieve aca-

demic success. The plan shall be submitted to the Governor, the General Assembly, and the Partnership by December 31, 2004.

- Section 15 (b) incorporating SEL into each district's educational program: Every Illinois school district shall develop a policy for incorporating social and emotional development into the district's educational program. The policy shall address teaching and assessing social and emotional skills and protocols for responding to children with social, emotional, or mental health problems, or a combination of such problems, that impact learning ability. Each district must submit this policy to the Illinois State Board of Education by August 31, 2004.

For schools that are already concerned about the social and emotional development of their students, this legislation provides the flexibility to include SEL in their school improvement plans. It also enables them to take time to teach skills necessary for success in school and in life.

The School Policies and Standards Committee has worked with members of the Illinois State Board of Education and CASEL to provide direction to schools as they design their policies for incorporating SEL into their educational programs. This committee is charged with several tasks:

1. To develop simple guidelines, including a self-assessment tool and reporting template, for school districts to develop and submit their policies on incorporating SEL into their educational program.
2. To develop a process for providing technical assistance to school districts in developing their policies.
3. To develop a process for reviewing school district submissions, and reviewing and analyzing the district policies.
4. To work with the Illinois State Board of Education to create a plan for incorporating social and emotional development into the Illinois Learning Standards.
5. To develop a plan for assessing the implementation of the social and emotional development standards.

The School Age Committee will develop a strategic plan for a comprehensive, coordinated system to address the social and emotional needs of school-age children ages 6 to 18 across the continuum of prevention and promotion, early intervention, and treatment. They are a multidisciplinary committee that is looking at many cross-cutting issues as they strive to prioritize recommendations and create a vision for their plan.

IMPLICATIONS FOR SCHOOL COUNSELORS

The work is new. It is exciting and full of promise for children's mental health. The implications for SEL are clear. The implications for school counselors are not. Certainly, the Illinois Developmental Model and the National Standards for School Counseling Programs support social emotional learning standards. The role definition and the professional standards for school counselors clearly state that counselors are trained to understand social-emotional development and that they act as mental health professionals in the schools. From the beginning, school counselors have been a part of the Children's Mental Health Task Force and now the Children's Mental Health Partnership. They have been recognized as mental health professionals working in the schools. With the focus of the Children's Mental Health Act on prevention, early intervention, and treatment, there is an opportunity for school counselors, school social workers, school psychologists, and school nurses to work collaboratively to insure that the social-emotional development of students is given top priority.

It is an exciting time in Illinois for children's mental health, for SEL and for school counseling. At last, barriers have been identified and recognition has been given to research that supports SEL as being critical to academic success and emotional well-being. The work has begun.

As we sit at the table to address the issues of underfunding, lack of resources, and fragmentation, there is a sense of hope despite the overwhelming task before us. In just 3 years children's mental health has been addressed and a task force report has been written. Legislation has been passed. Schools have been mandated to write SEL policies and to include them in their educational plan. The Illinois Board of Education has been mandated to create SEL standards. The Office of Mental Health has been allowed to use funds for children 0 to 18 years old. The state Departments of Public Aid, Human Services, and Children and Family Services worked together to create an initiative that would set up a hotline and screening program for low-income children with mental illnesses. Much has been accomplished. Illinois looks forward to creating a children's mental health plan that will provide a coordinated system to address the prevention, early intervention, and treatment needs of all Illinois children. Professional school counselors in Illinois are excited about the possibility of being acknowledged appropriately and being asked to do the work for which they were trained and for which they have a passion.

REFERENCES

Children's Mental Health Act. (2003). Public Act 93-0495. Retrieved September 2004 from www.ivpa.org

Collaborative for Academic Social and Emotional Learning. (2003). *Safe and sound: An educational leader's guide to evidence-based social and emotional learning (SEL) programs*. Chicago, IL: Author.

Goleman, D. (1995). *Emotional intelligence: Why it can matter more than IQ*. New York: Bantam.

Illinois Children's Mental Health Task Force. (2003). *Children's mental health: An urgent priority for Illinois*. Springfield, IL: Office of the Attorney General, State of Illinois. Retrieved September 2004 from www.ivpa.org

Illinois School Counseling Association, Illinois Counselor Educators and Supervisors, Illinois Counseling Association, Illinois Career Development Association. (1996). *Developmental Counseling Model for Illinois Schools: Guidelines for program development*. DeKalb, IL: Author. Retrieved September 2004 from www.ilschoolcounselor.org

Mental Health for Children Working Group. (2001, March). *White paper on mental health services for children and youth in Illinois*.

Appendix A
A Brief Historical
Perspective
of Emotional Intelligence

John Pellitteri
Queens College, CUNY

Although the term *emotional intelligence* has only been formally used for the last 15 years, the roots of emotional intelligence are ancient. As a psychological construct, emotional intelligence consists of emotions, which have a long philosophical history as well as a central place in the social sciences, and also consists of intelligence, which is a specialized field of study within theoretical and applied psychology. This section provides a brief history of emotions, intelligence, and their recent integration into emotional intelligence.

EMOTIONS

The centrality of emotions in human adaptation to the environment can be traced to the prehistoric era. The first humans, in an attempt to make sense of the weather and other natural occurrences in their surroundings, were believed to ascribe human emotions to such phenomena (i.e., thunder meant that the sky was angry). "Looking at all of nature as though it were alive is called *animism* and the projection of human attributes onto nature is called *anthropomorphism*" (Hergenhahn, 1992, p. 25). The energy, the movement, and the force of natural occurrences are qualities that can be similar to the dynamics and experience of human emotions. In this way, the perception of emotions in natural phenomena gives it the impression of being alive (the word e-motion suggests movement). In addition, physiological reactions to sensory stimuli (i.e., increased heart rate in response to a sudden flash of lightening) form the basis of human emotions, thus creating a similarity of internal bodily states and external environmental conditions.

As humans evolved, their capacity for reasoning and self-reflection developed. The ancient Greek philosophers, who formed the foundations of modern-day psychology, examined emotions along with other human attributes such as values and ethics with the main focus on intellectual functions such as reasoning. Emotions often were less central in their inquiries. Artistotle, however, viewed emotions as "amplifying any existing tendency, ... provid[ing] a motive for acting, ... [and] influenc[ing] how people perceive things" (Hergenhahn, 1992, p. 48). Aristotle's insights on emotion are relevant today and find support from psychological research. His notion of selective perception, which considers how emotional states influence what stimuli are perceived and processed, relates to findings from cognitive science (Wells & Mathews, 1994), emotion research (Isen, 1993; Schwarz, 2002), and psychoanalytic projective techniques (Bellak, 1993; Exner, 1993).

The 17th-century philosopher, Baruch Spinoza, distinguished emotion from passion, the latter of which was seen as disruptive and needed to be controlled by reason (Hergenhahn, 1992). An examination of Spinoza's ideas finds similarities to Freudian psychoanalysis (i.e., rational analysis of unconscious impulses). It also emphasizes the relationship between affect (emotions) and cognition (intellect or reason). This philosophical position continued a long-held view of emotions as being disruptive to pure reason. Emotions were considered to be "misguided judgments about life and our place in the world" (Solomon, 1993, p. 5). It was not until the Romantic period of the 18th and 19th centuries that this view of emotions and reason was challenged. The philosophers of this period formed the basis of humanistic-existential psychology which values feelings, uniqueness, and the holistic person. Thus, emotion was elevated to a more central and more positive role in human functioning.

In the late 19th century, William James, who was an early figure in American psychology, developed what was to be called the James–Lange theory of emotion (Carl George Lange independently developed an almost identical theory at the same time). Rather than see emotions as preceding and directing behavior, the James–Lange theory posits that behavior occurs first and that emotions result from our interpretation of our behavior. James considered how our perceptions of the environment lead to physiological sensations, which in turn form the basis of emotions (Solomon, 1993). This view finds support from a seminal social psychology research study by Schachter and Singer (1962), where participants who were physiologically aroused by norepinephrine interpreted the same physical states as distinctly different emotions (anger and joy) based on the affective cues from other people in the immediate environment. This study illustrates not only the physiological components to emotions but also the significance of the social-cognitive basis for the construction of emotions. The implications of James' theory is that we should act the way we want to feel. Someone who is smiling and laughing will likely attribute these behaviors to feeling happy. In terms of counseling, this relates to behavioral approaches where a change in behavior precedes changes in cognition and affect.

INTELLIGENCE

Psychology in the early 20th century was distinguished by the intelligence testing movement, which had its formal beginning in 1905 when Alfred Binet developed the first standardized intelligence test. This measure, commissioned by the French Ministry of Education, was designed to distinguish different levels of intellectual functioning to identify children with mental retardation. The Binet–Simon scale underwent several revisions and in 1916 L. M. Terman at Stanford University adapted the scale for use in the United States. The resulting Stanford–Binet Intelligence Scale is still one of the most widely used IQ measures today along with the Wechsler Intelligence Scale, which was first developed in 1939 (Anastasi & Urbina, 1997). These intelligence tests have had several revisions of test items, content, format, and most important, normative groups to provide current and valid results. World War I created the need to evaluate the intelligence and abilities of a large number of army recruits. Robert Yerkes, in response, developed group IQ tests, the Army Alpha (which required reading abilities) and the Army Beta (which did not depend on reading). The psychological testing movement, supported by the needs of the military, industry, and education, led to the development of numerous instruments designed to measure abilities, achievement, aptitude, interests, and personality (Kaplan & Saccuzzo, 1997).

The theoretical evolution of the construct of intelligence understandably influences its psychometric history. The dominant view at the initial phase of intelligence theory was that of Spearman in 1904, who proposed a unifactoral model, that is, one general structure or, g factor, as the overriding executive function of various subfactors of intelligence (Sternberg & Powell, 1982). E. L. Thorndike was the first major theorist to postulate the notion of different types of intelligence. Thorndike divided intelligence into three types: "Abstract intelligence was spoken of as ability to understand and manage ideas and abstractions, mechanical intelligence as the ability to understand and manage concrete objects of the physical environment, and social intelligence as ability to understand and manage people" (Thorndike & Stein, 1937, p. 275). It is social intelligence that becomes a theoretical basis for the current emotional intelligence construct. Thorndike contended, however, that social intelligence was difficult to measure because it consists of several different abilities, habits, or attitudes.

Researchers struggled with distinguishing social intelligence as separate from general intelligence and not merely an application of the g factor to social information. In the 1950s while little was done in the assessment of social intelligence, researchers and theorists expanded the construct to include concepts such as empathy, sensitivity, insight, perception, and interpersonal judgment (Ruisel, 1992). There was also an increase in research in cognitive processes and their relation to emotion (Omdahl, 1995). Wedeck's 1947 definition of social intelligence (as cited in Ruisel, 1992) as the ability to assess accurately feelings, moods, and motivations of others is surprisingly similar to the current definitions of emotional intelligence.

In 1983, Howard Gardner proposed an influential theory of multiple intelligence. His model postulates seven competencies (intelligences): linguistic, musical, logico-mathematic, spatial, body kinesthetic, interpersonal, and intrapersonal. Traditional IQ tends to represent functioning in linguistic, logico-mathematical, and spatial only. Social intelligence is represented in Gardner's model by *interpersonal* intelligence. One component in Gardner's theory that receives greater emphasis than in previous models is *intrapersonal* intelligence, which is the "capacity ... [to] access one's own feeling life" (Gardner, 1983, p. 239). It is from Gardner's conception of multiple types of intelligence that emotional intelligence emerges. Emotional intelligence can be placed within Gardner's intrapersonal and interpersonal intelligences with its emphasis on awareness of "one's own and other's emotions" (Salovey & Mayer, 1990, p. 189).

EMOTIONAL INTELLIGENCE

The history of emotional intelligence as a formal construct is significantly brief compared with the history of emotions and intelligence. The first formal presentation of emotional intelligence theory in a professional journal was the seminal article by Salovey and Mayer in 1990 in which they described the abilities-based emotional intelligence model. Mathews, Zeidner, and Roberts (2002) cited earlier uses of the term *emotional intelligence;* however, these were not presenting a coherent theory. In a series of scholarly publications (Mayer, DiPaolo, & Salovey, 1990; Mayer & Salovey, 1993, 1997; Mayer, Salovey, & Caruso, 2000; Salovey & Mayer, 1990) the authors developed the proposal that emotional intelligence was a type of intelligence that was distinct from IQ and involved the use of emotional information in a socially adaptive manner. Unlike social intelligence, which is difficult to measure and to distinguish from IQ, the Mayer and Salovey emotional intelligence model is more narrowly defined and operational. In addition, Mayer and Salovey's notion of emotions serving as an aid to judgment and decision making is in contrast to historical views of emotions as disruptive to reasoning. Mayer, Salovey, and Caruso have developed two abilities-based measure of EI: the Multifactoral Emotional Intelligence Scales (MEIS, Mayer, Caruso, & Salovey, 1999) and the Mayer-Salovey-Caruso Emotional Intelligence Test (MSCEIT, Mayer, Salovey, & Caruso, 2002). They have also attempted to bring conceptual clarity to the field by introducing the distinction between their abilities-based model and Goleman's (1995) and Bar-On's (1996) mixed models that blend traits and other related personality concepts (Mayer et al., 2000)

Building on the work of Mayer and Salovey, Goleman (1995) popularized emotional intelligence within the general public. His claims that emotional intelligence has greater predictive powers for success than IQ generated tremendous enthusiasm about the concept and has lead to widespread publications. Unfortunately, some of this enthusiasm about emotional intelligence has been misplaced and misguided without a firmly established empirical basis for such predictive claims (Mathews et al., 2002; Mayer et al., 2000). Goleman focused his applications of emotional intelligence to business setting (Goleman, 1998) and leadership (Goleman, Boyatzis, & McKee, 2002), and has developed a measurement instrument based on his own conception of emotional intelligence (Boyatzis, Goleman, & Rhee, 2000).

The third major figure in the emotional intelligence field is Bar-On (1996), whose measure, the EQi, was an initial attempt to measure various personality constructs based on his independent work on the concept Emotional Quotient. Bar-On (1997), however, did credit Mayer and Salovey as being one of the many influences in his thinking. His model based on the EQi has accumulated a large number of studies with international samples. Bar-On and Parker (2000) have edited the *Handbook of Emotional Intelligence* that incorporates various perspectives and concepts such as social intelligence, emotional competence, and alexithymia.

One of the early challenges in the emotional intelligence field has been to establish its validity. This has been made difficult by the various definitions of the construct and the inclusion of numerous related concepts. Mathews et al.

(2002) noted the breadth of emotional intelligence conceptualizations that can include many factors from the neural sensitivity of processing affective information, to personality traits, to higher order abstractions of meaning. Several authors (Davies, Stankov, & Roberts, 1998; Mathews et al., 2002; Hedlund & Sternberg, 2000) cautioned against the conceptual pitfalls of defining emotional intelligence too broadly and of the overlap with existing constructs of personality.

Another challenge has been the psychometric difficulties of measuring emotional intelligence. Some of the major challenges in the assessment of emotional intelligence include establishing criteria for "correct" responses on test items, considering the idiosyncrasies of various situations that may influence emotional responses, and actually accessing internal affective states. Schutte and Malouff (1999) published a survey of emotional intelligence measures and related concepts that, with the exception of the MEIS and MSCEIT, tend to be self-report tests. Instruments designed for use with children are relatively new and are particularly important given the necessity to validate the effectiveness of SEL programs in schools (Schutte & Malouff, 1999). Measures of the emotional intelligence concept of self-awareness for children are just beginning to be developed (Houtmeyers, 2002; Stern & Pellitteri, 2004).

As a synthesis of emotions and intelligence, the emotional intelligence construct integrates several areas of research and in doing so has numerous areas of potential application. Although Mathews et al. (2002), in a comprehensive review of the current scientific literature on emotional intelligence, cast doubts on its validity as an empirical construct, they noted how the "myth" of emotional intelligence can serve as an inspiration to those in education and draw attention to the importance of emotional factors. Whether emotional intelligence will ever be established as a long-lasting scientific construct in the future is uncertain. However, its current popularity creates potential to have a positive impact on the well-being of today's children and their school environments.

REFERENCES

Anastasi, A., & Urbina, S. (1997). *Psychological testing* (7th ed.). Upper Saddle River, NJ: Prentice Hall.

Bar-On, R. (1996, August). *The era of the EQ: Defining and assessing emotional intelligence.* Paper presented at the annual convention of the American Psychological Association, Toronto, Canada.

Bar-On, R. (1997). *Emotional Quotient Inventory user's manual.* Toronto, Canada: Multi-Health Systems.

Bar-On, R., & Parker, J. (Eds.). (2000). *The handbook of emotional intelligence.* San Francisco: Jossey-Bass.

Bellak, L. (1993). *The TAT, CAT, and SAT in clinical use* (5th ed.). Boston: Allyn & Bacon.
Boyatzis, R. E., Goleman, D., & Rhee, K. S. (2000). Clustering competencies in emotional intelligence: Insights from the Emotional Competence Inventory. In R. Bar-On & J. Parker (Eds.), *The handbook of emotional intelligence* (pp. 343–362). San Francisco: Jossey-Bass.
Davies, M., Stankov, L., & Roberts, R. (1998). Emotional intelligence: In search of an elusive construct. *Journal of Personality and Social Psychology, 75,* 989–1015.
Exner, J. E., Jr. (1993). *The Rorschach: A comprehensive system: Vol. 1: Basic foundations* (3rd ed.). New York: Wiley.
Gardner, H. (1983). *Frames of mind: The theory of multiple intelligences.* New York: Basic Books.
Goleman, D. (1995). *Emotional intelligence: Why it can matter more than IQ.* New York: Bantam.
Goleman, D. (1998). *Working with emotional intelligence.* New York: Bantam.
Goleman, D., Boyatzis, R., & McKee, A. (2002). *Primal leadership: Realizing the power of emotional intelligence.* Boston: Harvard Business School Press.
Hedlund, J., & Sternberg, R. (2000). Too many intelligences? Integrating social, emotional, and practical intelligence. In R. Bar-On & J. Parker (Eds.), *The handbook of emotional intelligence* (pp. 136–168). San Francisco: Jossey-Bass.
Hergenhahn, B. R. (1992). *An introduction to the history of psychology* (2nd ed.). Belmont, CA: Wadsworth.
Houtmeyers, K. A. (2002). Attachment relationships and emotional intelligence in preschoolers (doctoral dissertation, University of Windsor, 2002). *Dissertation Abstracts International: B. The Physical Sciences & Engineering, 62*(10-B), 4818.
Isen, A. (1993). Positive affect and decision making. In M. Lewis & J. M. Haviland (Eds.), *Handbook of emotions* (pp. 261–277). New York: Guilford.
Kaplan, R. M., & Saccuzzo, D. P. (1997). *Psychological testing: Principles, applications, and issues* (4th ed.). Pacific Grove, CA: Brook/Coles.
Mathews, G., Zeidner, M., & Roberts, R. (2002). *Emotional intelligence: Science and myth.* Cambridge, MA: MIT Press.
Mayer, J., Caruso, D., Salovey, P. (1999). Emotional Intelligence meets traditional standards for an intelligence. *Intelligence, 27,* 267–298.
Mayer, J. D., DiPaolo, M., & Salovey, P. (1990). Perceiving affective content in ambiguous visual stimuli: A component of emotional intelligence. *Journal of Personality Assessment, 54,* 772–781.
Mayer, J. D., & Salovey, P. (1993). The intelligence of emotional intelligence. *Intelligence, 17,* 433–442.
Mayer, J. D., & Salovey, P. (1997). What is emotional intelligence? In P. Salovey & D. J. Sluyter (Eds.), *Emotional development and emotional intelligence* (pp. 3–31). New York: HarperCollins.
Mayer, J., Salovey, P., & Caruso, D. (2000). Models of emotional intelligence. In R. Sternberg (Ed.), *Handbook of intelligence* (pp. 396–420). New York: Cambridge University Press.
Mayer, J., Salovey, P., & Caruso, D. (2002). *Mayer–Salovey–Caruso Emotional Intelligence Test manual.* Toronto, Canada: Multi-Health Systems.
Omdahl, B. L. (1995). *Cognitive appraisal, emotion, and empathy.* Hillsdale, NJ: Lawrence Erlbaum Associates.
Ruisel, I. (1992). Social intelligence: Conception and methodological problems. *Studia Psychologica, 34,* 281–296.
Salovey, P., & Mayer, J. (1990). Emotional intelligence. *Imagination, Cognition, and Personality, 9,* 185–211.

Schachter, S., & Singer, J. (1962). Cognitive, social, and physiological determinants of emotional states. *Psychological Review, 69,* 379–399.

Schutte, N. S., & Malouff, J. M. (1999). *Measuring emotional intelligence and related constructs.* Lewiston, NY: Mellen.

Schwarz, N. (2002). Situated cognition and the wisdom in feelings: Cognitive tuning. In L. F. Barrett & P. Salovey (Eds.), *The wisdom in feeling: Psychological processes in emotional intelligence* (pp. 144–166). New York: Guilford.

Solomon, R. (1993). The philosophy of emotions. In M. Lewis & J. M. Haviland (Eds.), *Handbook of emotions* (pp. 3–15). New York: Guilford.

Stern, R., & Pellitteri, J. S. (2004). *E.I. kids: A children's emotional awareness measure-administration and scoring manual.* Unpublished manuscript.

Sternberg, R., & Powell, J. (1982). Theories of intelligence. In R. Sternberg (Ed.), *Handbook of human intelligence* (pp. 975–1005). Cambridge, England: Cambridge University Press.

Thorndike, R., & Stein, S. (1937). An evaluation of the attempts to measure social intelligence. *The Psychological Bulletin, 34,* 275–285.

Wells, A., & Mathews, G. (1994). *Attention and emotion: A clinical perspective.* Hove, England: Lawrence Erlbaum Associates.

Appendix B
Web-Based Resources
for Social Emotional
Learning

Barbara Muller-Ackerman
Parsippany Counseling Center

6seconds – Emotional Intelligence Network with lesson plans, articles and many resources. www.6seconds.org/

American Counseling Association (ACA) – www.counseling.org

American School Counselor Association (ASCA) – www.schoolcounselor.org

The professional association for school counselors with role and position statements, publications and lesson plans. A division of ACA.

Center for 4th and 5th R's – Tom Lickona's site at SUNY Cortland for character education – www.cortland.edu/character/index.asp

Center for the Advancement of Ethics and Character at Boston University – www.bu.edu/education/caec/files/teacherresources.htm

Center for Social Emotional Education- www.csee.net Educational and professional development organization committed to K-12 SEE.

Character Counts – web site for the Josephson Institute for Ethics program for school, community and sport. www.charactercounts.org

Character Education Resource Guide – Indiana Department of Education guide with grade by grade lesson plans for implementing character education. http://doe.state.in.us/publications/pdf_citizenship/citizensguide.pdf

Collaborative for the Academic, Social and Emotional Learning. CASEL's homepage with programs, research and resources. www.casel.org

Committee for Children – producers of Second Step and Steps to Respect programs for character education, bullying and violence prevention. www.cfchildren.org

Consortium for Research on Emotional Intelligence in Organizations – www.eiconsortium.org

Don't Laugh at Me- program developed by Peter Yarrow and Operation Respect- free program to educators with downloads of the curriculum on site. www.dontlaugh.org

Emotionally Intelligent Parenting – web site for books, articles and resources for the application of emotional intelligence principles to parenting – www.eqparenting.com

National Association of School Psychologists- www.naspweb.org

National Association of Social Workers – www.naswdc.org

Positive Discipline – home page of Jane Nelson, author, with information on class and morning meetings www.positivediscipline.com

Project EXSEL-New York City project for social and emotional education under the auspices of Columbia University. http://pd.ilt.columbia.edu/projects/exsel/

Social Decision Making/Problem Solving Program – a character education program of merit from the New Jersey University of Medicine and Dentistry – http://130.219.58.44/sdm/

Utah Department of Education Character Education site – projects, resources and lessons. www.usoe.k12.ut.us/curr/char_ed

Author Index

Note: *f* indicates figure, *t* indicates table.

Subject Index

Note: *f* indicates figure, *t* indicates table.